Microservice Patterns and Best Practices

Explore patterns like CQRS and event sourcing to create scalable, maintainable, and testable microservices

Vinicius Feitosa Pacheco

BIRMINGHAM - MUMBAI

Microservice Patterns and Best Practices

Commissioning Editor: Merint Mathew
Acquisition Editor: Alok Dhuri
Content Development Editor: Akshada Iyer
Technical Editor: Adhithya Haridas
Copy Editor: Safis Editing
Project Coordinator: Prajakta Naik
Proofreader: Safis Editing
Indexer: Francy Puthiry
Graphics: Jisha Chirayil
Production Coordinator: Aparna Bhagat

First published: January 2018
Production reference: 1290118

Published by Packt Publishing Ltd.
Livery Place
35 Livery Street
Birmingham
B3 2PB, UK.

ISBN 978-1-78847-403-0

www.packtpub.com

To my mother, Vera Feitosa, for her sacrifices and for exemplifying the power of determination.

To my wife, Paola Katherine, for being my loving partner throughout our joint life journey.

To my friend and teacher, Claudio Cardozo, who gave me the opportunity to start my career and taught me how to win.

`mapt.io`

Mapt is an online digital library that gives you full access to over 5,000 books and videos, as well as industry leading tools to help you plan your personal development and advance your career. For more information, please visit our website.

Why subscribe?

- Spend less time learning and more time coding with practical eBooks and Videos from over 4,000 industry professionals

- Improve your learning with Skill Plans built especially for you

- Get a free eBook or video every month

- Mapt is fully searchable

- Copy and paste, print, and bookmark content

PacktPub.com

Did you know that Packt offers eBook versions of every book published, with PDF and ePub files available? You can upgrade to the eBook version at `www.PacktPub.com` and as a print book customer, you are entitled to a discount on the eBook copy. Get in touch with us at `service@packtpub.com` for more details.

At `www.PacktPub.com`, you can also read a collection of free technical articles, sign up for a range of free newsletters, and receive exclusive discounts and offers on Packt books and eBooks.

Contributors

About the author

Vinicius Feitosa Pacheco has been working as a software engineer since 2007. He has diverse experience with high-performance and high-availability software architectures, with an emphasis on microservices, and is passionate about teaching and talking about them.

In the last 4 years, he has worked as an instructor in the field of software engineering techniques (including design patterns) and programming languages, such as Python, Java, and Go. He has been a speaker at large conferences such as PyCon Argentina, Pycon Colombia, EuroPython, RubyConf Brazil, the MobileConf, and QConSP.

About the reviewer

Alexander Sofras is a software architect living in picturesque Surrey, England. He has been programming for most of his life, working on independent games, academic computer vision projects, and financial analytics software. Most recently, he has helped deliver a market-leading business intelligence platform to investment banks worldwide and maintains that interest with a passionate support of blockchain technology. When not working, he enjoys catching up with old friends, going to the theater, painting, and gaming.

Packt is searching for authors like you

If you're interested in becoming an author for Packt, please visit `authors.packtpub.com` and apply today. We have worked with thousands of developers and tech professionals, just like you, to help them share their insight with the global tech community. You can make a general application, apply for a specific hot topic that we are recruiting an author for, or submit your own idea.

Table of Contents

Preface

Microservices is a software architecture strategy that has been in use for some years, with the goal of making services more scalable. Monolithic applications are losing ground to service-oriented projects, owing to the need for today's businesses to grow rapidly and dynamically. By designing this new architectural model, object-oriented principles, standards, decoupling, and responsibilities have become fundamental beyond automated testing.

Knowledge of microservices will enable you to create maintainable and scalable applications. By the end of this book, you will be fully capable of creating interoperable microservices, testable and prepared for a great performance.

Who this book is for

This book is intended for readers who have experience with web development but want to improve their development techniques to create more maintainable and scalable applications. Readers are not expected to have development experience using microservices. The concepts and standards demonstrated in this book enable the reader to develop applications that are simple to understand and support a high volume of access.

What this book covers

Chapter 1, *Understanding the Microservices Concepts*, gives you an overview of microservice concepts. This chapter will help you to understand the concepts behind the architecture, for example, the client-first approach and domain definition.

Chapter 2, *The Microservice Tools*, takes you through the most common tools to be applied to microservices. Once you know your customers and how to define the domains of your application, it's time to make technical decisions—which programming language to use, which framework is appropriate, and how to validate whether your microservice template is functional or not.

Chapter 3, *Internal Patterns*, introduces you to internal microservice application patterns. We will address topics such as caching strategies, workers, queues, and asynchrony.

Chapter 4, *Microservice Ecosystem*, covers how to create a group of resilient and scalable microservices from a monolithic application. The chapter also focuses on how to separate microservices correctly in their respective containers and explains the distribution of the storage layer.

Chapter 5, *Shared Data Microservice Design Pattern*, covers a special case. Normally, microservices are totally independent in business, testing, communications, connections, and storage, but not in this pattern. The shared pattern is a special pattern for migration concepts, from monolithic to microservices; overall, it's a pattern for transitioning.

Chapter 6, *Aggregator Microservice Design Pattern*, covers the most simple and typical pattern, which basically consists of applying data orchestration to microservices.

Chapter 7, *Proxy Microservice Design Pattern*, covers the proxy pattern, which is very similar to the aggregator pattern. When thinking of the structure, it's used when it isn't necessary to join data to send it to the end user. Understanding the differences between the proxy pattern and the aggregator pattern, as well as the correct request redirection for the responsible microservice, is the goal of this chapter.

Chapter 8, *Chained Microservice Design Pattern*, covers the chained pattern, where the information that will be sent to the client can be consolidated into a chain. Explaining information consolidation is the main objective of this chapter.

Chapter 9, *Branch Microservice Design Pattern*, covers the branch pattern, which is a mix of the aggregator and chain patterns. It's normally used when, in the backend, a microservice doesn't have all the data to complete a task or should directly notify another microservice. This chapter explains when this pattern composition is useful and the ways in which it could be good for the business.

Chapter 10, *Asynchronous Messaging Microservice*, explains one of the most complex patterns: applying asynchronism at the microservice level. This chapter is about how microservices can communicate asynchronously using messaging tools.

Chapter 11, *Microservices Working Together*, is a conclusion on patterns. After learning all about the microservice patterns, we will see how to put all the microservices to work together.

Chapter 12, *Testing Microservices*, explains the most plausible possibilities for testing and how to make this part, which is so important, simple.

Chapter 13, *Monitoring Security and Deployment*, covers what is necessary and best practices to maintain microservices in production.

To get the most out of this book

Having some knowledge of OOP and package structure in Go (golang) will make reading this book more interesting.

Download the example code files

You can download the example code files for this book from your account at `www.packtpub.com`. If you purchased this book elsewhere, you can visit `www.packtpub.com/support` and register to have the files emailed directly to you.

You can download the code files by following these steps:

1. Log in or register at `www.packtpub.com`.
2. Select the **SUPPORT** tab.
3. Click on **Code Downloads & Errata**.
4. Enter the name of the book in the **Search** box and follow the onscreen instructions.

Once the file is downloaded, please make sure that you unzip or extract the folder using the latest version of:

- WinRAR/7-Zip for Windows
- Zipeg/iZip/UnRarX for Mac
- 7-Zip/PeaZip for Linux

The code bundle for the book is also hosted on GitHub at `https://github.com/PacktPublishing/Microservice-Patterns-and-Best-Practices`. We also have other code bundles from our rich catalog of books and videos available at `https://github.com/PacktPublishing/`. Check them out!

Download the color images

We also provide a PDF file that has color images of the screenshots/diagrams used in this book. You can download it here: `https://www.packtpub.com/sites/default/files/downloads/MicroservicePatternsandBestPractices_ColorImages.pdf`.

Conventions used

There are a number of text conventions used throughout this book.

`CodeInText`: Indicates code words in text, database table names, folder names, filenames, file extensions, pathnames, dummy URLs, user input, and Twitter handles. Here is an example: "The `config.py` file is where the settings for each development environment exist."

A block of code is set as follows:

```
class TestDevelopmentConfig(TestCase):

    def create_app(self):
        app.config.from_object('config.DevelopmentConfig')
        return app

    def test_app_is_development(self):
        self.assertTrue(app.config['DEBUG'] is True)
```

When we wish to draw your attention to a particular part of a code block, the relevant lines or items are set in bold:

```
@patch('views.rpc_command')
def test_sucess(self, rpc_command_mock):
    """Test to insert a News."""
```

Any command-line input or output is written as follows:

```
$ docker-compose -f docker-compose.yml up --build -d
```

Bold: Indicates a new term, an important word, or words that you see onscreen. For example, words in menus or dialog boxes appear in the text like this. Here is an example: "The following screenshot represents the interface of **DATADOG**:"

Warnings or important notes appear like this.

Tips and tricks appear like this.

Get in touch

Feedback from our readers is always welcome.

General feedback: Email `feedback@packtpub.com` and mention the book title in the subject of your message. If you have questions about any aspect of this book, please email us at `questions@packtpub.com`.

Errata: Although we have taken every care to ensure the accuracy of our content, mistakes do happen. If you have found a mistake in this book, we would be grateful if you would report this to us. Please visit `www.packtpub.com/submit-errata`, selecting your book, clicking on the Errata Submission Form link, and entering the details.

Piracy: If you come across any illegal copies of our works in any form on the Internet, we would be grateful if you would provide us with the location address or website name. Please contact us at `copyright@packtpub.com` with a link to the material.

If you are interested in becoming an author: If there is a topic that you have expertise in and you are interested in either writing or contributing to a book, please visit `authors.packtpub.com`.

Reviews

Please leave a review. Once you have read and used this book, why not leave a review on the site that you purchased it from? Potential readers can then see and use your unbiased opinion to make purchase decisions, we at Packt can understand what you think about our products, and our authors can see your feedback on their book. Thank you!

For more information about Packt, please visit `packtpub.com`.

1
Understanding the Microservices Concepts

In the programming world, design patterns are very common. This is no different when it comes to web development. With the internet popularity and then after Web 2.0, many patterns developed for the web were widely disseminated with the intention of making the development more dynamic and simple for new features.

Patterns such as **MVC** (**Model-View-Controller**), **HMVC** (**Hierarchical Model View Controller**), and **MTV** (**Model Template View**), among others, inspired the creation of various frameworks such as Django, Ruby on Rails, Spring MVC, and CodeIgniter, for example.

All these frameworks are excellent for creating web applications quickly and without great concern for application architecture. This is because much of the work is done by the framework. All these patterns were thought to be only applied to a web application with all the required business rules. Typically, these applications, where all business rules are on the same code base, are called **monoliths**.

For years, the monoliths absolutely reigned in the web development ecosystem. Many companies looking for space in the market validated products by creating software on these full-stack frameworks. Many monolithic software applications went to the internet and, over time, a word has emerged as a problem for these monolithic applications: success.

Success is a very problematic word for monolithic applications because of the following difficulties:

- Maintenance on the same code base can be complicated due to merges that are difficult to apply
- Implementing new features is increasingly complex and may take longer than expected
- Application scalability
- Deploying new features without impacting what is already online is challenging
- Architectural changes are always very complex

These are just some examples of the kinds of problems that may exist in a monolithic application. These difficulties are a good motivation to migrate monolithic application architecture to microservices. Increasingly, adopting microservices has been the path taken by the software engineering industry and most companies, where the word success has meant trouble for the provision of practice and scalable business. The advantages of the microservices architecture are many:

- An exclusive business domain for each microservice, facilitating the implementation of new features
- Better definition of business without cyclic dependency between them
- Independent deployment
- Simplicity to identify errors
- Technological independence among microservices
- Independence between teams
- Implementation of isolation
- Possible scalability for specific microservice

Showing you how to make the transition from a monolithic application to microservices, applying appropriate patterns, and showing you possible implementation misconceptions, is the aim of this book. All modifications will be applied to the same project, a news portal that has interactivity, a recommendation system, authentication, and an authorization system. Throughout the book, you will be shown every step of this migration when applying design patterns, and both internal and external migrations when it comes to the communication layer between microservices. Of course, to get to that point, you first need to understand some important concepts to efficiently implement the microservices.

Knowing the application

It is time to get to know the application that will be used throughout the book. This application will be the source of all explanations of concepts and all practical code that will be developed in the book. The base system is a news portal that consists of, basically, three areas:

- **News**: This is the news itself.
- **Recommendations**: These are responsible for storing user preferences and thus are able to offer specific news to users or even compose a completely unique home page according to the user profile.
- **User**: This is the basic registration information of a user.

All the application's business is on the same source code, that is, a monolithic software. The application was developed on the Django Framework, using PostgreSQL as a database, and Memcached as cache, which is only applied to the database layer.

With this structure, if there is an overload on the level of recommendations, all the applications must be scaled, and not only the part referring to the recommendations, because the application is monolithic. Another problem is that if one commits and incurs a problem, it propagates errors in segments that have no relationship with deficiency in the composition of domains. Something expensive for the application changes in the stack. If you want to change the type of cache used, then all other caches will be lost.

Domain-driven design

The OOP concepts can be applied to the design of microservices, not only in the internal design of the application but also in the architecture and the business division. When it comes to **Domain-Driven Design (DDD)**, it is no different.

DDD came from the book Domain-Driven Design written by Eric Evans. The Evans book is a large catalog of patterns, coming from over 20 years of the author's experience developing software using OOP. It is very important to note that OOP is not only inheritance, interfaces, or anything else of the type. OOP's main ideas are as follows:

- Code alignment with the business
- Favoring of reuse
- Minimal coupling

Evans's book is divided into four parts:

- Putting the domain model to work
- Model building blocks-driven design
- Refactoring to deeply understand the model
- Strategic design

All the preceding parts can be applied to microservices. Model building blocks-driven design and refactoring to deeply understand the model internally applies to microservices, that is, the code itself. The others can be applied either internally in the software, but can also be used to design microservices and their signatures.

The first part is emphatic about the need to use ubiquitous language for communication between those responsible for the business, and the engineering team responsible for the development. This language consists of terms that are part of everyday conversations between business experts and development teams. Everyone should use the same terms in spoken language, the source code, and the signing of microservices. This means that when the business specialist says, *The home page should seek breaking news with the title and description* the ubiquitous language applied in the code will be represented as follows:

- Microservice news
- Endpoint recent news
- Payload with attribute title and description

This type of communication will mitigate errors in understanding requirements and maintain the general knowledge about application unison. Another important point is that, with the ubiquitous language, identifying areas is simpler because, as interactions have standardized terms, a word may indicate something new.

The fourth part will clarify the boundaries of a microservice and ease of management between the parties. Besides having a ubiquitous language used in the development of a consistent and adequate microservice, some strategies are necessary for dealing with complex systems, where multiple pieces of software (developed by several teams) interact. Delimit the context in which each team works and what is the degree of interaction between these teams and these contexts? Of the many tools that the DDD provides us, three are more prominent for efficient microservices:

- **Context maps**: These are the communication paths between microservices with appropriate interactions between microservices teams. After the analysis of the areas are already defined, the team can choose to be dependent on another team for domain language.

- **Anti-corruption layer** (ACL): This is the function that translates foreign concepts for an internal model to provide loose coupling between the domains.
- **Interchange context**: This provides an environment for both teams and discusses the meaning of each foreign term and translates the languages of microservices.

Thinking about the application we are working on, the DDD would be very useful for avoiding misunderstandings in the interpretation of how microservices should work. A common misconception in news systems is about the terms user and author; both are users of the system, one as a player and another as publisher, but if a product owner says, "*The user published bad news*" we have a problem in communication between product teams and development teams. This may result in an inconsistent microservice within the business itself. Another problem is that the phrase spoken earlier by the product owner suggests an unwanted feature, which is a user who can publish materials. DDD is just thinking about defining the microservice domain and standardizing terms to generate consistent internal models and an API with solid meaning. The difference in meanings or representations for the same attribute is known as a **semantic gap**, and is exactly what we are dealing with throughout the chapter.

Besides the aspects mentioned previously, helping to create microservices intact, there is a feature of DDD which undoubtedly is the most important when it comes to designing microservices. The concept of bounded contexts is essential to determine the range of a microservice and in the end, the responsibility that the microservice has. The most important thing is understanding that without these, coupling limits will be high and concepts such as single responsibility can never be achieved.

Single responsibility principle

Another principle that is applied to microservices and comes from the OOP world is specifically the letter **S** in **SOLID**. What could be thought before the class level should now be through the application level, so that microservices can be really *micro* in terms of what really matters at the domain level.

The microservice domain cannot be large; on the contrary, it must be limited. The limits that were cited in DDD return to be applied now and with more intensity. Precisely, the limits in the microservice domain is what will make this application sensitive to changes and open to the perception of possible errors.

It is a very common difficulty in maintaining pure microservices in their domains. The natural tendency, either by habit or ignorance, is to try to group all the business rules or similar codes in the same microservice, without even understanding whether they are part of the same domain.

To illustrate, think of the application on which we are working, our news portal. News and recommendations virtually work together all the time. Recommendations always put together some news that has some of the related labels. At first, it makes sense, because as the recommendations are always related to the news, apparently this does not cause a problem and, moreover, could reduce problems such as network latency. The main concept could be represented by the following diagram:

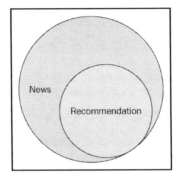

However, creating a microservice containing news and recommendations will generate unnecessary and very expensive engagement for future changes. In a simple demonstration exercise, we can think of a number of business changes with which this engagement would generate problems.

A new business requirement arose. Those responsible for thinking about the product had an idea to use recommendations to compose a personal home page according to the news that stands out most in our portal. So, the recommendations aren't just connected to the news anymore, but to the user too. With this new requirement, some problems relating to the coupling done previously will emerge at the level of deployment, scalability, and maintenance features code.

Based on the new requirement mentioned previously, it is clear that news and recommendations work together, but they are totally different domains from each other. Identifying areas to apply the principle of sole responsibility for each microservice is crucial to application architecture. The following diagram shows the main idea of the microservice distribution:

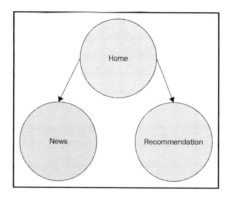

Working together and in concert, **Home** requests information either from **News** or **Recommendation**. There are some forms of data orchestration that we will come to later in the book, but now it is important to understand that **Home** can consult separate services and compose the received data conveniently.

The separation of **News** and **Recommendation** results in an application where the deploy becomes a simpler, more consistent code base and the fully defined and specific business domain for a purpose.

Explicitly published interface

The published interface is a term that usually generates a lot of confusion with the public interface. It is critical to understand the difference between the two terms: microservices and distributed source systems.

Think of a microservice. All internal microservice code will be used and shared among the development team; class methods are abstractions or attributes and can all be part of the public interface between teams. This is because of the convenience to notify and make changes in the event of possible refactoring. There is no point in generating a lot of bureaucracy at the development level, just for the features to gain speed in the implementation.

When it comes to the published interface, however, it is different. The published interface is what the microservice developers release. The published interface is what will be consumed by the internet. A good example is the **Single Sign-On (SSO)** API. Imagine that APIs suffer sudden changes to implement new features such as security and that these changes do not have a good system of alerts for all customers of these APIs. It is simply not appropriate to use this SSO service, because of updates, the API client suffers from incompatibilities.

Published interfaces should have more control and be more resilient to refactoring. Usually, they apply only to external application clients. The less possible changes in the level of the signatures, the better. The following diagram shows the possibility of maintaining the published interface signature:

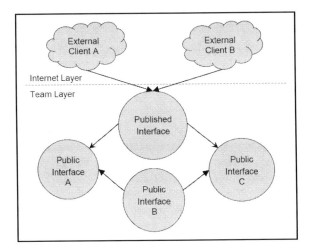

Some concepts are important for published interfaces, such as:

- **Published versioned interfaces**: An efficient version control to indicate when something, deprecated is key. Not only that, but it will also indicate what the new version is and when the deprecated version will be deactivated permanently.
- **Small published interfaces**: A large payload is much more susceptible to change than a more specialized payload. Applying the concepts of DDD on these payloads is very healthy.
- **Published external interfaces**: Do not create the concept of published interfaces for internal development teams. This creates a slow process of change and implementation features.

It is common to think of the concept of public interface versus published interface as something similar to the public versus private OOP, but they are actually different. The published interface does not mean depriving the client of resources, but rather directing the customer to consume adequate resources resiliently.

Independently deploy, upgrade, scale, and replace

Discussing this topic is very interesting and relevant to the microservices ecosystem. Deploy, upgrade, replace, and scale are great advantages that microservices have over monolithic systems, when it comes to most aspects of their functions.

Independent deployment

A standard aspect of the professional software development world is version control. This is because developers are pretty much working on features and maintenance of legacy code in the same application, at the same time.

In the end, a landmark (tag) is created in the application and this landmark is sent to production; this process is called deployment. At that same point, some problems may arise.

Let's consider a situation; in our news portal, one developer is working on an important feature for recommendations while another developer is working on fixing bugs. Both commit to hitting the same target. At the time of deployment, there is a major problem. The bug in news was not fixed successfully, which prevented the new feature from going into production. Software can be thoroughly tested, and even though much attention is given to each task, the unforeseen can still happen.

When it comes to microservices, this kind of problem is reduced drastically. Rethink the same scenario.

On our news portal, one developer is working for a few weeks on an important feature for the Recommendations microservice and another developer is working on a bug in the news microservice. Both commit to hitting the same target, each in their respective microservice; however, we still encounter a problem during deployment. The bug in news was not fixed successfully, which prevents the new version of the news microservice from going into production, but the Recommendations microservice is perfect and the new feature goes into production without any problems.

This is perhaps one of the main positive points when it comes to independent deployment. Of course, the complexity of maintaining the operation of multiple machine instances generates more complexity, but if you think about it, in a world of cloud computing, the complexity of multiple instances would be the same even though the application was monolithic, as the need for scalability is always real.

Later in the book, we see some patterns of deployment; we just focus on reducing complexity and practicality to perform deploys continuously.

Upgrade

There is an item that is mandatory for microservices to really be microservices; this item is an independent upgrade. Some rules must be followed to upgrade as independently as possible:

- **Never share libraries between microservices**: This means that each microservice has a stack that is totally independent of any other microservice. Sharing libraries is an error that generates high coupling and problems at the time of deployment. The microservices can start with the same stack, although it is usually best to analyze the domain and the data structure to see if the stack proposal is compatible or not. However, starting with the same stack does not mean keeping concurrent versioning. Another aspect that needs attention is to completely avoid creating business components on specific versions of a library stack. This approach prevents any technological developments in the microservice and means that, for example, security patches cannot be applied.

- **Strong delimitation of microservice domains**: We have already talked about bounded contexts, but it is worth reiterating again. The microservice limits are essential to determine whether the domain really is compatible with microservices architecture, or whether what is being designed is only a monolithic part decoupled from the rest. The loose coupling is what defines a microservice subject to upgrades and changes in the level of business without major conflicts with the ecosystem, in which the microservice is inserted.

- **Establish a client-server relationship between microservices**: This means that each microservice is a separate application and has complete autonomy over itself. When a microservice depends on another microservice's business resolutions, we have an alert point. The microservices can communicate with each other freely to ask for information, but never to solve business issues. When a microservice sends a message to another and is waiting for the answer to complete a task, there is an error. This error is critical and will result in scalability and transactional issues. When a microservice sends a message to another, there is a very strong idea there: asynchrony. As one microservice server performs tasks and provides information, another client microservice requests information. When the two faces—server and client—are intrinsically linked to a microservice, there is a design error.

- **Deploy in separate containers**: This approach not only facilitates the independent structure of a microservice, but also ensures that a fault in one microservice is totally individual, without disrupting an entire microservice pool. When we speak of separate containers, we are not necessarily talking about virtualization. The containers in question can be physical; it is a matter of the strategy and resources of a company, but the fact is that it is not healthy to keep more than one microservice in a container. It is important to remember that failures will occur, and when they occur, it is important to be prepared to mitigate the failures. Microservices as a group in a single container means that there will be a failure when a cyclomatic microservices burst occurs.

Separate containers are also essential for upgrading tools that are part of the stack, but that are not properly coded, such as databases and caches.

Scale

Scalability of speech is a common approach; see *The Scale Cube* which is discussed in the book *The Art of Scalability* from Martin L. Abbott and Michael T. Fisher. The concepts of the *Scale Cube* are fully applicable to microservices, and web applications in general, that need to be scalable:

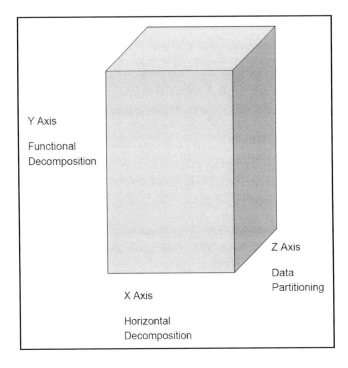

The concept of a scale cube shows that there are basically three forms of scalability: *x*-axis, *y*-axis, and *z*-axis. To better understand each of these three approaches, we will use some diagrams.

The x-axis

On the *x*-axis, this strategy targets the horizontal scalability with the same application server replicated *n* times in full and in a balanced order of $1/n$.

The problem with this strategy is that resources such as databases and caches will be required, since the number of applications that accesses these features gradually increases, as necessary, to scale. For this strategy, caches require more memory and databases need a pool of greater connections, something that does not always result in a benefit:

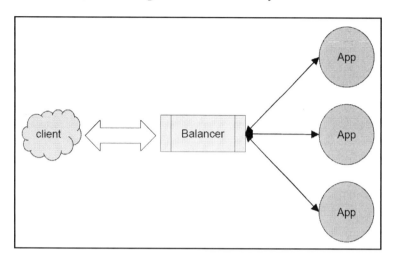

The y-axis

In this strategy, a verb or route is used by the balancer to identify where to go with the request. The following image represents the *y*-axis:

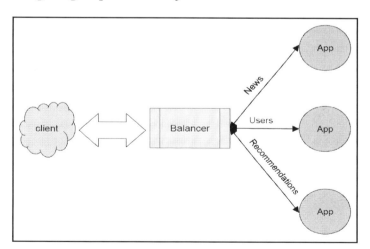

The principle does not seem to be very scalable, but it is exactly the junction with the *y*-axis and *x*-axis that is used to scale microservices.

This join between *y*-axis and *x*-axis allows us, occasionally, to bring scalability to just part of the microservices. In the following diagram, it can be seen that `News` was the most scaled microservice, followed by `Recommendations`, but `Users` have no major changes. This type of scalability technique greatly reduces the drawbacks of shared resource access, as each microservice structure manages and uses only its own resources, such as caches and databases. Take a look at the following diagram:

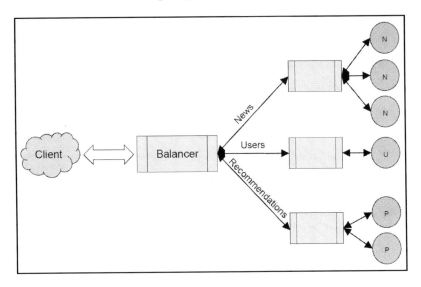

The z-axis

The z-axis is very similar to the *x*-axis when it comes to scalability structure, as it distributes exactly the same code on each server. The big difference is that each server responds to a specific subset of data. In this strategy, the search is providing not only scalability regarding the application, but also the data you use.

The following diagram shows a little example:

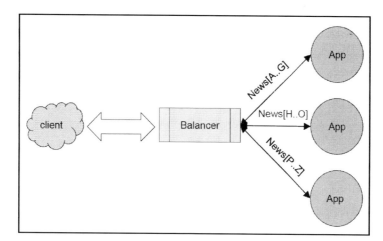

This strategy is not entirely ruled out when it comes to microservices, but its use is a little different. The applicability ends up not being on the verbs, but on geolocation. This means that, in a global application, the database of a microservice is distributed by region and is preferably available for this region, that is, people who access the website in Europe will, preferably, see the European news.

The definition of how microservices are scaled is directly linked to business strategy. From a technical point of view, the focus is to provide a flexible software strategy allowing changes as they certainly occur.

Replace

Updates to microservices are normal, but sometimes these updates may compromise the health of a microservice. New features can cause the microservice to absorb many responsibilities that go beyond the original domain idea.

A common mistake is adding new features and invalidating old ones without removing them completely. Some features of the development processes become more clear when a new microservice is created that is intended to replace an old one.

This process may seem more time consuming, however, it is very healthy for the application as a whole. Rethink whether old features still make sense, remove any zombie code which has no more relevance to the business, becoming consumers of resources and aggregators of complexity.

The replace process, when it comes to microservices, is very simple, as shown in the following diagram:

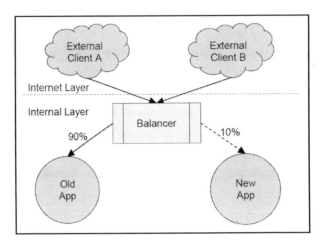

The concept applied to the replacement process is very simple. With control as the balancing layer, which will direct **90%** of the requests for the old microservice and **10%** for the new microservice, it is possible to monitor and analyze how mature a new application is and if no feature has been forgotten or has unwanted side effects.

This approach reduces the error effect on production, and provides real data on the new application. As the new microservice gains maturity and confidence in the availability of features, a higher percentage of requests is released for the new microservice. Importantly, the microservices, due to the size of the small business scope and low coupling, are easily replaceable. A total replacement service is a natural process when it comes to evolution, both in business and as a stack.

Light weight communication

In monolithic systems, many projects fail to be successful in the move to microservices architecture just because of problems in the communication layer. Of course, when we talk about containers, distributed applications, and business domain partitioning, some terms may amaze you—these terms are latency and data translation.

Communication in a monolithic application is made up of internal components, such as methods, functions, attributes, and parameters. In this ecosystem, latency and data translation are irrelevant. In the world of microservices, they are topics that must be thoroughly analyzed.

There are two methods of communication between microservices:

- Synchronous
- Asynchronous

It is important to understand how each of these forms works. Let's see how:

	One-to-One	One-to-Many
Synchronous	Request/response	-
Asynchronous	Notification	Publish/subscribe
	Request/async response	Publish/async responses

Have a look at the preceding table; the type of communication adopted will vary according to the need of the domain. For direct and sequential systems, a synchronous communication approach may be more appropriate. In the case of tasks that do not need an immediate response, the asynchronous approach can be the most appropriate.

Synchronous

When it comes to the communication layer between microservices, synchronous is certainly the most widely used approach. Within this topic, some protocols are well known and others less so. The range of direct protocols is as follows:

- HTTP
- TCP
- WebSockets
- Sockets
- RPC
- SOAP

Arguably, the most commonly implemented is HTTP. Many microservices use HTTP to communicate with each other, where as the HTTP is typically used with JSON.

The problem with this approach is that, with HTTP, JSON can generate an unwanted processing time to send and translate the information. Some teams that use JSON with HTTP only adopt the *keep alive* strategy for app-to-app communication and conventional connections to APIs.

When it comes to HTTP, API with JSON is practically normative. However, for internal communication between microservices, this is quite questionable. A good approach, in this case, considering problems of latency and data translation, is the use of binary traffic for communication between microservices.

There are some very interesting options for this approach: Avro, Protocol Buffer with CPRM, and Thrift are some examples. Another important point is that with binary we are not tied to any specific technology, and changing the communication interface with this technology is extremely simple.

Asynchronous

In some direct communications between microservices, timing may be important, but there are other times where the process can simply be asynchronous; there's no need for an immediate response or confirmation of success, all that is required is to simply run a task. For this approach, the message broker is just perfect.

Some software applications appear a good choice for message brokers, such as RabbitMQ, ActiveMQ, ZeroMQ, Kafka, and Redis. Each of these options has its own peculiarities, some are faster, others are more resilient. Again, the business setting is going to determine which technology is used.

Potentially heterogeneous/polyglot

There is no single solution for everything in software development. It's a phrase I've heard a few times and it's the truth. A very interesting feature of a well-composed microservice is the possibility of a microservice with completely different technology from another microservice. This heterogeneous strand of microservices gives the total engineering team the ability and freedom to seek the most appropriate solution to a problem.

With multilingual microservices, it is important to understand that there is an increase of complexity with regards to deploy and stack maintenance. However, the compensation provided by the heterogeneous applications is very valuable.

Documentation of communication

Communication between teams, whether technical teams or business teams, is something that is, relatively complex. At other times, the technical communication between various teams such as frontend, backend, and mobile can be costly, and can delay some deliveries, commits, or the functionality of a feature. However, fluid communication with no noise is critical to the success of any project.

Writing good documentation, either in internal code or a simple document, is the best way to standardize knowledge among teams. The Swagger API is a good alternative solution for such problems:

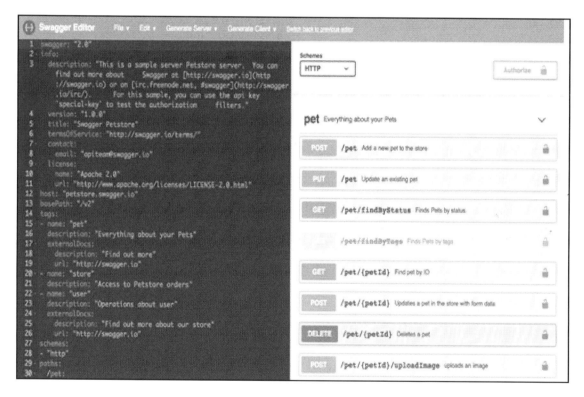

With a simple configuration file, all of the APIs can be developed together with full integration between the team that develops requirements and the team that develops solutions.

Endpoints for web applications

As we have already seen with the published interfaces, it is now important to define the content of these endpoints and their size.

An important topic that is not always addressed is the componentization of the endpoints that are exposed. Think about a microservice responsible for user information. Some development teams decided to create a large endpoint that provides all possible information stored about a user. This type of endpoint, one `getUser` type, may seem simple for development, but not for scalability.

A great deal of useless information for those who consume the API may be being passed, or is heavily specific information to transmit and expensive to be generated by the microservice. Thinking practically, the most sensible approach is to create an information API more fragmented and diverse, and if a `getUser` is necessary, create an orchestrator of the smaller information and pass on a single endpoint. The following diagram is a good example of this:

This type of strategy is called endpoint builder, where the heavy point of information actually is compositions of other lighter data sources.

Endpoints for mobile applications

Problems such as speed and weight information in the web world are not very common; we cannot say the same for the mobile world.

The componentization endpoints providing a lightweight and mature API for mobile applications is critical to business success. No one wants the battery completely consumed because an application has expensive endpoints.

With the mobile ecosystem, APIs with a `getUser`, as mentioned in the preceding topic, are totally impractical. The definition of the limits of a microservice is not just what constitutes the microservice domain, but also exposing of the data of this domain.

Caching at the client level

A caching strategy is one of the most important items for discussion when it comes to web applications; with microservices it is no different.

When we speak of cache at the client level, it means that the request only passes to be processed on the backend, if really necessary. In other words, it tries to block direct access to the backend to requests that have already been implemented in the recent past.

A very useful tool for this strategy is the Varnish Cache, defined as: *the Varnish Cache accelerator is a web application also known as reverse HTTP proxy caching*. In the following diagram, we can see the operation of Varnish Cache:

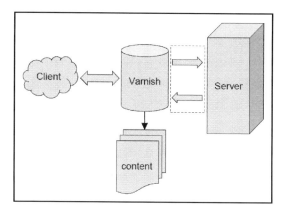

The requests come from various types of web clients. **Varnish** Cache passes the request to the **Server** the first time only and stores the received data from the **Server**. If a second request for the same information already in the **Varnish** Cache is made, then **Varnish** Cache will answer the request, leaving the **Server** free of such access.

The **Varnish** Cache can store a number of different types of information in memory, but it is critical and targets the transmitted data. If the information is not componentized, **Varnish** always let the request go to the **Server**; you will have no way of knowing if the request is the same type.

Throttling for your client

Microservices that are well designed are highly scalable, but it does mean having infinite resources. With cloud-computer-limited resources, it is very relative, but the cost to provide a service can become so high that it prevents the same.

Thinking about it, some steps can be taken to reduce the cost of consumption. One, as mentioned earlier, is the implementation of an efficient cache. However, that's not all; at times, throttling is necessary to block the high consumption of resources.

It is not feasible that a client of a microservice as a web page runs a very high number of requests for the microservice, or that the same page is not mature enough to handle data already received.

For this, simple throttling that keeps the reference of who consumes the information and the data transferred to the client is very effective for reducing the consumption of microservices.

Some throttling policies can be applied:

- Number of requests per minute from the same client
- Number of requests per second from the same client
- Number of requests per minute from the same client for similar information
- Number of requests per second for the same client for the same information

With these, it is possible to limit such potential blunders as inadequate data manipulation, irresponsible Ajax requests, and less sophisticated attack attempts.

Identifying anemic domains

Microservices that do not have a sufficiently mature business layer to solve their own tasks are examples of software built on an anemic domain.

The identification of an anemic domain can be done by making a few simple observations:

- The microservice cannot perform the tasks itself with only the data received
- The microservice needs to fetch data in more than one endpoint to perform a task
- The microservice does not have a self-sufficient entity model

- The microservice waits for the completion of a task in another microservice to follow up what you need to do
- The microservice needs to share resources with other external microservices; these resources can be cached to the sample database

If the microservice being developed is one of those items, then it can be a weak area. If a microservice has two or more characteristics of those listed, then it is definitely an anemic domain.

Anemic domains are very harmful to the microservices ecosystem, because they have a tendency to be multiplied in order to correct the technical debt generated by the deficiency in the composition of their respective domains.

Identifying the fat domains

In many cases, the microservices perform more tasks than they should. Apparently all is well and deployment is simplified, but in fact, the domain is fat. Microservices do not have that name because they are a small application, but because they have a small and simple business domain. When a microservice has limitations in certain fields, it means that the application was initially constructed on a small monolith.

Thinking about our application, the news portal, a good candidate for a microservice is users. It makes perfect sense to build a microservice administering user data. However, usually, in a monolithic application, the layer on the users has a strong connection with **AAA (Authentication, Authorization, and Accounting)**.

When it comes to microservice data, users, and AAA are an undesired coupling. This is mainly because the whole process of AAA is not restricted only to end users, but for clients such as mobile, frontend, and consumer APIs. In this case, the User microservice represents a fat domain.

The division of this fat domain can be held in two parts; the first part is `AAAService` and the second is `UserService`. Another approach is the AAA responsibility for a gateway API. The functional scalability and features of implementation with these separate domains is much more interesting for the growth of the product as a whole.

Understanding the size and limits of the domains is clearly critical to the growth and scalability of the final product.

Identifying microservice domains for the business

This is the time to understand the business domain that will be developed in the book. The domains are contained in our monolithic application. Let's recap how it is composed. Our monolithic Django is organized into three Django apps that are as follows:

- News
- Recommendations
- Users

It is important to understand that in this context, because of how Django is designed, Users and AAA are coupled, and we have seen that this is not good when it comes to microservices.

Another point is that news will not necessarily result in a single microservice; we can create microservices-varied news with the type of news. This would facilitate the targeting of APIs and scalability for each different type of news content. On our portal, we have sports, politics, and celebrity news. If a new theme is developed, a new News microservice will be created for this theme. This approach enables something like z-axis scalability for that part of the application.

At first, our domains will be divided into the following categories:

- SportNewsService
- PoliticsNewsService
- FamousNewsService
- RecomendationService
- UsersService
- AAAService (Optional)

Of course, new fields can be added and others can be removed; limiting the view of this microservice is our big target.

From domain to entity

Given the domains that we have in our application, it is time to define the entities. When we speak of entities microservices it is important to note that any transactional need among microservices can mean a design error.

A process asynchronous message by the broker can be used to sanitize the database, but that does not mean that there is a transaction. Trying to establish a type of transaction between microservices that are completely separated may be a big mistake.

Our old application had the following entities:

- News:
    - ID – `UniqueID`
    - Author – `FK user_id`
    - Title
    - Description
    - Content
    - Labels – News subjects
    - Type – New type (Sports, Famous, Politics)
    - `CreatedAt`
    - `UpdatedAt`
    - `PublishedAt`
- Recommendations:
    - `Label`
    - `user_id`
- Users:
    - ID
    - Name
    - Email

In addition to these entities, there is a range of tables that complement the user's information for the purpose of providing permissions and access permissions.

With the transformation of monolithic architecture for microservices architecture, the data model and design of these entities will also change.

First, we know that all the news segments will not be unique. This implies the removal of the *Type*:

- News Service:
    - ID
    - Author
    - Title
    - Description
    - Content
    - Labels
    - CreatedAt
    - UpdatedAt
    - PublishedAt

Another change is that users will no longer have the responsibility for authentication and authorization.

Summary

The goal of this chapter was to show you the basics of the development of a scalable microservice architecture, either from the point of view of the fields or from a strictly technical perspective.

We have addressed topics such as using Domain-Driven Design in microservices, *The Scale Cube*, the single-responsibility principle, and published interfaces in order to provide the minimum required theoretical knowledge, so you can apply it in a practical way in the upcoming chapters.

In the next chapter, we'll begin defining our stack using the concepts that we have already learned so far.

2
The Microservice Tools

Some issues are always questionable or controversial when it comes to choosing a microservice stack. Much is discussed regarding the performance, practicality, cost, and scalability. Most of what is discussed is background views; many of these are valid opinions and many others not so much.

Obviously, the history of the development team should be considered in any technical decisions regarding the stack and implementation. However, at times, it is necessary to leave some comfort zones behind to develop a product. A comfort zone can be a programming language, a protocol, a framework, or a database, and they can limit a developer's ability to move at speed. The developed application then becomes more and more scalable.

In this chapter, you will be working on points that should be examined for internal discussions and development teams. In the end, it is always important to understand that the development stack is not an amusement park; to develop the best product, we should always be considering the aspects of cost and scalability.

Some criticisms will be made throughout this chapter. None of these criticisms seek to depreciate or affirm the best technology to be applied. All analysis is performed here with the full focus on the end product of this book, which is a news portal using the microservice architecture.

In this chapter, we'll look at the following:

- Programming languages
- Microservices frameworks
- Binary communication
- Message broker

- Caching tools
- Fail alert tools
- Locale proof performance

Programming languages

Discussing programming languages is something that can be controversial, primarily because many developers tackle programming languages in a great hurry. However, programming languages should be seen as what they really are, a working tool. Every tool has a specific purpose and programming languages are no different.

It is just an analysis focused on our business, the news portal, which we will use to get to the point of how to select a language.

A big plus point for microservices is the heterogeneity of applications. In other words, it is not necessary to think of a single stack to apply to all business areas. We can thus define each microservice stack that applies, including when it comes to a programming language.

Basically, any programming language that meets the internet can be used in microservices. The difference is due to the requirements and domain boundaries that must be encoded. Some domain indicators can help us in this process.

If a microservice has strong mathematical processing load requirements, or where immutability of values is something positive, functional languages would be an interesting way to go. If there is a demand for processing large masses of data, then a compiled language with a robust virtual machine may be the answer.

Remember that missing this strategy could compromise the project deadline or even the entire application architecture. The fact is that several aspects should be analyzed before any definition, such as:

- Proficiency
- Performance
- Development practicality
- Ecosystem
- Scalability cost

Proficiency

The first goal for a software developer is to achieve proficiency in any programming language or paradigm. Achieving a good level of proficiency is not easy, and some languages may have a steeper learning curve than others.

Problems arise when proficiency in a language ends up creating a comfort zone from which a developer or team finds it difficult to leave. In contrast, a myth must be overthrown: that one programming language is much easier than the other. Obviously, a language may prove simpler than another at first, but in the end what will count is the practice time and the number of scenarios experienced by a developer with a programming language.

Another myth that must be fought is that all languages are equal at their core and that only the syntax changes. This is one of the worst possible errors that can be committed. Languages can be quite different in internal design and performance, although they have similar syntaxes.

Proficiency is something that should be considered when deciding which language to apply for a microservice. However, it should not be as decisive as this one.

Performance

This is a key requirement in choosing a programming language for a microservice. When we talk about performance for microservices, there are many points where performance can be a problem: the network communication layer, access to the database, where the servers are available. All these points can be problematic for microservices. The programming language cannot be another can of slowness.

When the target is microservice performance, no matter the skill of the development team, it should be used for best second language benchmarks and stress tests.

Something that often creates misunderstanding is considering the speed of a development team to implement a feature and performance requirement. Performance is related to a metric similar to how a code behaves when responding to a request or performing a task. Definitely, personal or team performance is not included in this metric.

Development of practicality

This is the requirement responsible for measuring the speed applied to a feature going into production. Development of practicality touches two teams: the development team that already exists and the development team that can come into existence.

As has been said before, the word *success* can be a problem for an application and consequently for the product owners. Keeping the base code simple and understandable is fundamental to facilitating code changes and for implementing new features.

Good programming practices can help us to understand the legacy code, but often the language itself, because the verbiage is not very friendly.

There are scenarios where a programming language, given its characteristics, is extremely performative. But the cost of time to implement something new, though it may be simple, can be very expensive.

Think of a scenario where a start-up has just launched its product. The product is also a **Minimum Viable Product** (**MVP**) and was launched in the market to go through public validation in general. If this MVP succeeds, it is essential to publish new features as quickly as possible. In this case, the performance is not the problem, but the practicality of new interactions on the code.

When we are developing microservices and we decide to use this programming language it is an important aspect to be noted.

Ecosystem

The ecosystem of a programming language is a crucial one.

We all know that parts of the frameworks are almost essential to gain speed and simplicity in the development of any application. With microservices, the scenario is identical.

It is feasible that features are not developed by something being blocked on the technical side. Of course, the microservices architecture is providing a plurality of very broad tool options. However, understanding the possible drawbacks when choosing a programming language, and therefore inheriting its ecosystem, is critical to the engineering team responsible for the implementation.

There are cases where a programming language is very performative, but the ecosystem that would win on development speed compromises performance. This type of situation is far more common than you think.

Another point is when a language is very simple, but the frameworks are not mature enough; you end up generating unnecessary complexity.

Observing the ecosystem of a programming language, and understanding the risks it is assumed we gain by inheritance, is fundamental to the adoption of a language.

Scalability cost

The cost of scaling an application is linked to two major factors. The first is the speed of the selected stack used to implement the software. Specifically, the speed and capacity of processing algorithms and answering requests. The second factor is the ability to scale the application of the business part. How long is it applied to features and especially the predictability of new features? The time to create something new or redesigning something that already exists is also expensive.

With microservices architecture, the cost of scalability is usually related to the concept of having smaller areas and parts which are less integrated. Even then this cost is very important.

Think of two applications, one with strong interactivity with the end user, such as an online game or editing documents in real time. Another application is fully illustrative, has an editorial part, but is not open to all users; a newspaper or streaming provider are good examples.

The application of real-time data processing and response time to requests must be fast and dynamic. In the second, application processing, it is not something that has much relevance, as the information may be in a cache or statically stored.

The cost will be high when you do not understand the nature of the microservice to be developed.

Making choices for our application

Because this is the point to choose a programming language for microservices and applications in general, we will apply this knowledge to select which programming language we use in each area of our service.

We know that our news portal has the following areas:

- SportNewsService
- PoliticsNewsService
- FamousNewsService
- RecommendationService
- UsersService

Given our fields of business, we can divide them by similarity of features. SportNewsService, PoliticsNewsService, and FamousNewsService have similar behavior. These microservices are news providers and are more focused on the consumption of data than receiving information.

These microservices may have an identical starting stack, which does not mean they should always be identical or that they need evolve in the same direction. Regarding the programming language, performance is not as crucial, but the speed of change and implementation of new features is crucial.

RecommendationService is very different from the other microservices. There is no direct interaction between the end user and the application. Nor is there a direct interaction between the editorial area and this software. RecommendationService is a support microservice; there are other microservices and all the interactions and operations are on the technical side. Loading and interaction occur completely asynchronously, but processing will certainly be higher than in other microservices. However, this is not a real-time application.

UserServices is a microservice with dynamic interaction on all sides, both for the end user as well as the editorial layer. The information from UserService may also be consumed by the other microservices such as RecommendationService. It is noteworthy that on this layer, caches can be dangerous, providing wrong information if they are not correctly invalidated. As UserService is a microservice that supports a direct relationship with the internet, it leads us to a programming language that has the speed of response for requests, processing speed, simplicity in implementing features, and good asynchrony APIs.

With the characteristics of each sector in mind, it is the time to think in a completely practical way to select a programming language that applies to each microservice. Let's consider each of the five aspects mentioned at the beginning of the chapter associated with the nature of the issues.

Comparing programming languages is complex, but in this case, we need to make choices. Many languages could be compared. However, for our application, we have chosen five for the comparison based on popularity, personal experience, documentation, and actual cases of applicability. The languages are Java, C#, Python, JavaScript, and Go.

Java

Java caters perfectly to the object-oriented paradigm. It is very performative, which reduces the cost of scalability. With the developments presented in the language, Java is not as verbose as before but still has a sharp verbiage, requiring developers to have the great proficiency to maintain the code and implement new features. Regarding the ecosystem, Java Virtual Machine is fantastic, mature, and very stable, but the frameworks are usually not as simple as they could be.

C#

Just like Java, C# perfectly meets the OOP paradigm. It is very performative, reducing the cost of scalability. C# has a similar verbiage to Java, with some additional practicalities. Proficiency with C# must also be high to generate speed in development. The ecosystem is very mature, with performers and not as complex frameworks.

Python

Python does not have the syntactic features of Java, C#, and OOP, but it caters well to the paradigm. As a fully interpreted language, it is not as performant as the other languages mentioned previously, which means more servers are required to support the same load that interpreted languages do not support. However, the higher cost of scalability is fully compensated when it comes to code maintenance and new features development, due to the simplicity of the language. A developer needs a fairly short amount of time to achieve proficiency in the language. The ecosystem is full of simple frameworks. Within the same ecosystem, there is a range of options for language interpreters, which helps in additional performance gains.

JavaScript

Undoubtedly, JavaScript is the language that generates less friction between the frontend and backend, as the backend JavaScript is optional, and the frontend is practically mandatory. It is a language with a good level of complexity. The developer needs to know the internal behavior of JavaScript well to not make bizarre mistakes. The paradigm that best applies to JavaScript is functional. The ecosystem has vast frameworks, too many in some cases, generating complexity especially regarding the builds. It has good performance, but it requires good proficiency to maintain the code and write new features.

Go

Go is a compiled programming language and has great performance. No doubt it is one of the languages that has seen growing popularity in recent years. Go is a language with the imperative paradigm, although very few developers understand that there is some level of OOP. The ecosystem's main characteristic is a standard robust library, making frameworks in some cases unnecessary. But the ecosystem is not perfect, with problems in simple things like version control. Go has simple and easily readable syntax. The main feature of the Go syntax is the convenience that it applies and how it handles concurrent programming.

To make it easier to compare, we will use the following chart as support:

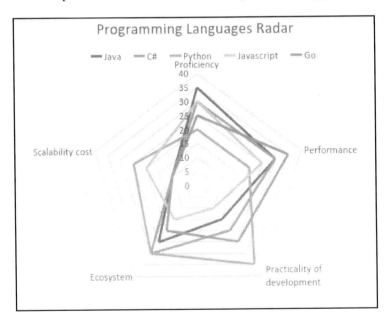

In the case of our news portal, these are the languages that will be applied:

- `SportNewsService`, `PoliticsNewsService`, and `FamousNewsService`: These microservices make use of Python. It is the typical scenario where language applies very well. The lower performance of Python will not be a problem even if the portal receives many hits.
- `RecommendationService`: This application also uses Python. This choice is fully related to a connection between performance and practicality in using other tools that will make the stack of our microservices. A microservice like this does not have the requirement of being real time; we can use something that has simplified APIs and is not as disruptive to the rest of the ecosystem.
- `UserService`: These microservices apply Go. `UserService` is a microservice that interacts with users as well as providing information to other application microservices.

The fact is that there is no perfect tool for everything. All languages have shown positive and negative points. With the great technological plurality that we can apply to the microservices architecture, managing the stack that best applies in each scenario is our role in this case.

Microservice frameworks

When dealing with frameworks, we have to think that because of the technological diversity of our frameworks, we will have at least three frameworks instead of one to keep our ecosystem.

Of course, we could have kept all microservices in the same stack. However, searching for the best overall performance for each domain, we opted for a more plural stack.

Obviously, at first, the impression is that the complexity will be higher than expected. But this type of complexity is matched by the performance most suitable for each case.

Basically, we chose three different programming languages to use on our news portal. Python, Go, and C# are those languages. It is time to think about which frameworks we will use for each of these languages, thus taking another step in shaping our development stack for each microservice.

Python

In the world of Python, there is a multitude of interesting frameworks; Bottle, Pyramid, Flask, Sanic, JaPronto, Tornado, and Twisted are some examples. The most famous that has more support from the community is Django.

Django is the same framework that was used to build our news portal in the monolithic version. It is a very good tool for full-stack applications and has, the main characteristic, and the simplicity to mount this type of software.

However, for microservices, I do not think it's the best framework for this purpose. Firstly, because the exposure of APIs is not native to Django. The ability to create an API with Django comes from a Django app called **Django Framework Rest**. In order to maintain the standard structure of the Django framework, the design of a simple API was a bit compromised. Django provides the developer with the entire development stack, which is not always what you want when developing microservices. A more simplistic and more flexible framework for compositions can be interesting.

In the Python ecosystem, there are other frameworks that work very well when it comes to APIs. Flask is a good example. An API, `Hello world`, is made in a very simple way.

Installing Flask with the command:

```
$ pip install flask
```

Writing the endpoint is very simple:

```
# file: app.py
# import de dependencies
from flask import Flask, jsonify
```

Instantiating the framework:

```
app = Flask(__name__)
```

Declaring the route:

```
@app.route('/')
def hello():
    #Prepare the json to return
    return jsonify({'hello': 'world'})
```

Executing the main app:

```
if __name__ == '__main__':
    app.run()
```

The preceding code is enough to return the message **hello world** in JSON format.

Other frameworks were inspired by Flask and worship the same simplicity and very similar syntax. A good example is Sanic.

Sanic can be installed with the command:

```
$ pip install sanic
```

The syntax is almost identical to Flask, as can be seen in the following code:

```
# file: app.py
```

Importing the dependencies:

```
from sanic import Sanic
from sanic.response import json
```

Instantiating the framework:

```
app = Sanic()
```

Declaring the route:

```
@app.route("/")
async def test(request):
    #Prepare the json to return
    return json({"hello": "world"})
```

Executing the main app:

```
if __name__ == "__main__":
    app.run(host="0.0.0.0", port=8000)
```

The big difference between Flask and Sanic is the performance. The performance of Sanic is much higher than Flask due to use of newer features in Python and the possibility of the exchange of the Sanic framework. However, Sanic is still not as mature and experienced in the market as Flask.

Another plus point for Flask is the integration with other tools like Swagger. Using the two together, our APIs would be not only written but also documented appropriately.

For microservices using Python as a programming language, performance is not the most important requirement, but practicality. Use this framework as Flask microservices.

Go

This is a totally different Python case. While most Python frameworks help with performance and try to provide the best possible environment for development, Go is not the same. Usually, frameworks with many features end up compromising the performance of the language.

Logs

When it comes to logs, they are virtually unanimous. You may refer to the `logrus` document (`https://github.com/Sirupsen/logrus`). It is a very mature and flexible logging library for Go, having hooks for different tools, ranging from the `syslog` to the InfluxDB for example.

The `logrus` has main features, that is, speed up on record logs and practicality of implementation.

Handlers

Creating routes to APIs in Go is very simple, but using native handlers' options can generate certain complexities, especially regarding the validations. The native muxer does not have a lot of flexibility, so the best option is to seek more productive tool handlers.

Go has a multitude of options for handlers, and perhaps the most explored library model because of the characteristic of writing the low-level language.

When it comes to performance for routers in Go, at the time of release of this book, there is nothing more performative than fasthttp: (`https://github.com/valyala/fasthttp`). This is a library written using Go that provides low-level language. Fasthttp metrics are outstanding.

Here are the numbers running tests locally to provision static files:

```
Running 10s test @ http://localhost:8080
  4 threads and 16 connections
  Thread Stats   Avg      Stdev     Max   +/- Stdev
    Latency   447.99us    1.59ms  27.20ms   94.79%
    Req/Sec    37.13k     3.99k   47.86k    76.00%
  1478457 requests in 10.02s, 1.03GB read
Requests/sec: 147597.06
Transfer/sec:    105.15MB
```

As it can be seen, the number of requests per second exceeds 140,000. However, writing the routes using fasthttp can be as complex as with the native library. Due to this problem, there are some frameworks that do interface for fasthttp. One of these interfaces is the fasthttprouter (`https://github.com/buaazp/fasthttprouter`), which ultimately creates a number of development facilities without overly compromising the good performance of fasthttp.

Writing routes with extreme performance is very seductive, but we need a balance between performance and stability; here we have a point needing attention. Fasthttp, as well as all its aid interfaces, modifies the native standard of the handler Go to implement the context itself. If there really is a big performance problem, using fasthttp may be something to think about. I do not think this is our case. Therefore, it is recommended to use something that has more compatibility with the standard Go interface.

The most famous option is **gorilla/mux** (`https://github.com/gorilla/mux`). Without a doubt, it is one of the most mature and experienced libraries for Go.

Middleware

For the composition of our middleware, use
Negroni (`https://github.com/urfave/negroni`). In addition to being a very mature tool, it has complete compatibility with the Mux Gorilla and the native API Go.

Tests

For unit testing, use the testify: (`https://github.com/stretchr/testify`). It is a simple library which accrues in both assertions and mocks. For functional testing, use the default Go library.

Package manager

If the Go ecosystem has a weak point, it is this. Go dependency management has always been something that requires a lot of attention.

If you do not know, the official repository of the Go dependencies is Git. Exactly, all Git, no matter if it's GitHub, Bitbucket, or any other. The problem is that when downloading a dependency using the Go command (`go get ...`), the version that will come to the application is always the one in the master repository. So there is no strict control of additions.

A package manager will use godep (`https://github.com/tools/godep`). This is a simple tool, which controls the versions used in the project guarding a JSON file with the repository URL and hash Git history.

Golang ORMs

A feature which is adopted by the Gophers, the name was given to developers using Go, is not using ORMs. Often the preference is to use only the communication driver in the database.

Often Gophers dispense the using of an ORM to adopt just a tool that helps to make more practical information from the database in a Go struct. A tool of this type of relational database is SQLX (`https://github.com/jmoiron/sqlx`).

SQLX does not work like ORM; it is only library to create a more friendly interface for native Go packages to communicate with the database/SQL.

If the chosen database application is to be NoSQL, it will hardly be adopting any data interpretation tools, as the most practical method is to use only the available driver.

Binary communication – direct communication between services

Much is discussed about microservices communication; topics such as protocols, layers, types, and package sizes are widely discussed when it comes to the subject.

The point is that communication between microservices is the most critical topic for project success. It is very clear that the amount of positive factors increases with microservices architecture, but how to make the communication that does not encumber the performance of a product to the end user is the key point.

It does not help that all the practicalities of developing and deploying the product do not scale or the end user experience is compromised.

There is a lot of literature and study material on the subject, but the challenge still remains. And oddly enough, even with all the available material, making mistakes in this part of the project is extremely easy.

There are only two forms of communication between microservices. These forms are synchronous and asynchronous. The most common is asynchronous communication between microservices, as it is easier to scale but it is harder to understand possible error points. Using synchronous forms of communication between microservices, it is easier to understand the possible errors in this area, but it is more difficult to scale. In this segment, we will deal with synchronous communication.

Understanding the aspect

The first step is to understand the functioning of the microservice to know what kind of communication best applies. Take, for example, the microservice recommendations. It is a microservice that has no direct communication with the customer, but traces a user's profile. No other application point expects an immediate response arising from this microservice. Thus, the communication model for this microservice is asynchronous.

Very well! We saw that `RecommendationService` is not a synchronous case; then what is?

The answer is `UserService`. When a user enters a given API that communicates with `UserService`, this user sees the change immediately. When a microservice requests some information on the requested `UserService`, we want the most current information possible and immediately. Yes, `UserService` is a service where synchronous communication can be applied.

But how can we create a good layer of synchronous communication between microservices? The answer is right in the next section.

Tools for synchronous communication

The most common form of direct communication between microservices is using the HTTP protocol with Rest and passing JavaScript Object Notation, the famous JSON. Communication works great for APIs, providing endpoints for external consumption. However, communication using HTTP with JSON has a high cost in relation to performance.

First, this is because in the case of communication between microservices, it would be more appropriate to optimize than the HTTP protocol creating some sort of pipeline or keeping the connection alive. The problem is the control of the connection timeout, which shouldn't be very strict, and in addition could start to close doors, threads, or processes with a simple silent error. The second problem with this approach is the serialization time of JSON sent. Normally this is not an inexpensive process. Finally, we have the packet size sent to the HTTP protocol. In addition to JSON, there are a number of HTTP headers that should be interpreted further which may be discarded. Look closer; there's no need to elaborate on protocols between microservices, the only concern should be to maintain a single layer for sending and receiving messages. Therefore, the HTTP protocol with JSON to communicate between microservices can be a serious slow point within the project and, despite the practicality of implementation of the protocol, the optimization is complex to understand yet not very significant.

Many would propose the implementation of communication sockets or WebSockets but, in the end, the customization process of these communication layers is very similar to the classic HTTP.

Synchronous communication layers between microservices must complete three basic tasks:

- Report practice and direct the desired messages
- Send simple, lightweight packages and fast serialization
- Be practical to maintain the signature of communication endpoints

A proposal that meets the aforementioned requirements communicates using binary or small-size packages.

Something important to point out when it comes to working with this type of protocol is that, usually, they are incompatible with each other. This means that the option chosen as the tool for serialization and submission of these small-sized packages should be compatible with the stack of all microservices.

Some of the most popular options on the market are:

- MessagePack (http://msgpack.org/)
- gRPC (https://grpc.io/)
- Apache Avro (https://avro.apache.org/)
- Apache Thrift (https://thrift.apache.org/)

Let us understand how each of these options works to see what best fits on our news portal.

MessagePack

The MessagePack or MsgPack is a type of serializer for binary information, but, as the official tool's own website says, *"It's like JSON, but fast and small."*

The proposed MsgPack is serializing data quickly and with reduced size, thus offering a more efficient package for communication between microservices. At first, the MsgPack was not more efficient than the other serializers, but this problem has been overcome with this change.

When it comes to compatibility between the programming languages, MsgPack is very good; it just has a library of the most well-known languages of the market. The offer goes from Python libraries to Racket, for example.

The MsgPack does not have a native tool in the shipping package; it is left to the developer. This can be a problem because a layer of communication between microservices that supports multilingual stacks still needs to be found.

gRPC

The gRPC has a more complete proposal than MsgPack because it is composed of the data serializer Protobuf, as a layer between communication services making use of RPC.

For serialization, create a .proto file with the information about what will be serialized for RPC communication following a client/server model if needed.

The following code can be seen as an example of a .protocol file, that was extracted from the official site tool:

The greeting service definition:

```
service Greeter {
```

Sends a greeting:

```
    rpc SayHello (HelloRequest) returns (HelloReply) {}
}
```

The request message containing the user's name:

```
        message HelloRequest {
            string name = 1;
        }
```

The response message containing the greetings:

```
        message HelloReply {
            string message = 1;
        }
```

The file `.proto` has a specific form of writing. The positive aspect of a file like this is that the signing of the communication layer is normalized because, at some level, the file created as the serialization template and creating clients/servers ends up serving as the documentation of endpoints.

After the file is created, to create the communication part you need only run a command line. The following example creates the client/server in Python:

```
    $ python -m grpc_tools.protoc -I../../protos --python_out=. --
grpc_python_out=. ../../protos/file_name.proto
```

The command may seem a little intimidating at first but is enough to generate a client and server RPC of communication. The gRPC has evolved a lot and received strong investment.

With regards to the compatibility, gRPC does not meet the same requirements that MsgPack does, but has compatibility with the most commonly used languages in the market.

Apache Avro

Avro is one of the most mature and experienced serialization systems for binary. As with gRPC, Avro also has a communication layer using RPC.

Avro uses a .avsc file, which is defined in JSON format, for the serialization process. The file may be composed of both types that provide JSON, or more complex types from Avro itself.

Even being very mature as a tool, Avro is the poorest in terms of native compatibility with other programming languages other than Java, Ruby, C++, C#, and Python. As the project is open source, there is a whole range of drivers that provide compatibility with Avro that come from the community.

Apache Thrift

Thrift is a project created by Facebook and maintained by the Apache Software Foundation. It has a good level of compatibility with the languages most commonly used in the market of programming.

Thrift has the communication layer with RPC and a part of serialization using a file .thrift as a template. The file .thrift has notation and types similar to the C++ language in which Thrift was developed.

An example of file .thrift can be viewed in the following:

```
typedef i32 MyInteger

const i32 INT32CONSTANT = 9853
const map<string,string> MAPCONSTANT = {'hello':'world',
       'goodnight':'moon'}

enum Operation {
   ADD = 1,
   SUBTRACT = 2,
   MULTIPLY = 3,
   DIVIDE = 4
}

struct Work {
   1: i32 num1 = 0,
   2: i32 num2,
   3: Operation op,
   4: optional string comment,
}

exception InvalidOperation {
   1: i32 whatOp,
   2: string why
}
```

```
service Calculator extends shared.SharedService {
  void ping(),
  i32 add(1:i32 num1, 2:i32 num2),
  i32 calculate(1:i32 logid, 2:Work w) throws
      (1:InvalidOperation ouch),
  oneway void zip()
}
```

Do not worry about the file contents. The important thing is realizing the flexibility that is offered by the RPC Thrift composition. An interesting point to note is the following line of code:

```
service Calculator extends shared.SharedService { ...
```

Thrift allows the use of inheritance among the template files, which will be used by code generators.

To create the client/server using Thrift, simply use the following command line:

```
$ thrift -r --gen py file_name.thrift
```

The preceding line will create a client and server in the Python programming language.

Among the options presented, the most common at the moment are Thrift and gRPC, and any one of these tools is a good deployment option for direct communication between microservices.

Direct communication alerts

Direct communication between microservices may result in a problem known as **Death Star**. The Death Star is an anti-pattern where there is communication between the recursion microservices, and making progress becomes extremely complicated or expensive for a product.

With the communication tools we saw previously, it is very easy to establish conversations between microservices with low latency. The common anti-pattern is to allow microservices to exchange messages with each other freely, if they have no information to process a specific task.

This is where we have an alert. If a microservice always needs to communicate with another to complete a task, it is a high coupling signal and we have failed in our DDD process. This engagement results in a Death Star. For clarity, consider the following scenario.

Imagine that we have four microservices. The microservices are A, B, C, and D. A request was made asking for information about A, but it does not have all the information content. This content is in B and C, but C does not have all of the information, so it asks D. B is not able to complete the task assigned to him and asks for data from C. However, D needs the data in A. The following is a diagrammatic representation of this process:

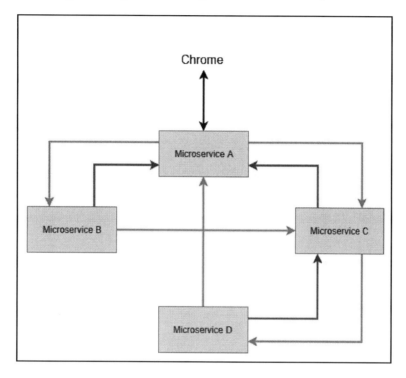

In the end, a simple request generates a very complex flow, where any failure is difficult to monitor. Apparently, it may seem natural, but over time and with the creation of new microservices, it makes this ecosystem unsustainable.

The microservices must be sufficiently well defined in their respective responsibilities for this type of messaging to be minimized.

No matter how fast the communication and serialization information is, if the product is not humanly intelligible and understandable, it will be very difficult to maintain the ecosystem of microservices, especially with regards to error control.

Message broker – Async communication between services

In the previous topic, we talked about synchronous communication between microservices using binary and alternatives to REST. This topic will deal with the communication between microservices using message broker, that is, a messaging system with a physical element, a communication layer, and a message bus.

With messaging systems, it is impossible to reproduce the Death Star. The design of the Death Star in a more robust application would be something like the following:

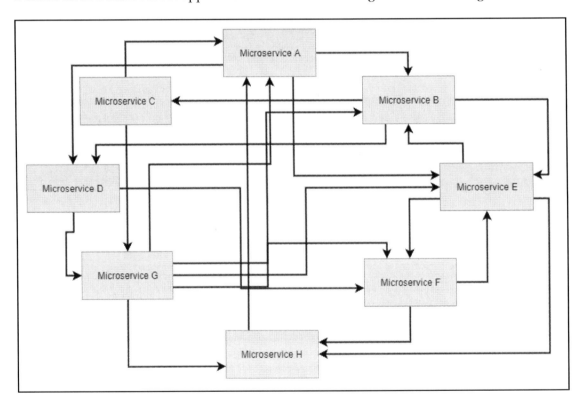

The diagram of a messaging system is totally different, similar to the one shown in the following:

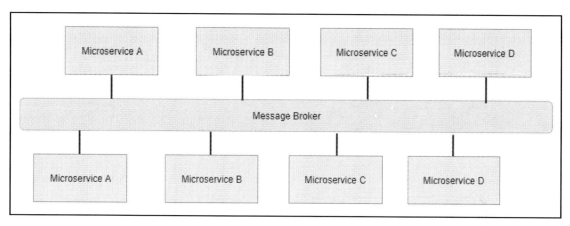

The message bus can be used for both synchronous and asynchronous communication, but certainly, the major point of emphasis of the message bus is in asynchronous communication.

You may wonder, if the messaging diagram is simpler and you can use this type of tool for synchronous communication, why not use this messaging for all types of communication between microservices?

The answer to this question is quite simple. A message bus is a physical component within the stack of microservices. It needs to be scaled just like any other physical component-based data storage and cache. This means that with a high-volume message, the synchronous mode of communication could be committed to an unwanted delay in the responses of the processes.

It is critical to the engineering team to understand where to correctly apply each tool without compromising the stack because of an apparent ease.

Within the various message brokers, there are some that stand out more, such as:

- ActiveMQ
- RabbitMQ
- Kafka

Let us understand the functioning of each of them a little better.

ActiveMQ

ActiveMQ is extremely traditional and very experienced. For years it was like the standard message bus in the Java world. There is no doubting the maturity and robustness of ActiveMQ.

It supports the programming languages used in the market. The ActiveMQ problem is related to the most common communication protocol, STOMP. Most mature libraries use ActiveMQ STOMP, which is not one of the models of sending more message performers. The ActiveMQ has been working on OpenWire for a solution in place of STOMP, but so far it is only available for Java, C, C++, and C#.

The ActiveMQ is very easy to implement, has been undergoing constant evolution, and has good documentation. If our application, the news portal, was developed on the Java platform, or any other that supports OpenWire, ActiveMQ is a case to be considered carefully.

RabbitMQ

RabbitMQ uses AMQP, by default, as the communication protocol, which makes this a very performative tool for the delivery of messages. RabbitMQ documentation is incredible and has native support for the languages most used in the market programming.

Among the many message brokers, RabbitMQ stands out because of its practicality of implementation, flexibility to be coupled with other tools, and its simple and intuitive API.

The following code shows how simple it is to create a system of `Hello World` in Python with RabbitMQ:

```python
# import the tool communicate with RabbitMQ
import pika
# create the connection
connection = pika.BlockingConnection(
  pika.ConnectionParameters(host='localhost'))
# get a channel from RabbitMQ
channel = connection.channel()
# declare the queue
channel.queue_declare(queue='hello')
# publish the message
channel.basic_publish(exchange='',
                routing_key='hello',
                body='Hello World!')
print(" [x] Sent 'Hello World!'")
```

```
# close the connection
connection.close()
```

With the preceding example, we took the official RabbitMQ site, we are responsible for sending the message `Hello World` queue for the `hello`. The following is the code that gets the message:

```
# import the tool communicate with RabbitMQ
import pika
# create the connection
connection = pika.BlockingConnection(
pika.ConnectionParameters(host='localhost'))

# get a channel from RabbitMQ
channel = connection.channel()

# declare the queue
channel.queue_declare(queue='hello')
# create a method where we'll work with the message received
def callback(ch, method, properties, body):
  print(" [x] Received %r" % body)

# consume the message from the queue passing to the method
      created above
channel.basic_consume(callback,
                      queue='hello',
                      no_ack=True)

print(' [*] Waiting for messages. To exit press CTRL+C')

# keep alive the consumer until interrupt the process
channel.start_consuming()
```

The code is very simple and readable. Another feature of RabbitMQ is the practical tool for scalability. There are performance tests that indicate the ability of RabbitMQ in supporting 20,000 messages per second for each node.

Kafka

Kafka is not the simplest message broker on the market, especially with regards to the understanding of its inner workings. However, it is by far the most scalable and is message broker performative for the delivery of messages.

In the past, unlike ActiveMQ and RabbitMQ, Kafka was not sending transactional messages, which could be a problem in applications where losing any kind of information was a high cost. But in the most recent versions of Kafka this problem has been solved, and currently, there are transactional shipping options.

In Kafka, the numbers are really impressive. Some benchmarks indicate that Kafka supports, without difficulty, over 100,000 messages per second for each node.

Another strong point of Kafka is the ability to integrate with various other tools like Apache Spark. Kafka has good documentation. However, Kafka does not have a wide range of supported programming languages.

For cases where performance needs to reach high levels, Kafka is more than a suitable option.

 For our news portal, we adopt RabbitMQ due to compatibility and the good performance that the tool has, compatible with the current situation of our application.

Caching tools

For microservices and modern web applications, the cache is not the only tool that exempts the database. It is a matter of strategy. Something that can be widely used to make the application much more performative than it would be without caches. But choosing well and setting the cache layer are crucial to success.

There are cache strategies consisting of using the cache as a loading point for the database. Observe the following diagram:

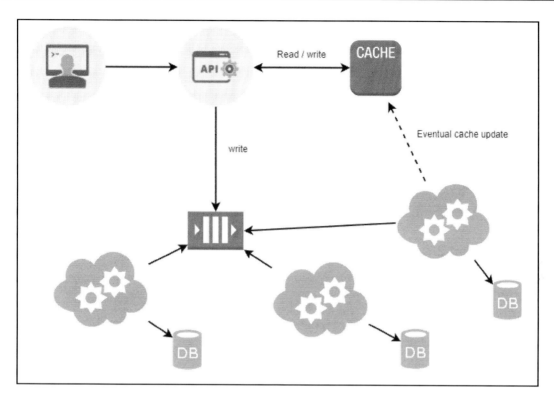

In the preceding diagram, we see that the requests arrive for our API, but are not directly processed and sent to the database. All valid requests are cached and simultaneously put in a row.

Consumers read the queue and process the information. Only after processing the information is the data stored in the database. Eventually, it is rewritten in the cache for data updates that are being consolidated in the database. With this strategy, any information requested by the API will be placed directly in the cache before it passes through the database, so that the database has the time required for processing.

For the end user, 200 is the HTTP response that is sent as soon as the data is stored in the cache, and not only after the registration of the information in the database, but also as this process occurs in an asynchronous way.

To have the possibility of this kind of strategy, we have to analyze the tools we have available. The best known on the market are:

- Memcached
- Redis

Let's look at the features of each.

Memcached

When it comes to Memcached, caching is one of the most known and mature markets. It has a key scheme/value storage for very efficient memory.

For the classic process of using cache, Memcached is simple and practical to use. The performance of Memcached is fully linked to the use of memory. If Memcached uses the disc to register any data, the performance is seriously compromised; moreover, Memcached does not have any record of disk capacity and always depends on third-party tools for this.

Redis

Redis can be practically considered as a new standard for the market when it comes to cache. Redis is effectively a database key/value, but because of stupendous performance, it has ended up being adopted as a caching tool.

The Redis documentation is very good and easy to understand; even a simple concept is equipped with many features such as pub/sub and queues.

Because of its convenience, flexibility, and internal working model, Redis has practically relegated all other caching systems to the condition of the legacy project.

Control of the Redis memory usage is very powerful. Most cache systems are very efficient to write and read data from memory, but not to purge the data and return memory to use. Redis again stands out in this respect, having good performance to return memory for use after purging data.

Unlike Memcached, Redis has native and extremely configurable persistence. Redis has two types of storage form, which are RDB and AOF.

The RDB model makes data persistent by using snapshots. This means that, within a configurable period of time, the information in memory is persisted on disk. The following is an example of a Redis configuration file using the RDB model of persistence:

```
save 60 1000
stop-writes-on-bgsave-error no
rdbcompression yes
dbfilename dump.rdb
```

The settings are simple and intuitive. First, we have to save the configuration itself:

```
save 60 1000
```

The preceding line indicates that Redis should do the snapshot to persist the data home for 60 seconds, if at least 1,000 keys are changed. Changing the line to something like:

```
save 900 1
```

Is the same as saying to Redis persist a snapshot every 15 minutes, if at least one key is modified.

The second line of our sample configuration is as follows:

```
stop-writes-on-bgsave-error no
```

It is telling Redis, even in case of error, to move on with the process and persistence attempts. The default value of this setting is yes, but if the development team decided to monitor the persistence of Redis the best option is no.

Usually, Redis compresses the data to be persisted to save disk usage; this setting is:

```
rdbcompression yes
```

But if the performance is critical, with respect to the cache, this value can be modified to no. But the amount of disk consumed by Redis will be much higher.

Finally, we have the filename which will be persisted data by Redis:

```
dbfilename dump.rdb
```

This name is the default name in the configuration file but can be modified without major concerns.

The other model is the persistence of AOF. This model is safer with respect to keeping the recorded data. However, there is a higher cost performance for Redis. Under a configuration template for AOF:

```
appendonly no
appendfsync everysec
```

The first line of this example presents the command appendonly. This command indicates whether the AOF persistence mode must be active or not.

In the second line of the sample configuration we have:

```
appendfsync everysec
```

The policy `appendfsync` active fsync tells the operating system to perform persistence in the fastest possible disk and not to buffer. The `appendfsync` has three configuration modes— `no`, `everysec`, and `always`, as shown in the following:

- **no**: Disables `appendfsync`
- **everysec**: This indicates that the storage of data should be performed as quickly as possible; usually this process is delayed by one second
- **always**: This indicates an even faster persistence process, preferably immediately

You may be wondering why we are seeing this part of Redis persistence. The motivation is simple; we must know exactly what power we gain from the persistent cache and how we can apply it.

Some development teams are also using Redis as a message broker. The tool is very fast in this way, but definitely not the most appropriate for this task, due to the fact that there are no transactions in the delivery of messages. With so many, messages between microservices could be lost. The situation where Redis expertly performs its function is as a cache.

Fail alert tools

Just as we prepare our product to be successful, we must also prepare for failures. There is nothing worse in microservices than silent errors. Receiving faulty alerts as soon as possible is critical, which is considered to be a healthy microservices ecosystem.

There are at least four major points of failure when it comes to microservices. If these points are covered, we can say that about 70% of the application is safe. These points are as follows:

- Performance
- Build
- Components
- Implementation failures

Let's understand what each of these risk points are and how we can receive failure alerts as soon as possible.

Performance

Let's look a little further at some very interesting tools to prove the performance of our endpoints. Local test endpoints help to anticipate performance issues that we would only see in production.

After sending the microservices to the production environment, some tools can be used to monitor the implementation of the performance as a whole. There are both free, as well as paid tools, and some very effective tools like New Relic and Datadog. Both are very simple to implement and have a dashboard rich in information:

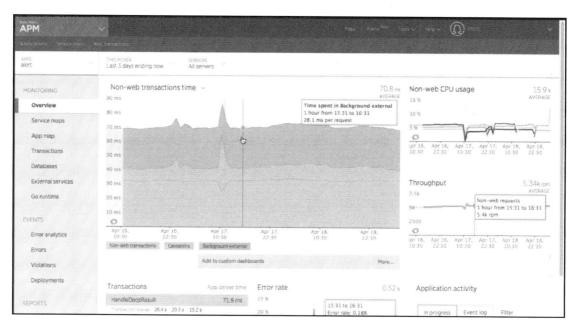

The following screenshot represents the interface of **DATADOG**:

Obviously, there are options for performance monitoring that are totally free, as we have the traditional Graphite with Grafana and Prometheus. The free options require more settings than those mentioned previously to provide similar results.

From the free options, Prometheus deserves a special mention because of its wealth of information and practical implementation. Along with Graphite, Prometheus also integrates with Grafana for displaying graphics performance. The following screenshot represents the use of Prometheus:

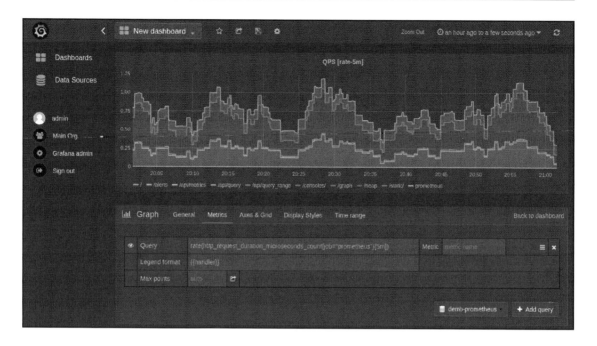

Build

This is a very important point because this is the last step in which a failure can be located without affecting the end user. One of the pillars of microservices architecture is processing automation. To build and deploy is no different.

The time to build is usually the last stage before moving the application to a particular environment, a quality environment, or stage production.

In microservices, all must have high coverage for unit testing, functional testing, and integration testing. It seems obvious to say, but many development teams do not end up paying too much attention to automated testing and suffer for it later.

To automate the application build process, and consequently, the application deployment, is fundamentally a good continuous integration tool or CI. In this respect, one of the most mature, complete, and efficient tools is Jenkins. Jenkins is a free and open source project. It is extremely configurable, being able to fully automate processes.

There are other options like Travis. Travis works online with a CI and is completely free for open source projects. Something interesting in Travis, is the great compatibility that it has with GitHub.

The most important factor of working with a CI is properly setting up the application testing process, because, as has been said before, this is the last stage to capture failures before affecting the end user of our product. The CI is the best place for the integration of microservices tests.

Components

The strong characteristic of microservices architecture is the large number of components that can fail. Containers, databases, caches, and message brokers serve as examples of failure points.

Imagine the scenario where the application begins to fail, simply because the hard drive of a database is faulty in some physical component. The time of action in applications where there is no monitoring for this type of problem is usually high because normally the application and the development and support teams always start investigating failures on the software side. Only after confirming that the fault is not in the software do teams seek problems in physical components.

There are tools like pens-sentinel to provide more resilience to the pens, but not all the physical components have that kind of support.

A simple solution is to create a health check endpoint within each microservice. This endpoint is not only responsible for validating the microservice instance, whether it is running, but also all the components that the microservice is connected to. Tools like Nagios and Zabbix are also very useful for making aid work to health check endpoints.

Implementation gaps

In some cases, automated tests may not have been well written and do not cover all cases, or some external component, such as an API vendor, starts throwing errors in the application.

Often these errors are silent, and we only realize after a user reports the error. But questions remain as to how many users have experienced this error and not reported it. What value loss level mistake did the product have?

These questions have no answers and are almost impossible to quantify. To capture this kind of problem as quickly as possible all the time, we need to monitor the internal failures of the application.

For this type of monitoring, there are a number of tools, but the more prominent is Sentry. Sentry has very interesting features:

- See the impact of new deployments in real time
- Provide support to specific users interrupted by an error
- Detect and thwart fraud as it's attempted: unusual amounts of failures on purchases, authentication, and other critical areas
- External integrations

Sentry has a cost and unfortunately, there is no free option that is effective.

With the four fault points covered by warning systems, we are safe to continue with our development and put into production our microservices with the automated and continuous process.

The databases

The programming with languages and development frameworks, this type of database is not good enough to cover all the uses of application scenarios.

To choose to use a database is necessary to assess the functioning and microservice operation mode in question. There are situations where the relational database makes sense, at other times one NoSQL can be better, and there are, of course, situations where none of these databases are sufficient and we need to use the database using graphs. This is exactly the situation in our news portal.

It would be very simple to say that SQL is sufficient for all, but it definitely is not. Think of our microservices to see what kind of database is best for each. The following application has these areas:

- `SportNewsService`
- `PoliticsNewsService`
- `FamousNewsService`
- `RecommendationService`
- `UsersService`

For microservices that directly show news, if you think about it, there is a direct relationship system. The purpose of these microservices is to simply and quickly bring out the news theme by batch. This behavior is very close to NoSQL, where the relational structure is weak and the speed of basic operations such as searches are faster.

For services and the features previously mentioned, use one database NoSQL, which in this case will be the MongoDB. This choice includes good documentation, and performance benchmarks of implementation simplicity and cost.

`UsersService` is totally different. A user's credentials for an application is only a login and a password, but there is other data that is related to this login and password. This will be the case for any possible registration data or default preference. So, we have information-relevant relationships in this area, but the best option is to use a conventional SQL.

The `UsersService` can use a database such as MariaDB, MySQL, Oracle, SQL Server, or PostgreSQL, for example. In the case of our application, use PostgreSQL due to compatibility features, maturity, and compatibility with the rest of the stack already selected.

There is another microservice with an entirely different function from the previous microservices. The `RecommendationService` should establish the relationship between preferences and users, but not only that. You should also be able to provide what or how many users are interested in the same topic. You can create this type of relationship with a conventional SQL database. However, over time, increasingly complex queries will emerge, and possibly a microservices understanding of speed, as well as maintenance, can be compromised by a bad choice in the stack of conception.

For `RecommendationService`, a good option is to adopt the database Neo4J. The quality of work with graphs and simplicity of the tool is exactly what we are looking for in this microservice.

The big target when it comes to the database, is again, understanding how the fields behave and not putting in any comfort zones at the time of choice. The most important thing is always to choose the best tool for each case.

Locale proof performance

One of the worst situations that can occur when we are working with microservices architecture is to put a code in production and see that the performance is poor. The work to bring the code back to the development environment, knowing that production in the project is compromised and the users are going through a bad experience, when it is something that could have been analyzed on the technical side, is extremely frustrating.

The problem now in production could have been predicted, and even solved in the development environment. To register this type of metric, there are many tools that can prove performance in the local environment.

Obviously, the local behavior will not perfectly reflect the production environment. There are many factors to be considered such as network latency, the machine where it was held for deployment and production, and communication with external tools. However, we can take local metrics to highlight a new algorithm or functionality that has compromised the overall performance of the application.

For local application metrics, there are some tools:

- Apache Benchmark
- WRK
- Locust

Each tool has specific features, but all serve the same purpose which is to get metrics about the endpoints.

Apache Benchmark

Apache Benchmark is better known as **AB**, and that's what we'll call it.

AB runs from the command line and is very useful to prove the speed and response of endpoints.

Running a local performance test is very simple, as can be seen in the following example:

```
$ ab -c 100 -n 10000 http://localhost:5000/
```

The preceding command line invokes AB to run 10,000 requests (-n 10000), simulating 100 concurrent users (-c 100), and calling the local route in door 5,000 (http:// localhost: 5000/). The displayed result will be something like the following screenshot:

```
Server Software:        Werkzeug/0.12.2
Server Hostname:        localhost
Server Port:            5000

Document Path:          /
Document Length:        11 bytes

Concurrency Level:      100
Time taken for tests:   2.247 seconds
Complete requests:      1000
Failed requests:        0
Total transferred:      165000 bytes
HTML transferred:       11000 bytes
Requests per second:    444.99 [#/sec] (mean)
Time per request:       224.722 [ms] (mean)
Time per request:       2.247 [ms] (mean, across all concurrent requests)
Transfer rate:          71.70 [Kbytes/sec] received

Connection Times (ms)
              min  mean[+/-sd] median   max
Connect:        0    0    0.1      0       1
Processing:    59  210   37.5    221     231
Waiting:       53  210   38.2    221     231
Total:         59  210   37.5    221     232
```

The result shows the server that performed the processing (Werzeug / 0.12.2), the hostname (localhost), the port (5000), and another set of information.

The most important data generated by AB is:

- Request per second: 444.99
- Time per request: 224.722 ms (mean)
- Time per request: 2.247 ms (mean, across all concurrent requests)

These three pieces of information at the end of the test process indicate the local application performance. As we can see in this case, the application used in this test returns 444.99 requests per second when you have 100 concurrent users and 10,000 charging requests.

Obviously, this is the most simple test scenario that can be done with AB. The tool has a number of other features, such as exporting graphics performance tests performed, and simulating all the verbs that the REST API can run on HTTPS certificates and simulate. These are only a few other attributes that AB offers as a resource.

WRK

Similar to AB, the WRK is also a tool executed by the command line and serves the same purpose as the AB. The following screenshot represents the WRK tool:

---

wrk - a HTTP benchmarking tool

wrk is a modern HTTP benchmarking tool capable of generating significant load when run on a single multi-core CPU. It combines a multithreaded design with scalable event notification systems such as epoll and kqueue.

An optional LuaJIT script can perform HTTP request generation, response processing, and custom reporting. Details are available in SCRIPTING and several examples are located in scripts/.

Basic Usage

```
wrk -t12 -c400 -d30s http://127.0.0.1:8080/index.html
```

This runs a benchmark for 30 seconds, using 12 threads, and keeping 400 HTTP connections open.

Output:

```
Running 30s test @ http://127.0.0.1:8080/index.html
  12 threads and 400 connections
  Thread Stats   Avg      Stdev     Max   +/- Stdev
    Latency   635.91us    0.89ms  12.92ms   93.69%
    Req/Sec    56.20k     8.07k   62.00k    86.54%
  22464657 requests in 30.00s, 17.76GB read
Requests/sec: 748868.53
Transfer/sec:    606.33MB
```

To run WRK is also very simple. Just use the following command:

```
$ wrk -c 100 -d 10 -t 4 http://localhost:5000/
```

However, WRK has some different characteristics compared to AB. The preceding command means that WRK will run a performance test for ten seconds (**d 10**), with 100 concurrent users (**c 100**), and will request four threads from the operating system for this task (**-t 4**).

Quickly observing the command line, it can be perceived that there is no limitation or requests load statement to be executed; WRK does not work that way. The WRK test proposed is to perform load stress for a period of time.

Ten seconds after executing the command line that is a little higher, WRK will return the information, shown in the following screenshot:

```
Running 10s test @ http://localhost:5000/
  4 threads and 100 connections
  Thread Stats   Avg      Stdev     Max   +/- Stdev
    Latency   268.68ms   73.98ms 678.53ms   89.14%
    Req/Sec    92.41     25.42   141.00     69.17%
  3688 requests in 10.09s, 594.26KB read
Requests/sec:    365.55
Transfer/sec:     58.90KB
```

Clearly, the returned data is more concise. But suffice to know that the behavior before a temporal change is made to our application.

Again, it is good to point out the local test feature and not necessarily the result of WRK is evidence that reflects the reality of an application in production. However, WRK offers good numbers to have a metric of application.

From the data generated by WRK, we can see that after the 10 seconds test with a 100 concurrent users and using four threads, our application in the local environment has the following numbers:

- Requests/sec: 365.55
- 268.68ms latency (mean)

The WRK figures are somewhat lower than those provided by AB; this is clearly the result of the test performed by each type of tool.

WRK is very flexible for running tests, including accepting the use of scripts in the Lua programming language to perform some specific tasks.

WRK is one of my favorite tools for local performance tests. The type of test performed by WRK is very close to reality and offers numbers very close to actual results.

Locust

Out of the tools listed as an example for local metrics APIs, Locust has only one visual interface. Another interesting feature is the possibility to prove to multiple endpoints simultaneously.

The Locust's interface is very simple and easy to understand. You can tell how many concurrent users will soon be used in the interface data input. After the start of the process with Locust, the iron fist begins to show the GUI HTTP verb used, the path where the request was directed, the number of requests made during the test, and a series number for the metrics collected from multiple websites.

The GUI can be seen in detail in the following screenshot:

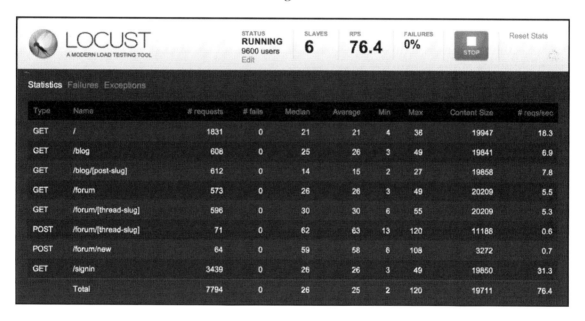

Using the Locust is very simple. The first step is the installation. Unlike AB and WRK, the installation of Locust is done through `pypi`, the Python installation package. Use the following command:

```
$ pip install locustio
```

After installation, you must create a configuration file called `locustfile.py` with the following contents:

```
# import all necessary modules to run the Locust:
 from locust import HttpLocust, TaskSet, task

    # create a class with TaskSet as inheritance
    class WebsiteTasks(TaskSet):
    # Create all the tasks that will be metrify using the @taks decorator
    @task
    # the name function will be the endpoint name in the Locust
    def index(self):
        # set to the client the application path with the HTTP
          verb        # in this case "get"
        self.client.get("/")
        @task
        def about(self):
           self.client.get("/about/")

    # create a class setting the main task end the time wait for each
 request
        class WebsiteUser(HttpLocust):
         task_set = WebsiteTasks
         min_wait = 5000
         max_wait = 15000
```

After the configuration file is created, it is time to run Locust. To do this, it is necessary to use the following command line:

```
$ locust -f locustfile.py
```

Locust will provide a URL to access the visual interface. Then the metrics can be verified.

Initially, Locust's configuration may seem more complex than the other applications shown in this section. However, after the initial process, the course of the test is very simple. As in AB and WRK, Locust has many features for deeper testing.

Summary

In this chapter, we learned the importance of making choices about the microservices stack. At first, it may seem very complex to make this kind of decision, but if we have in mind the definitions of the areas we want to develop, this process loses complexity.

We have seen that programming language, frameworks, and databases have defined purposes and we should never disregard this fact. A simple illustration is: trains are not made to fly. This does not mean that any tool is acceptable for any given purpose; it is simply not appropriate for a task for which it was not designed.

We have also seen the importance of caches, established how quick and agile communication between microservices occurs, and the importance of fault alerts in several layers of our microservices.

Finally, we know some tools that help us to prove the performance of microservices still in the local environment.

Armed with the knowledge acquired in this chapter, we are able to move on to the next, and to create our microservices effectively.

In Chapter 3, *Internal Patterns*, we'll start to code our first microservice.

3
Internal Patterns

In the first two chapters, we obtained a range of substantial information. We covered concepts such as the **Domain-Driven Design (DDD)**, caching, and database among other items essential to the development of efficient and scalable microservices. In this chapter, we need to cover more theoretical content, especially when it comes to patterns for the development of microservices.

Now, let's look at patterns, anti-patterns, tools, and code structure options for microservices. In this chapter, we will work on the applicability of caches, queues, asynchrony, and workers. The time has come to start writing our application and to put the theory to practice. Let's take up one of our microservices and apply the knowledge acquired so far to it. By the end of this chapter, you will know the two patterns that are extremely useful for microservices—CQRS and event sourcing.

In this chapter, we'll look at the following:

- Developing the structure
- Caching strategies
- CQRS – query strategy
- Event sourcing – data integrity

Developing the structure

In the previous chapters, we defined our domains, which are as follows:

- `SportNewsService`
- `PoliticsNewsService`

- FamousNewsService
- RecomendationService
- UsersService

The first step is to choose a domain to apply our techniques. To do this, we will use the UsersService. This domain is quite interesting because it has unique characteristics and is an excellent case to apply the techniques learned here.

Let's gather the tools that we will use for the composition of UsersService. At first, we will use only one database table, but we know that the rest will be created.

Database

Our database is a PostgreSQL and the structure of the first table is extremely simple, as seen in the following screenshot:

```
                                     Table "public.users"
 Column   |  Type   |                      Modifiers                       | Storage  | Stats target | Description
----------+---------+------------------------------------------------------+----------+--------------+-------------
 id       | integer | not null default nextval('users_id_seq'::regclass)   | plain    |              |
 name     | text    | not null                                             | extended |              |
 email    | text    | not null                                             | extended |              |
 password | text    | not null                                             | extended |              |
Indexes:
    "users_pkey" PRIMARY KEY, btree (id)
```

In the table users, we have an ID that is the unique identification key, username, user email, and user password.

Programming language and tools

Our UsersService will be written in Go; the tools we use in this programming language have already been described in Chapter 2, *The Microservice Tools*. However, it is necessary to download the dependencies of the project to start development. This is done using the following commands:

```
$ go get github.com/gorilla/mux
$ go get github.com/lib/pq
$ go get github.com/codegangsta/negroni
$ go get github.com/jmoiron/sqlx
```

Muxer is responsible for application handles and is our initial dependency. The gorilla/mux will be responsible for the `UsersService` synchronous communication layer, at first. This communication will be with HTTP/JSON.

The PQ is the interface responsible for communication between our software and the PostgreSQL database. We will have a look at how it functions in this chapter.

The **Negroni** is our middleware manager. At this stage of the application, the sole responsibility is to manage the application logs.

The SQLX is our executor of queries in the database and since this is very common in Go, it'll be no different to use in ORMs in our microservice. However, the application of the values returned from the queries about our structs will be run by SLQX.

Project structure

The main characteristic of microservices is their simplicity of structure. This simplicity does not mean the absence of robustness, but it means it is easy to read and understand the project development.

Our `UsersService` is also simple enough to make future modifications. You can be sure that this project is going to change a few times in your life cycle.

The structure of our project in the first version is as follows:

- `models.go`
- `app.go`
- `main.go`

Let's see each of them and how they function.

The models.go file

Starting with the models is always interesting, because it is the best place to understand the business of a project.

At first, we declare the package on which we are working, and then the imports required for the project, as follows:

```
package main

import (
    "github.com/jmoiron/sqlx"
    "golang.org/x/crypto/bcrypt"
)
```

Then, we make the declaration of our entity, `Users`. Go does not have classes, but instead uses structs. The final behavior is very similar to the OOP, of course, but there are peculiarities.

- `User` is the struct responsible to represent the database entity:

```
type User struct {
    ID       int    `json:"id" db:"id"`
    Name     string `json:"name" db:"name"`
    Email    string `json:"email" db:"email"`
    Password string `json:"password" db:"password"`
}
```

So, we have created the five basic CRUD operations, specifically: `five-create`, `read one`, `read list`, `update`, and `delete`.

- To get a return, just update the `User` instance with the data from `db`:

```
func (u *User) get(db *sqlx.DB) error {
    return db.Get(u, "SELECT name, email FROM users WHERE id=$1",
        u.ID)
}
```

The `get` method returns only one user. The data to search, in the case of the ID, is passed inside the memory reference of the struct, as can be seen by the syntax, `u.ID`. Something interesting to note here is that access to the database in PostgreSQL is through dependency injection, passed as a parameter in the `get` method.

- Update the data in the `db` using the instance values:

```
func (u *User) update(db *sqlx.DB) error {
    hashedPassword, err := bcrypt.GenerateFromPassword(
        []byte(u.Password),
        bcrypt.DefaultCost,
    )
    if err != nil {
```

```
        return err
    }
    _, err = db.Exec("UPDATE users SET name=$1, email=$2,
     password=$3 WHERE id=$4", u.Name, u.Email,
     string(hashedPassword), u.ID)
    return err
}
```

The update method is very similar in structure to the get method. The values for persistence are passed within the pointer *Users, and access to the database is for dependency injection. In addition to the query, which is obviously different from the query in the method get, there is the mechanism to crypto the password. To ensure that the password does not get exposed in the database, we use the bcrypt Go library to create a hash from the password passed to the method.

- Delete the date from the db using the instance values:

```
func (u *User) delete(db *sqlx.DB) error {
    _, err := db.Exec("DELETE FROM users WHERE id=$1", u.ID)
    return err
}
```

The delete method has the same structure as that of the get method. Note the _, err := db.Exec(...) declaration. This type of syntactic construction may seem strange, but it's necessary. Go does not throw an exception; it simply returns an error if it exists. This type of control seems absurd, but you can see that there is a lot of elegance in this code structure.

- Create a new user in the db using the instance values:

```
func (u *User) create(db *sqlx.DB) error {
    hashedPassword, err := bcrypt.GenerateFromPassword(
        []byte(u.Password),
        bcrypt.DefaultCost,
    )
    if err != nil {
        return err
    }
    return db.QueryRow(
        "INSERT INTO users(name, email, password) VALUES($1, $2, $3)
        RETURNING id", u.Name, u.Email,
        string(hashedPassword)).Scan(&u.ID)
}
```

In the `update` method, we make the treatment of password for insertion in the database, as shown in the following code:

- `List` returns a list of users. This could be applied pagination:

```
func list(db *sqlx.DB, start, count int) ([]User, error) {
   users := []User{}
   err := db.Select(&users, "SELECT id, name,
    email FROM users LIMIT $1 OFFSET $2", count, start)
   if err != nil {
     return nil, err
   }
   return users, nil
}
```

Finally, the most different point within our model. Primarily because `list` is not a method, but a function, this type of approach is common among Go developers. A method is only created if you change or use something of an instance or struct. When there is any type of alteration or use of data which creates a function, the `list` function simply returns a list of users receiving parameters for possible information paginations.

Finally, our archive, `models.go`, is as follows:

```
package main
import (
  "github.com/jmoiron/sqlx"
  "golang.org/x/crypto/bcrypt"
)
```

`User` is the `struct` responsible for representing the database entity:

```
type User struct {
   ID           int      `json:"id" db:"id"`
   Name         string `json:"name" db:"name"`
   Email        string `json:"email" db:"email"`
   Password string `json:"password" db:"password"`
}
```

`Get` returns just the update `User` instance with the data from db:

```
func (u *User) get(db *sqlx.DB) error {
   return db.Get(u, "SELECT name, email FROM users WHERE id=$1",
    u.ID)
}
```

Update the data in the db using the instance values:

```
func (u *User) update(db *sqlx.DB) error {
  hashedPassword, err := bcrypt.GenerateFromPassword(
    []byte(u.Password), bcrypt.DefaultCost)
  if err != nil {
    return err
  }
  _, err = db.Exec("UPDATE users SET name=$1, email=$2,
   password=$3 WHERE id=$4", u.Name, u.Email,
   string(hashedPassword), u.ID)
  return err
}
```

Delete the date from the db using the instance values:

```
func (u *User) delete(db *sqlx.DB) error {
  _, err := db.Exec("DELETE FROM users WHERE id=$1", u.ID)
  return err
}
```

Create a new user in the db using the instance values:

```
func (u *User) create(db *sqlx.DB) error {
  hashedPassword, err := bcrypt.GenerateFromPassword(
    []byte(u.Password), bcrypt.DefaultCost)
  if err != nil {
    return err
  }
  return db.QueryRow(
    "INSERT INTO users(name, email, password) VALUES($1, $2, $3)
     RETURNING id", u.Name, u.Email,
     string(hashedPassword)).Scan(&u.ID)
}
```

List returns a list of users. This could be applied pagination:

```
func list(db *sqlx.DB, start, count int) ([]User, error) {
  users := []User{}
  err := db.Select(&users, "SELECT id, name,
   email FROM users LIMIT $1 OFFSET $2", count, start)
  if err != nil {
    return nil, err
  }
  return users, nil
}
```

The app.go file

The file app.go is responsible for receiving data and sending it to our data storage. When we read this file, it seems to do too much or is badly divided, but it is very important to understand the characteristics of the language with which we are working.

Go is an imperative programming language—just writing clear, simple, and objective code is the focus of the developers. Patterns like MVC projects and complex structures of settings are not always applied in Go, especially when you program in the purest way possible. This does not mean that such patterns cannot be applied, quite the contrary. However, patterns like MVC are used in the structures of the Go files, only when there is a real need.

Let's take a look at our file app. go. Again, we have the declaration of the package where we are working and the imports that will be used in the file:

```
package main
import (
  "database/sql"
  "encoding/json"
  "fmt"
  "log"
  "net/http"
  "strconv"

  "github.com/codegangsta/negroni"
  "github.com/gorilla/mux"
  "github.com/jmoiron/sqlx"
  _ "github.com/lib/pq"
)
```

There is a point of attention on imports, Imports _ "github.com/lib/pq". The underscore sign before import means that we are invoking the init method inside of this library, but we're not going to make any direct reference to the library within the code.

Similar to the file models. go, we have a declaration of a struct. Struct App is composed of two elements—a memory reference to the SQLX and a memory reference to our router.

App is the struct with app configuration values:

```
type App struct {
  DB               *sqlx.DB
  Router           *mux.Router
}
```

The first struct method, `App`, is the `Initialize`. In our case, we've already got the connection with the database instantiated.

Initializes create the DB connection and prepares all the routes:

```
func (a *App) Initialize(db *sqlx.DB) {
    a.DB = db
    a.Router = mux.NewRouter()
    a.initializeRoutes()
}
```

After initializing the connections, it's now time to define the routes in the `initializeRoutes` method, as follows:

```
func (a *App) initializeRoutes() {
    a.Router.HandleFunc("/users", a.getUsers).Methods("GET")
    a.Router.HandleFunc("/user", a.createUser).Methods("POST")
    a.Router.HandleFunc("/user/{id:[0-9]+}",
     a.getUser).Methods("GET")
    a.Router.HandleFunc("/user/{id:[0-9]+}",
     a.updateUser).Methods("PUT")
    a.Router.HandleFunc("/user/{id:[0-9]+}",
     a.deleteUser).Methods("DELETE")
}
```

The definition of the routes is very clear and simple, because it is a simple CRUD. The following is the method that will be used to initialize the microservice. The `Run` method activates the Negroni, which is our controller of middleware, passes the router to it, and activates the server Go native.

Run initializes the server:

```
func (a *App) Run(addr string) {
    n := negroni.Classic()
    n.UseHandler(a.Router)
    log.Fatal(http.ListenAndServe(addr, n))
}
```

To avoid code duplication, let's create two helper functions inside the `App.go` file. These functions are `respondWithError` and `respondWithJSON`. The first function is responsible for passing to the HTTP layer, error codes that can be generated within the application, such as `404`, `500`, and all codes that should be reported.

The second function is responsible for creating the JSONs that must be answered for each request:

```
func respondWithError(w http.ResponseWriter, code int, message
  string) {
  respondWithJSON(w, code, map[string]string{"error": message})
}
func respondWithJSON(w http.ResponseWriter, code int, payload
  interface{}) {
  response, _ := json.Marshal(payload)

  w.Header().Set("Content-Type", "application/json")
  w.WriteHeader(code)
  w.Write(response)
}
```

Now, let's create our CRUD methods. The first method that we'll create will be responsible for fetching a single user; let's call it `getUser`. This method will translate the last ID in the request by checking if it is possible to be used for searching in the database. If it is not possible to throw an HTTP error, a `User` instance is created, and the `get` method of the model is called. If the user is not found in the database, or if there is any kind of problem with the database, the corresponding HTTP error code will be sent. In the end, if everything's okay, JSON will be sent in response to the request:

```
func (a *App) getUser(w http.ResponseWriter, r *http.Request) {
  vars := mux.Vars(r)
  id, err := strconv.Atoi(vars["id"])
  if err != nil {
          respondWithError(w, http.StatusBadRequest, "Invalid
    product ID")
          return
  }

  user := User{ID: id}
  if err := user.get(a.DB); err != nil {
    switch err {
      case sql.ErrNoRows:
        respondWithError(w, http.StatusNotFound, "User not found")
      default:
        respondWithError(w, http.StatusInternalServerError,
  err.Error())
```

```
    }
    return
}

respondWithJSON(w, http.StatusOK, user)
}
```

The next method of the `app.go` file has a purpose much like the `getUser`. However, we want to get many users at once. Let's call this the `getUsers` method. This method receives count and starts as parameters to search pagination, normalizing the possible values of a misguided search. Then, it uses the `list` method, which is in the `models.go` file, and passes in the instance of the database connection and the values for search pagination. If we do not have any mistakes, we send the JSON in response to the request:

```
func (a *App) getUsers(w http.ResponseWriter, r *http.Request) {
    count, _ := strconv.Atoi(r.FormValue("count"))
    start, _ := strconv.Atoi(r.FormValue("start"))

    if count > 10 || count < 1 {
        count = 10
    }
    if start < 0 {
        start = 0
    }

    users, err := list(a.DB, start, count)
    if err != nil {
        respondWithError(w, http.StatusInternalServerError, err.Error())
        return
    }

    respondWithJSON(w, http.StatusOK, users)
}
```

Now, we move on to the methods that generate changes in the database. The first method that we see is `createUser`. In this method, we translate JSON into the body of the request sent to an instance of the user. The user instance calls the `create` method of the model to persist the data. If no error occurs, the HTTP 201 code is not returned, indicating that the user was created successfully:

```
func (a *App) createUser(w http.ResponseWriter, r *http.Request) {
    var user User
    decoder := json.NewDecoder(r.Body)
    if err := decoder.Decode(&user); err != nil {
        respondWithError(w, http.StatusBadRequest, "Invalid request
payload")
```

```
    return
  }
  defer r.Body.Close()

  if err := user.create(a.DB); err != nil {
    fmt.Println(err.Error())
    respondWithError(w, http.StatusInternalServerError, err.Error())
    return
  }

  respondWithJSON(w, http.StatusCreated, user)
}
```

After the method responsible for creating a user, let's write the method responsible for editing a user. We will call this the updateUser method. In this method, we get the ID of the user that should be modified, translate the body of the request received in JSON for the instance, and then call the update method to modify the data instance. If there is no error, we will send the corresponding HTTP code:

```
func (a *App) updateUser(w http.ResponseWriter, r *http.Request) {
  vars := mux.Vars(r)
  id, err := strconv.Atoi(vars["id"])
  if err != nil {
    respondWithError(w, http.StatusBadRequest, "Invalid product ID")
    return
  }

  var user User
  decoder := json.NewDecoder(r.Body)
  if err := decoder.Decode(&user); err != nil {
    respondWithError(w, http.StatusBadRequest, "Invalid resquest
payload")
    return
  }
  defer r.Body.Close()
  user.ID = id

  if err := user.update(a.DB); err != nil {
    respondWithError(w, http.StatusInternalServerError, err.Error())
    return
  }

  respondWithJSON(w, http.StatusOK, user)
}
```

Finally, let's write the last method of our CRUD, which is responsible for removing a user from the database. Let's call this method `deleteUser`. In this method, we get the `id` as a parameter and use this data to create an instance of the user. Once the instance is created, the delete method of the instance is called. If there are no errors, the corresponding HTTP code is sent:

```go
func (a *App) deleteUser(w http.ResponseWriter, r *http.Request) {
    vars := mux.Vars(r)
    id, err := strconv.Atoi(vars["id"])
    if err != nil {
        respondWithError(w, http.StatusBadRequest, "Invalid User ID")
        return
    }

    user := User{ID: id}
    if err := user.delete(a.DB); err != nil {
        respondWithError(w, http.StatusInternalServerError, err.Error())
        return
    }

    respondWithJSON(w, http.StatusOK, map[string]string{"result":
"success"})
}
```

Finally, our `app.go` file looks as follows:

```go
package main

import (
    "database/sql"
    "encoding/json"
    "fmt"
    "log"
    "net/http"
    "strconv"

    "github.com/codegangsta/negroni"
    "github.com/gorilla/mux"
    "github.com/jmoiron/sqlx"
    _ "github.com/lib/pq"
)
```

App is the struct with app configuration values:

```
type App struct {
  DB                *sqlx.DB
  Router            *mux.Router
}
```

Initialize creates the DB connection and prepares all the routes:

```
func (a *App) Initialize(db *sqlx.DB) {

  a.DB = db
  a.Router = mux.NewRouter()
  a.initializeRoutes()
}

func (a *App) initializeRoutes() {
  a.Router.HandleFunc("/users", a.getUsers).Methods("GET")
  a.Router.HandleFunc("/user", a.createUser).Methods("POST")
  a.Router.HandleFunc("/user/{id:[0-9]+}",
    a.getUser).Methods("GET")
  a.Router.HandleFunc("/user/{id:[0-9]+}",
    a.updateUser).Methods("PUT")
  a.Router.HandleFunc("/user/{id:[0-9]+}",
    a.deleteUser).Methods("DELETE")
}
```

Run initializes the server:

```
func (a *App) Run(addr string) {
  n := negroni.Classic()
  n.UseHandler(a.Router)
  log.Fatal(http.ListenAndServe(addr, n))
}

func (a *App) getUser(w http.ResponseWriter, r *http.Request) {
  vars := mux.Vars(r)
  id, err := strconv.Atoi(vars["id"])
  if err != nil {
    respondWithError(w, http.StatusBadRequest, "Invalid product ID")
    return
  }

  user := User{ID: id}
  if err := user.get(a.DB); err != nil {
    switch err {
      case sql.ErrNoRows:
          respondWithError(w, http.StatusNotFound, "User not found")
```

```
        default:
            respondWithError(w, http.StatusInternalServerError,
err.Error())
        }
        return
    }


    respondWithJSON(w, http.StatusOK, user)
}

func (a *App) getUsers(w http.ResponseWriter, r *http.Request) {
    count, _ := strconv.Atoi(r.FormValue("count"))
    start, _ := strconv.Atoi(r.FormValue("start"))

    if count > 10 || count < 1 {
        count = 10
    }
    if start < 0 {
            start = 0
    }

    users, err := list(a.DB, start, count)
    if err != nil {
        respondWithError(w, http.StatusInternalServerError, err.Error())
        return
    }

    respondWithJSON(w, http.StatusOK, users)
}

func (a *App) createUser(w http.ResponseWriter, r *http.Request) {
    var user User
    decoder := json.NewDecoder(r.Body)
    if err := decoder.Decode(&user); err != nil {
        respondWithError(w, http.StatusBadRequest, "Invalid request
payload")
        return
    }
    defer r.Body.Close()

    if err := user.create(a.DB); err != nil {
        fmt.Println(err.Error())
        respondWithError(w, http.StatusInternalServerError, err.Error())
        return
    }

    respondWithJSON(w, http.StatusCreated, user)
```

```go
    }

    func (a *App) updateUser(w http.ResponseWriter, r *http.Request) {
      vars := mux.Vars(r)
      id, err := strconv.Atoi(vars["id"])
      if err != nil {
        respondWithError(w, http.StatusBadRequest, "Invalid product ID")
        return
      }

      var user User
      decoder := json.NewDecoder(r.Body)
      if err := decoder.Decode(&user); err != nil {
        respondWithError(w, http.StatusBadRequest, "Invalid resquest
payload")
        return
      }
      defer r.Body.Close()
      user.ID = id

      if err := user.update(a.DB); err != nil {
        respondWithError(w, http.StatusInternalServerError, err.Error())
        return
      }

      respondWithJSON(w, http.StatusOK, user)
    }

    func (a *App) deleteUser(w http.ResponseWriter, r *http.Request) {
      vars := mux.Vars(r)
      id, err := strconv.Atoi(vars["id"])
      if err != nil {
        respondWithError(w, http.StatusBadRequest, "Invalid User ID")
        return
      }

      user := User{ID: id}
      if err := user.delete(a.DB); err != nil {
        respondWithError(w, http.StatusInternalServerError, err.Error())
        return
      }

      respondWithJSON(w, http.StatusOK, map[string]string{"result":
"success"})
    }

    func respondWithError(w http.ResponseWriter, code int, message string)
{
```

```
    respondWithJSON(w, code, map[string]string{"error": message})
}

func respondWithJSON(w http.ResponseWriter, code int,
 payload interface{}) {
  response, _ := json.Marshal(payload)

  w.Header().Set("Content-Type", "application/json")
  w.WriteHeader(code)
  w.Write(response)
}
```

The code may look big, but it's actually fairly concise within the concept of our microservice.

The main.go file

Now that you have a basic understanding of our project, let's take a look at the `main.go` file. This is the file responsible for sending settings necessary for the operation of our microservice to our app and for running the microservice itself. As can be seen in the following code, we instantiate a connection to the database from the beginning. This instance is the database that will be used in every application:

```
package main
import (
  "fmt"
  "github.com/jmoiron/sqlx"
  _ "github.com/lib/pq"
  "log"
  "os"
)

func main() {
  connectionString := fmt.Sprintf(
    "user=%s password=%s dbname=%s sslmode=disable",
    os.Getenv("APP_DB_USERNAME"),
    os.Getenv("APP_DB_PASSWORD"),
    os.Getenv("APP_DB_NAME"),
  )

  db, err := sqlx.Open("postgres", connectionString)
  if err != nil {
    log.Fatal(err)
  }
```

```
    a := App{}
    a.Initialize(cache, db)
    a.Run(":8080")
}
```

Unlike the `app.go` file, `main.go` is leaner. In Go, the whole application is initialized by executing a function, `main`. In our microservice, it is no different. Our main method sends to the `App` instance what is necessary to connect the database. At the end of the `Run` method, it runs the application server on port `8080`.

Caching strategies

There are some strategies of caches for web applications. These same strategies can be applied for microservices. The most common strategy for caching is when we store the information in a cache after a query. In the following diagram, we receive a request through our API and we will, in the application, make the data query. The first search is performed in the cache and, if the data is not in the cache, the search is performed in the database. To return the query from the database, the value is recorded in the cache:

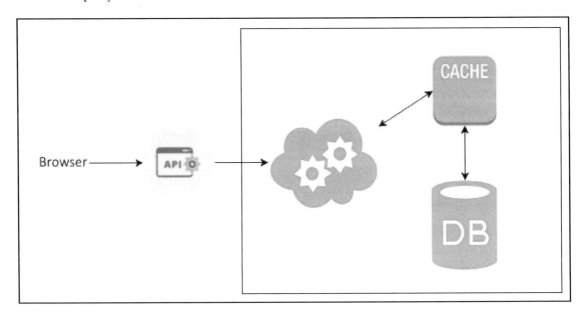

This kind of strategy is the simplest cache that can be applied. We see the changes we should make in our application to have the cache layer.

Applying cache

The first step is to download dependency with Redis as the connection driver:

```
$ go get github.com/garyburd/redigo/redis
```

The Redigo is our communication interface with Redis. We will use Redis as a cache tool of our microservice.

Now, we will create the cache.go file. This file is responsible for delivering us a configured instance of the cache. Similar to the other files we've ever created, let's declare the package where we are working and the dependencies, as follows:

```go
package main

import (
  "log"
  "time"

  redigo "github.com/garyburd/redigo/redis"
)
```

Then, we create an interface to create a pool of connections to the Redis and a struct with all the settings of the connection. Note that the instance of our pool will also be in the struct.

Pool is the interface to pool of Redis:

```go
type Pool interface {
  Get() redigo.Conn
}
```

Cache is the struct with cache configuration:

```go
type Cache struct {

    Enable          bool

    MaxIdle         int

    MaxActive       int

    IdleTimeoutSecs int

    Address         string

    Auth            string
```

```
    DB              string

    Pool            *redigo.Pool


}
```

Now, we'll create the method of our struct responsible for giving us a new connection pool. Redigo has a struct called `Pool`, which, when configured correctly, returns exactly what we need. In our cache configuration, we have the option **Enable**. If the option is enabled, we will apply the settings to return connection pooling; if it is not enabled, we simply ignore this process and return null. This implies that the pool will be validated at final; if something is wrong, we launch a fatal error and stop the server, followed by provisioning the service:

```go
// NewCachePool return a new instance of the redis pool
func (cache *Cache) NewCachePool() *redigo.Pool {
  if cache.Enable {
    pool := &redigo.Pool{
      MaxIdle: cache.MaxIdle,
      MaxActive: cache.MaxActive,
      IdleTimeout: time.Second * time.Duration(cache.IdleTimeoutSecs),
      Dial: func() (redigo.Conn, error) {
        c, err := redigo.Dial("tcp", cache.Address)
        if err != nil {
          return nil, err
        }
        if _, err = c.Do("AUTH", cache.Auth); err != nil {
          c.Close()
          return nil, err
        }
        if _, err = c.Do("SELECT", cache.DB); err != nil {
          c.Close()
          return nil, err
        }
        return c, err
      },
      TestOnBorrow: func(c redigo.Conn, t time.Time) error {
        _, err := c.Do("PING")
        return err
      },
    }
    c := pool.Get() // Test connection during init
    if _, err := c.Do("PING"); err != nil {
      log.Fatal("Cannot connect to Redis: ", err)
    }
    return pool
  }
```

```
      return nil
    }
```

Now, we create the method that searches our cache and that enters the data in our cache. The getValue method receives, as a parameter, the search key in the cache. The setValue function receives, as parameters, the key and the value that should be inserted in the cache:

```
func (cache *Cache) getValue(key interface{}) (string, error) {
    if cache.Enable {
            conn := cache.Pool.Get()
            defer conn.Close()
            value, err := redigo.String(conn.Do("GET", key))
            return value, err
    }
    return "", nil
}

func (cache *Cache) setValue(key interface{}, value interface{}) error {
    if cache.Enable {
            conn := cache.Pool.Get()
            defer conn.Close()
            _, err := redigo.String(conn.Do("SET", key, value))
            return err
    }
    return nil
}
```

In this way, our file, cache. go, is mounted and ready to be used in our application. However, we have to make some changes to our cache file before it is used. We will start by changing our file main.go.

In the file main.go, let's add a new import. When we import flags, we can receive information directly from the command line, and use them in our configuration of Redis:

```
import (
  "flag"
  "fmt"
  "github.com/jmoiron/sqlx"
  _ "github.com/lib/pq"
  "log"
  "os"
)
```

What we must do now is add the options that can be passed to the command line. This change also happens in the file main.go. First, we create an instance of our Cache, then add to the pointer of this instance, the settings. All settings have a default value if no argument is passed on the command line.

The order of the settings is as follows:

1. **Address**: This is where Redis runs
2. **Auth**: This is the password used to connect to the Redis
3. **DB**: This is the Redis Bank that will be used as cache
4. **MaxIdle**: This denotes the maximum number of connections that can be idle
5. **MaxActive**: This denotes the maximum number of connections that can be active
6. **IdleTimeoutSecs**: This is the time a connection timeout leads to enter activity

At the end of all settings, we'll create a new pool of connections with the NewCachePool method and pass the pointer to our cache instance, as follows:

```go
func main() {
 cache := Cache{Enable: true}
 flag.StringVar(
            &cache.Address,
            "redis_address",
            os.Getenv("APP_RD_ADDRESS"),
            "Redis Address",
 )

 flag.StringVar(
            &cache.Auth,
            "redis_auth",
            os.Getenv("APP_RD_AUTH"),
            "Redis Auth",
 )
 flag.StringVar(
            &cache.DB,
            "redis_db_name",
            os.Getenv("APP_RD_DBNAME"),
            "Redis DB name",
 )
 flag.IntVar(
            &cache.MaxIdle,
            "redis_max_idle",
            10,
            "Redis Max Idle",
 )
```

```
flag.IntVar(
            &cache.MaxActive,
            "redis_max_active",
            100,
            "Redis Max Active",
)
flag.IntVar(
            &cache.IdleTimeoutSecs,
            "redis_timeout",
            60,
            "Redis timeout in seconds",
)
flag.Parse()
cache.Pool = cache.NewCachePool()
...
```

Another change that should be made within `main.go` is to pass the App cache to the `initialize` method:

```
...
a.Initialize(
    cache,
    db,
)
...
```

We edit the `app.go` file to effectively use the cache according to the diagram given earlier. The first change is in the struct of the App, because it happens to store the cache:

```
type App struct {
    DB         *sqlx.DB
    Router *mux.Router
    Cache    Cache
}
```

Now, we should make sure that the `initialize` method receives the cache and passes the value to the instance of the App:

```
func (a *App) Initialize(cache Cache, db *sqlx.DB) {

    a.Cache = cache
    a.DB = db
    a.Router = mux.NewRouter()
    a.initializeRoutes()
}
```

Now, we can apply the cache in any part of the App; let's modify the getUser method to use the cache structure that we talked about earlier. Two parts of the method should be changed, so that the cache is applied.

First, rather than seek user data directly in PostgreSQL, we check if the data is already in the cache. If the data is already in the cache, we're not even going to get the data in the base.

The second amendment is that if the data is not in cache, perform a search in the database, and register this same data into the cache before returning a response to the request. In this way, in a subsequent search, the data will be in the cache, and the query on the database will not be performed:

```
func (a *App) getUser(w http.ResponseWriter, r *http.Request) {
  vars := mux.Vars(r)
  id, err := strconv.Atoi(vars["id"])
  if err != nil {
    respondWithError(w, http.StatusBadRequest, "Invalid product ID")
    return
  }

  if value, err := a.Cache.getValue(id); err == nil && len(value) != 0 {
    w.Header().Set("Content-Type", "application/json")
    w.WriteHeader(http.StatusOK)
    w.Write([]byte(value))
    return
  }

  user := User{ID: id}
  if err := user.get(a.DB); err != nil {
    switch err {
      case sql.ErrNoRows:
        respondWithError(w, http.StatusNotFound, "User not found")
      default:
        respondWithError(w, http.StatusInternalServerError, err.Error())
    }
    return
  }

  response, _ := json.Marshal(user)
  if err := a.Cache.setValue(user.ID, response); err != nil {
    respondWithError(w, http.StatusInternalServerError, err.Error())
    return
  }

  w.Header().Set("Content-Type", "application/json")
  w.WriteHeader(http.StatusOK)
```

```
    w.Write(response)
    }
```

With the preceding amendments, after consultation in the database, the cache is replaced by query values and responds without the need for access to the database. This approach is sufficient for most cases but, in some scenarios, where the load of requests is high or the database may be very demanding, even having a cache, the database can become a point of slowness. The next cache strategy is very interesting for this kind of problem.

Caching first

A very useful cache strategy performance is **caching first**. This strategy is to use the cache as the first level of the database. The process can be considered quite simple. All common operations on the database are performed primarily in the cache, and sent in a queue at the same time that the workers begin to consume this queue and normalize the data in a real database:

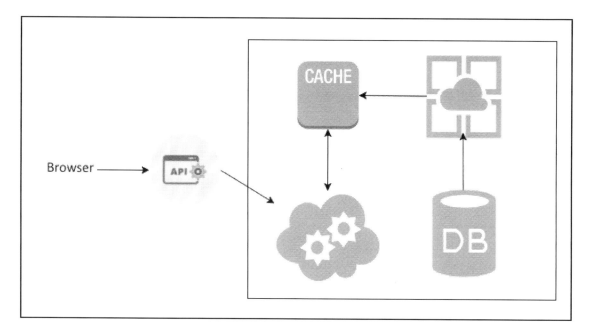

To apply this technique, it is essential to use queues and asynchrony for consuming data. Something highly recommended with this approach is the use of cache with persistence.

In the next topic in this chapter, we will continue working to implement the strategy of caching first.

Enqueuing tasks

We know that we want to use the cache as a draft database, where all information can be consumed immediately, and only later consolidate our data in the database effectively.

Let's understand a little about the internal flow of persistence by looking at the following points:

1. This executes a request to the application.
2. Information sent to the application is registered in two places when it comes to POST/PUT/DELETE. The first is the cache, where it will be all the information sent in the request. The second place is the queue, where it will be an identification key to the cached information.
3. The workers start and check if there is some content in the queue.
4. If there is content in the queue, the workers seek the data in the cache.
5. After searching the data in the cache, the data is persisted in the database.
6. This step is only for when the request is a GET. In this case, step 2 will only cache to fetch the data. If you can't find the data in the cache, step 6 runs by going to the database for the search. To return data, the searches are recorded in the cache.

It is important to make it clear that the mere sending to the cache and queue is sufficient to return a message to the client, which is a message of success or failure. Take a look at the following diagram:

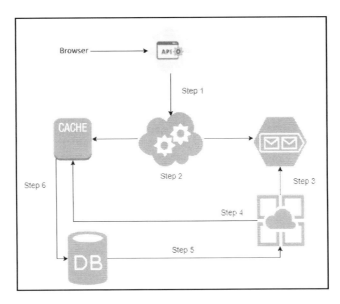

Now that you understand the concept, let's modify our code to apply it. The `main.go` file is the point of application, as well as the place where all the settings are obtained. In this file, we will declare the names of the queues that are used in our process. The following are the imports, and we will create the following constants:

```
const (
    createUsersQueue = "CREATE_USER"
    updateUsersQueuc - "UPDATE_USER"
    deleteUsersQueue = "DELETE_USER"
)
```

These constants are used in other parts of the application to send data to the queue.

In the file `cache. go`, we will create a new method for the instance from the cache. This method is responsible for storing the keys in the queues:

```
func (cache *Cache) enqueueValue(queue string, uuid int) error {
    if cache.Enable {
            conn := cache.Pool.Get()
            defer conn.Close()
            _, err := conn.Do("RPUSH", queue, uuid)
            return err
    }
    return nil
}
```

The next step is to modify the `createUser` method in the `app.go` file. This method removes every part of persistence that stemmed from the database. The only access we should have is to the PostgreSQL at this point is the capture of a new sequence to be applied to the instance of the entity.

After assigning the ID entity, we register in the cache using the ID as the key and the entity in JSON format as the value. Then, we send the key to the queue CREATE_USER. Take a look at the following example:

```
func (a *App) createUser(w http.ResponseWriter, r *http.Request) {
    var user User
    decoder := json.NewDecoder(r.Body)
    if err := decoder.Decode(&user); err != nil {
            respondWithError(w, http.StatusBadRequest, "Invalid
request payload")
            return
    }
    defer r.Body.Close()

    // get sequence from Postgres
```

```
     a.DB.Get(&user.ID, "SELECT nextval('users_id_seq')")

     JSONByte, _ := json.Marshal(user)
     if err := a.Cache.setValue(user.ID, string(JSONByte)); err != nil {
               respondWithError(w, http.StatusInternalServerError,
err.Error())
               return
     }

     if err := a.Cache.enqueueValue(createUsersQueue, user.ID); err != nil
{
               respondWithError(w, http.StatusInternalServerError,
err.Error())
               return
     }

     respondWithJSON(w, http.StatusCreated, user)
}
```

Now, we have the data in the queue and the cache before the record in the database. If a query is performed right now, the data will be returned from the cache and not from the base.

The next step is to register the information in the cache only database, but we will cover that a little later in the chapter.

Asynchronism and workers

Our information is already in a queue, but not yet stored in the database. This is due to the fact that we are not consuming the information that is in the queue, but sending it to the database instead.

The processes of recovering the data that is in the queue and that of sending them to a normalized database must be asynchronous. In the end, it's like we have two applications within the same software. The first part of the application is responsible for receiving the data, while the second part is responsible for processing the data.

Let's see how we conduct this process in the application code. We will first create a file named `workers.go`. Then, we will declare the package where we are working and the imports, as seen in the following code:

```
     package main

     import (
```

```
    "encoding/json"
    redigo "github.com/garyburd/redigo/redis"
    "github.com/jmoiron/sqlx"
    "log"
    "sync"
)
```

After the opening statements, let's write the struct that will meet all the workers. The struct contains the instance cache settings, and the database instance ID of the worker and the queue that the worker will consume.

Worker is the struct with worker configuration values:

```
type Worker struct {
  cache Cache
  db        *sqlx.DB
  id        int
  queue string
}
```

Let's create a `newWorker`function, which will be responsible for initializing the worker that will receive all data as a parameter to the struct of the worker:

```
func newWorker(id int, db *sqlx.DB, cache Cache,
queue string) Worker {
  return Worker{cache: cache, db: db, id: id, queue: queue}
}
```

The next step is to create the method `process` that belongs to the worker. This is the method that will run the queue and send data to the database. If the process fails, the method will resend the data which will be held for the queue.

The `process` method receives the ID of the worker. Within the method, there is an infinite loop where a cached connection is requested to the connection pool and two variables, `channel` and `uuid`, are declared. Both variables are populated with the information from the queue. In our case, the channel exists only to fulfil the subscription Redigo API. What we are going to use is the variable `uuid`.

We will use the `BLPOP` function of Redis to consume the queue. With `uuid` populated, we use the `GET` function of Redis to get the data in the cache. On the basis of the information retrieved, we will instantiate a user using the struct. Then, we'll call the `create` method of the own instance of the user to register the new user in the database:

```
func (w Worker) process(id int) {
  for {
```

```
conn := w.cache.Pool.Get()
var channel string
var uuid int
if reply, err := redigo.Values(conn.Do("BLPOP", w.queue,
 30+id)); err == nil {

  if _, err := redigo.Scan(reply, &channel, &uuid); err != nil {
    w.cache.enqueueValue(w.queue, uuid)
    continue
  }

  values, err := redigo.String(conn.Do("GET", uuid))
  if err != nil {
    w.cache.enqueueValue(w.queue, uuid)
    continue
  }

  user := User{}
  if err := json.Unmarshal([]byte(values), &user); err != nil {
    w.cache.enqueueValue(w.queue, uuid)
    continue
  }

  log.Println(user)
  if err := user.create(w.db); err != nil {
    w.cache.enqueueValue(w.queue, uuid)
    continue
  }

} else if err != redigo.ErrNil {
    log.Fatal(err)
}
conn.Close()
  }
}
```

Now, staying in the workers.go file, write the UsersToDB function, which creates a number of workers that we wish for the queue to instantiate additionally, and initialize the workers asynchronously.

UsersToDB creates workers to consume the queues:

```
func UsersToDB(numWorkers int, db *sqlx.DB, cache Cache,
 queue string) {
 var wg sync.WaitGroup
 for i := 0; i < numWorkers; i++ {
    wg.Add(1)
```

```
        go func(id int, db *sqlx.DB, cache Cache, queue string) {
            worker := newWorker(i, db, cache, queue)
            worker.process(i)
            defer wg.Done()
        }(i, db, cache, queue)
    }
    wg.Wait()
}
```

The following is the final result of the `workers.go` file:

```
package main

import (
    "encoding/json"
    redigo "github.com/garyburd/redigo/redis"
    "github.com/jmoiron/sqlx"
    "log"
    "sync"
)
```

`Worker` is the struct with worker configuration values:

```
type Worker struct {
    cache Cache
    db        *sqlx.DB
    id        int
    queue string
}
```

`UsersToDB` create workers to consume the queues:

```
func UsersToDB(numWorkers int, db *sqlx.DB, cache Cache,
 queue string) {
    var wg sync.WaitGroup
    for i := 0; i < numWorkers; i++ {
        wg.Add(1)
        go func(id int, db *sqlx.DB, cache Cache, queue string) {
            worker := newWorker(i, db, cache, queue)
            worker.process(i)
            defer wg.Done()
        }(i, db, cache, queue)
    }
    wg.Wait()
}

func newWorker(id int, db *sqlx.DB, cache Cache,
 queue string) Worker {
```

```
    return Worker{cache: cache, db: db, id: id, queue: queue}
}

func (w Worker) process(id int) {
  for {
    conn := w.cache.Pool.Get()
    var channel string
    var uuid int
    if reply, err := redigo.Values(conn.Do("BLPOP", w.queue,
     30+id)); err == nil {

        if _, err := redigo.Scan(reply, &channel, &uuid); err != nil {
          w.cache.enqueueValue(w.queue, uuid)
          continue
        }

        values, err := redigo.String(conn.Do("GET", uuid))
        if err != nil {
          w.cache.enqueueValue(w.queue, uuid)
          continue
        }

        user := User{}
        if err := json.Unmarshal([]byte(values), &user); err != nil {
          w.cache.enqueueValue(w.queue, uuid)
          continue
        }

        log.Println(user)
        if err := user.create(w.db); err != nil {
          w.cache.enqueueValue(w.queue, uuid)
          continue
        }

    } else if err != redigo.ErrNil {
        log.Fatal(err)
    }
    conn.Close()
  }
}
```

However, to invoke our workers, we should do a little editing in the `main.go` file. Recall that the `main.go` file is the one that initializes the microservice. Two new items have been added to the main function. There is also the possibility of receiving the number of workers by queue via the command line to initialize the application, and initialization of the workers itself, using the prefix `go`, as shown in the following code:

```go
func main() {
    var numWorkers int
    cache := Cache{Enable: true}
    flag.StringVar(
        &cache.Address,
        "redis_address",
        os.Getenv("APP_RD_ADDRESS"),
        "Redis Address",
    )
    flag.StringVar(
        &cache.Auth,
        "redis_auth",
        os.Getenv("APP_RD_AUTH"),
        "Redis Auth",
    )
    flag.StringVar(
        &cache.DB,
        "redis_db_name",
        os.Getenv("APP_RD_DBNAME"),
        "Redis DB name",
    )
    flag.IntVar(
        &cache.MaxIdle,
        "redis_max_idle",
        10,
        "Redis Max Idle",
    )
    flag.IntVar(
        &cache.MaxActive,
        "redis_max_active",
        100,
        "Redis Max Active"
    )
    flag.IntVar(
        &cache.IdleTimeoutSecs,
        "redis_timeout",
        60,
        "Redis timeout in seconds"
    )
    flag.IntVar(
        &numWorkers,
```

```
        "num_workers",
        10,
        "Number of workers to consume queue"
    )
    flag.Parse()
    cache.Pool = cache.NewCachePool()

    connectionString := fmt.Sprintf(
        "user=%s password=%s dbname=%s sslmode=disable",
        os.Getenv("APP_DB_USERNAME"),
        os.Getenv("APP_DB_PASSWORD"),
        os.Getenv("APP_DB_NAME"),
    )

    db, err := sqlx.Open("postgres", connectionString)
    if err != nil {
        log.Fatal(err)
    }

    go UsersToDB(numWorkers, db, cache, createUsersQueue)
    go UsersToDB(numWorkers, db, cache, updateUsersQueue)
    go UsersToDB(numWorkers, db, cache, deleteUsersQueue)

    a := App{}
    a.Initialize(cache, db)
    a.Run(":8080")
}
```

At last, we have our application using the caching first strategy. In case of UsersService, this strategy works very well, because the user ID is always something simple to obtain and calculate. A positive point is that everything we need to adopt this strategy is already in the application. There's no need to add something new to the stack. However, along with the advantages, there are some downsides as well.

Imagine if the ID to retrieve the cache is very difficult to obtain or calculate. Think also of the case where the identification key can be composed. How do we deal with this kind of obstacle to implement the caching first strategy?

For this type of problem, it is better to adopt another pattern. The **Command Query Responsibility Segregation (CQRS)** is a great option when the search scenario and maintenance is more complex.

We'll explain this pattern in the next section of this chapter.

CQRS – query strategy

CQRS is a very important concept and one that you need to know. I always say that every architect has a toolbox and CQRS is the kind of tool that needs to be present in your box.

What is CQRS?

CQRS means Command Query Responsibility Segregation. As the name implies, it is about separating the responsibility of writing and reading of data. CQRS is a *code pattern* and not an *architectural pattern*.

Let's understand the classic scenarios of everyday life and, then, we will see how CQRS could be applied as a solution.

With the growth of the internet, we cannot think of creating applications for a few users; most of the new applications have premises of scalability, performance, and availability. How can an application work well with both tens and thousands of users simultaneously? It is complex to create a model that meets those needs. Databases, when required, can become a bottleneck.

Let's consider a financial credit system. People use this to get fast credit for special purchases in stores. The access to data change can at times be easy one moment or intense another moment.

The answer to this type of problem may lie in scaling the application in *n* servers. We can migrate to cloud-computing and create a script autoscaling to scale, as per demand.

The concept of scalability of the application will solve some problems of availability, such as supporting many users simultaneously without compromising the performance of the application.

Will just scaling the application servers solve all our problems?

Deadlocks, timeouts, and slowness mean that your database may be in too much demand.

More instances of an application is not a guarantee that the application will always be available. In this scenario, the application is totally dependent on the availability of the database.

Database scalability can be much more complex and expensive than scaling application servers. However, it is usually due to database consumption that applications have performance problems.

Complex queries can be performed to obtain database data. ORMs can add even more complexity to the data filtering process by mapping entities and **filtering data** by using joins in different tables.

Content obsolescence could be true. A limited set of data is constantly consulted and changed by a large number of users. This means that one data displayed on the screen may already have been changed by another. It is possible to state that all information displayed may already be obsolete.

Understanding CQRS

To have multiple servers consuming a single database that serves as both reading and writing can lead to many points of slowness in manipulating data and cause various problems in performance. The whole process of the business rule that will get the display data takes extra time in processing. Finally, we still have to consider the fact that the data displayed can be out of date.

The CQRS teaches us the division of responsibility for writing and reading data, both conceptual and using different physical storages. This means that there will be separate means for recording and retrieving data from the databases. Queries are done synchronously in a separate denormalized database, and writes asynchronously to a normalized database. Caching first is still a type of CQRS implementation at the conceptual level.

Definitely, the CQRS does not have to be applied in every process of an application, only when there is a real need for optimization. A DDD-based modeling a **Bounded Context** (`http://www.microsofttranslator.com/bv.aspx?from=ptto=enr=truea=`
`http%3A%2F%2Fwww.eduardopires.net.br%2F2016%2F03%2Fddd-bounded-context%2F`) may implement the CQRS, while others do not.

The implementation of CQRS can be very simple or very complex, depending on the need of the application. Regardless of how it is implemented, CQRS always brings in extra complexity, and so it is necessary to evaluate the scenarios in which it is really required to work with this pattern. The basic idea is to segregate the responsibilities of the application in two parts. The **Command** will be responsible for modifying the state of the data in the application, and the **Query** that is the operation responsible for retrieving information from the database.

We could think of it as similar to separating CommandStack responsibilities and QueryStack in an *n*-tier architecture.

- **QueryStack** is relatively simple, as it is the responsibility of it to retrieve data that is almost ready for display. We can say that QueryStack is a synchronous layer that retrieves data from a *denormal* reading.

This bank may be a denormalized NoSQL as MongoDB (`https://www.microsofttranslator.com/bv.aspx?from=ptto=ena=https%3A%2F%2Fwww.mongodb.com%2F`), Redis (`https://www.microsofttranslator.com/bv.aspx?from=ptto=ena=http%3A%2F%2Fredis.io%2F`), RavenDB (`https://www.microsofttranslator.com/bv.aspx?from=ptto=ena=https%3A%2F%2Fravendb.net%2F`), or any other on the market. The *denormal* concept can be applied with one table per view, or as a *flat query* that returns all the data needed to be displayed.

The use of a *flat query* in an unnormalized bank avoids the need for joins, making queries much faster. We must accept that there will be duplication of data in order to meet this model.

- **CommandStack:** CommandStack is potentially asynchronous. It is in CommandStack where entities, business rules, and other processes will be. Thinking in DDD, the domain belongs to this segment of the application. CommandStack follows a *behavior-centric* approach where all business intention is initially triggered by the client. We use the concept of commands to represent a business intent. The commands declared are of imperative form, are raised asynchronously in the form of events, are interpreted by `CommandHandlers`, and return a success or failure.

Whenever a command is triggered and changes the state of an entity in writing, a database process should be raised for the agents that will update the data needed in the backseat reading.

Synchronization: The following are some strategies to keep the foundations of reading and recording synchronized, and it is necessary to choose the one that best meets your scenario:

- **Automatic updating**: All changes in the state of a given recording database raise a synchronous process to update on the bench
- **Update possible**: All state changes of a given recording database trigger an asynchronous process to update the reading bank, offering an eventual data consistency
- **Controlled update**: A regular process and schedule is raised to synchronize the databases

- **Update on demand**: Every query checks the consistency of the read base compared to the recording, and forces an update if it is out of date

Any update is one of the most used strategies, because it assumes that any given displayed data may already be out of date, so it is not necessary to impose a synchronous update process.

Queueing: Many CQRS implementations may require a message broker for the processing of commands and events. In this case, we have an implementation, as shown in the following diagram:

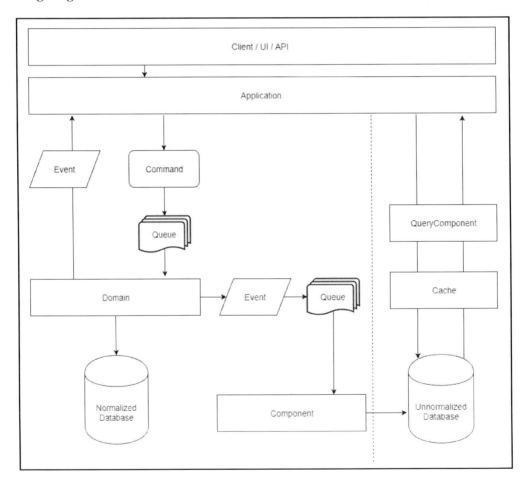

Advantages and disvantages of implementing CQRS

The CQRS presents a different concept from the classic monolithic, where the whole process of writing and reading passes through the same layers and compete with each other in the processing of business rules and database usage. The concepts that are involved with CQRS provide us with greater scalability and availability. It is important to list some of the following positive aspects:

- The commands are asynchronous and processed in the queue so as to reduce the waiting time
- Writing and reading data do not compete for the same resources
- Queries on QueryStack are made separately and independently and do not depend on CommandStack processing
- It is possible to scale the CommandStack processes and QueryStack processes separately
- Expressive domain representation using the ubiquitous language in business intentions and other DDD concepts

The CQRS has many advantages for an application, but we must also talk about some disadvantages:

- CQRS is not easy. There is extra complexity in your application as well as a clear understanding of the domain and the ubiquitous language.
- Further attention is required when using the eventual consistency model. This concept is not mandatory, but requires more attention.
- Depending on the implementation, especially if you use the strategy of eventual consistency, it is common to adopt the use of a message broker. This increases application complexity and component monitoring.

It is important to note that CQRS is not an architectural pattern and can be understood as a form of *componentizing* part of your application. A common misconception is that CQRS should always be used in conjunction with event sourcing. Event sourcing has a strong connection with CQRS, and is easily implemented, since we also have CQRS. However, it is possible to implement event sourcing independent of CQRS.

Definitely, CQRS is an incredible pattern and it should be explored in any type of application, especially with microservices. The flexibility of scalability and the high availability we gain from adopting the pattern outweigh any additional complexity.

Event sourcing – data integrity

Before going directly onto the theme of event sourcing, it is necessary to understand the functioning of most standard applications.

Whenever we run the command UPDATE in the database, we perform a modification to our current representation in the database. With that, whenever we do a query on the database, we seek the current state of a record. This behavior is called state mutation. Let's use an example to make it clearer.

State mutation

Suppose we have a table responsible for administering the access level of a user. The table is composed as follows:

ID	user_name	status	user_manager
1	John Doe	admin	Manager1

As we look at the preceding table, we see that the user John Doe is an administrator and this status was applied by Manager1. After a period of time, it was found that John Doe could never have been the admin of the application and an UPDATE is performed on this row in the table:

```
UPDATE status_user set status='normal_user', user_manager='Manage2' WHERE
ID=1;
```

This change results in some modifications in line with ID = 1:

ID	user_name	status	user_manager
1	John Doe	normal_user	Manager2

In this case, Manager2 was responsible for the change in the status of the user. The current status of the user John Doe is normal_user, but what was the previous status? Who was responsible for making John Doe an application administrator for some period of time?

The default behavior adopted to record changes in the database does not allow us to know the trajectory of a record within the application—we always know only the current state of the registry. To supply to this kind of need, I want to get to know the entire history of a record that enters event sourcing.

Understanding event sourcing

The idea of event sourcing is a little different. Each change in the current state of your database would be a new event in a stream that only allows inclusion. Each update on the table would generate a new line, the change of status. If you have changed to an incorrect status, a new line would be generated by correcting this status. So, we'd have all the changes until you reach the current time of permission for the user.

From the beginning, in the `status_user` table using the concept of event sourcing, the records would be as follows:

ID	user_name	status	user_manager
1	John Doe	admin	Manager1
1	John Doe	normal_user	Manager2

If a new status change is applied to the user `John Doe`, a new line would be generated by keeping track of the changes. Event sourcing uses the *append only* model for database records.

Event sourcing has positives and negatives. Among the positive points are the historical maintenance records, while negatives include exponential growth in the database records' editing operations. For this reason, it is very common to see event sourcing being used with CQRS, precisely, not to encumber the searches in the database due to a large number of the same record.

Summary

This was a great chapter. Finally, we began writing our application, and applied both basic concepts as well as an advanced cache. We now understand the behaviors and concepts of the patterns, CQRS, and event sourcing.

Now, we're ready to move on and continue to build our application.

In the next chapter, we'll keep working on our microservice code and start the environment configuration.

4
Microservice Ecosystem

There are some things we don't know when we write software. For example, whether the software will be a success or not. However, some things will not be right when we write an application and put it into production; there will be failures.

Someone, at some point, said that there can be no software without bugs; at best, the software may have an unknown bug. Unfortunately, this statement is true; we could say that it's a phrase that is almost 100% accurate.

Often, the applications that we write have high test coverage; the domain business also features automated tests and all the integrations as well. Apparently, everything is fine. However, when we talk about microservices, we should add a few potential risk points, for example, network connection, errors in the load balance, and faults in the external service consumption.

Okay, our microservices, at some point, will fail, either due to a bug introduced by the development team or as a result of integration with other services. However, if we are going to have flaws in our application, we should fail with success.

You may be asking: is it possible to fail successfully? The answer to this question is a resounding yes.

Failing successfully means that when a failure occurs, not having services unavailable or any non-availability was partial and not systemic. Quick retrieval problems are another feature that is successful.

In terms of good results at the time of failure, we will take some steps to address this on the stack in which we are working. In this chapter, we will cover the following topics:

- Separation in containers
- Data distribution
- Reaction mechanisms against failures

Separating containers

It is very important to understand how failures happen in order to know how to prevent them. Let's start thinking about common practices in monolithic applications that are routinely taken for microservices architecture. This example will help us understand how to react before the failure.

A common approach is to place the entire structure of an application in a single repository. What I mean is that software code, database, cache, and all the other features of the application, will be on the same machine. I've lost count of the number of times I have come across this scenario.

The following image shows that the **cache**, database, **API**, and **Business Logic** layer are in the same place. At first glance, there's nothing wrong with that. With everything in the same machine, problems such as latency, packet loss, and complexity to deploy are minified:

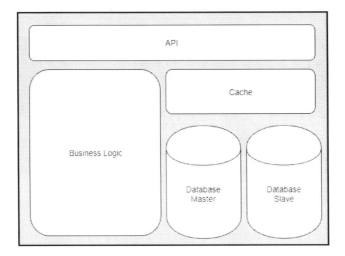

Now, imagine the scenario where the container begins to fail. It is very difficult to clearly identify which component is responsible for the failure of the container. It will take a considerable amount of time to conduct this identification. A flaw in the cache can simply make any application collapse. The degradation process is gradual, and by the time you realize the systemic failure of the container, it may be too late.

As all components are attached and there is no way to treat them in isolation, the entire application will be restarted. There will be no graceful system capable of supporting this activity, and data can be lost, in addition to generating some level of inconsistency.

What once seemed to be positive due to the reduction of complexity in the deployment and the mitigation of latency and packet loss, is now shown as an option where resilience is easily corrupted. Keeping the entire application stack in a single physical component means that all software layers will play by the same features of the component. At this point, failures that could be mitigated are created by our own options.

With this systemic failure, not only has the availability of the application been compromised, but the credibility of the product in the eyes of customers and investors may be affected. The following image represents a failure when the cache has an error and the databases are overloaded, creating a system collapse:

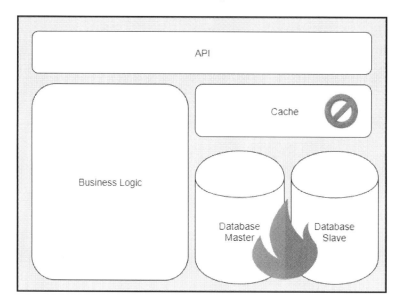

This isn't even the worst-case scenario. Remember the worst word for an application of this type: success. With success comes the need to scale the application. This means we need to multiply the capacity availability, but we won't improve the resilience. We are saying that high availability will be linked to the amount of hits supported, but not about staying available, even if internal failures occur.

This may not be an option for our application. Often, in the ecosystem of the bad practice of microservices, monolithic architecture is repeated. For some software engineers, microservices architecture consists only of separating the business logic from the application. This is a tremendous mistake. The components of the application must also be designed in a scalable manner and, therefore, be quick to modify or reset in an extreme situation.

Layered services architecture

This is a very common anti-pattern when we think of the separation that must be performed on the application. Many engineers confuse the separation of components of the stack with the separation of the logic layer, and, with that, end up generating an anemic domain without any representation in the business.

In the following diagram, we can see this bad practice. The software is composed of three physical components that are not required. The separation of the application is extremely granular. In this diagram, the **Orchestrator** and **DataAccess** don't make sense.

The essential business needs to access the data. Soon, there will be no logic in creating this separation. Another point is that if the **Orchestrator** directly accesses the data, it means that it has some level of intelligence regarding the business of application, which I don't have.

The **Orchestrator** is also completely unnecessary because there is no data to be orchestrated since there is only one layer of business.

This sort of granularity is a very common mistake in microservices architecture and is exactly what we want to avoid at all costs. Such granularity creates complexity, which only deploys the cost of maintaining working physical components and communication costs between the many layers. The following diagram represents the layered services architecture:

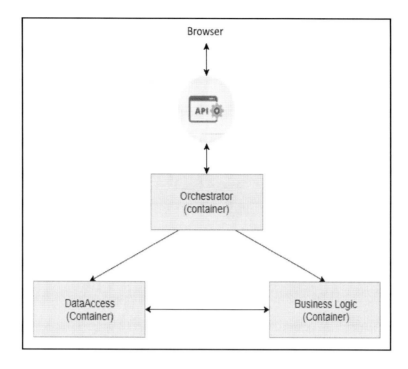

Our next step is to generate a separation that makes sense in our application. It is great to have an image of the preceding diagram in our minds. This is something that we shouldn't repeat under any circumstances.

Separating UsersService

The separation of the components of a microservice can be done in many ways. If we are using physical or virtual containers, the separation should be carried out in a healthy way for the application, enabling scalability, resilience, availability, and each part of the versioning microservice.

Something that I highly recommend is using Docker to divide the components. Firstly, it is very easy to automate; secondly, it is easy to reproduce the same stack of production in other environments, including the right to development, thus avoiding unpleasant surprises.

In all our microservices, let's use Docker as a tool for the creation of application containers. This book sets out to fully explain the use of Docker, but also lets us show its applicability in our microservices.

Before we begin to code Docker, let's explore how our application looks after the separation of the component, as shown in the following diagram:

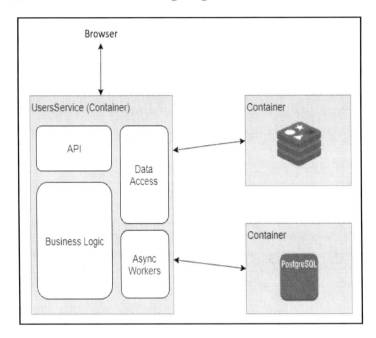

We will make the necessary changes to our project, for this diagram represents the reality of our microservice.

Creating Dockerfile

First, let's create the file `Dockerfile` in `UsersService` itself. This file is responsible for assembling the image of our container and compiling the application.

The `FROM` policy is responsible for indicating which operating system will be used for our application. In this case, we will use a `golang:latest`, which is an Ubuntu with Go properly installed.

APP Dockerfile
For more control, you can copy and build manually
from `golang:latest`.

The `LABEL` policy serves to tell you what the name of our application and version is:

```
LABEL Name=userservice Version=0.0.1
```

With the `RUN` policy, we are creating the default workspace directories of Go. These directories are `src`, `pkg`, and `bin`. To create them, use the `mkdir -p` command shown here, which creates all the directories, indicated by the end of the statement:

```
RUN mkdir -p /go/src \
   && mkdir -p /go/bin \
   && mkdir -p /go/pkg
```

Then, we will use the `ENV` command twice. The first time is to create the `GOPATH` application; without `GOPATH`, the Go application cannot go through the build process. Then, we will use `ENV` to associate `GOPATH` to the `PATH` of the operating system of our container, as shown in the following code snippet:

```
ENV GOPATH=/go
ENV PATH=$GOPATH/bin:$PATH
```

Again, we will use the `RUN` command with `mkdir -p`, but now to create the directory of our application, as follows:

```
# now copy your app to the proper build path
RUN mkdir -p $GOPATH/src/app
```

Then, use `ADD` to indicate the container location on our application within the operating system of the container. Similarly, we will use `WORKDIR` to say that this is our working directory, as shown here:

```
ADD . $GOPATH/src/app
WORKDIR $GOPATH/src/app
```

We will use `RUN` to run the build of our application process. The binary generated will have the name `main` and will be run by the `CMD` policy, as follows:

```
RUN go build -o main .
CMD ["/go/src/app/main"]
```

At the end of our `Dockerfile`, we are exposing the `3000` port for access to application endpoints:

```
EXPOSE 3000
```

Finally, this is the complete `Dockerfile` of our application:

```
# APP Dockerfile
# For more control, you can copy and build manually
FROM golang:latest

LABEL Name=userservice Version=0.0.1

RUN mkdir -p /go/src \
   && mkdir -p /go/bin \
   && mkdir -p /go/pkg
ENV GOPATH=/go
ENV PATH=$GOPATH/bin:$PATH

# now copy your app to the proper build path
RUN mkdir -p $GOPATH/src/app
ADD . $GOPATH/src/app

WORKDIR $GOPATH/src/app
RUN go build -o main .
CMD ["/go/src/app/main"]
EXPOSE 3000
```

After the creation of the `Dockerfile` for the microservice, we will create the `Dockerfile` for our PostgreSQL database.

First, we will create a new directory in our application named `db`. In this, we will create the `Dockerfile` directory for PostgreSQL.

As you can see in the following code block, this file is a lot less complex than the one you created earlier. Simply define the repository where PostgreSQL will be downloaded using the `FROM` policy and, when running the build process of the container, it should also execute the `create.sql`file:

```
FROM postgres

# run create.sql on init
ADD create.sql /docker-entrypoint-initdb.d
```

We ordered the `create.sql` file in time to build the container. What file is that? That's exactly what we will see now.

Within the `db` directory we created recently, let us add another file other than `Dockerfile` itself. This is the `create.sql` file responsible for setting our databases for testing, development, and production:

```
CREATE DATABASE users_prod;
CREATE DATABASE users_dev;
CREATE DATABASE users_test;
```

Now that we have our two `Dockerfile` files, let's get back to our `main` directory and create the microservice file that will be used to orchestrate the first moment in our containers.

For the orchestration, let's use Docker Compose. So, in the main directory of our application, we will create the `docker-compose.yml` file. This is a YAML file and must comply with the standard syntax.

At the beginning of the file, we will declare the version of Docker Compose we used and open the syntax for the services, as shown in the following code:

```
version: '2.1'
services:
```

The first service that lets us declare is the Redis. This service is composed of the name of the container, the image that will be used, the communication port, and a test to verify that the service is running:

```
redis:
    container_name: redis
    image: redis
    ports:
     - "6379:6379"
    healthcheck:
      test: exit 0
```

The second service is the database, our PostgreSQL. This service is composed of the name of the container, the directory where the `Dockerfile` is, the gateway to communicate with the database, environment variables, and a test policy to verify that the service is running. Something that is strongly pointed out is the change of password and the user database. Let's look at the following code:

```
users-service-db:
    container_name: users-service-db
    build: ./db
```

```
ports:
  - 5435:5432 # expose ports - HOST:CONTAINER
environment:
  - POSTGRES_USER=postgres
  - POSTGRES_PASSWORD=postgres
healthcheck:
  test: exit 0
```

The third service is our microservice. The `UsersService` microservice is composed of the name of the container, the downloadable image where the `Dockerfile` is, and the environment variables of this service that depend on the access door and the access links.

Something interesting to note is that we are now using a connection string for each database that will be created in the `create.sql` file that is in the db , as shown in the following code snippet:

```
userservice:
    container_name: userservice
    image: userservice
    build: .
    environment:
        - APP_RD_ADDRESS=redis:6379
        - APP_RD_AUTH=password
        - APP_RD_DBNAME=0
        - APP_SETTINGS=project.config.DevelopmentConfig
        - DATABASE_URL=postgres://postgres:postgres@users-service-
db:5432/users_prod?sslmode=disable
        - DATABASE_DEV_URL=postgres://postgres:postgres@users-service-
db:5432/users_dev?sslmode=disable
        - DATABASE_TEST_URL=postgres://postgres:postgres@users-service-
db:5432/users_test?sslmode=disable
    depends_on:
      users-service-db:
        condition: service_healthy
      redis:
        condition: service_healthy
    ports:
      - 8080:3000
    links:
      - users-service-db
      - redis
```

Finally, our `Docker-compose.yml` is as follows:

```
version: '2.1'

services:
```

```
  redis:
    container_name: redis
    image: redis
    ports:
      - "6379:6379"
    healthcheck:
      test: exit 0

  users-service-db:
    container_name: users-service-db
    build: ./db
    ports:
      - 5435:5432 # expose ports - HOST:CONTAINER
    environment:
      - POSTGRES_USER=postgres
      - POSTGRES_PASSWORD=postgres
    healthcheck:
      test: exit 0

  userservice:
    container_name: userservice
    image: userservice
    build: .
    environment:
      - APP_RD_ADDRESS=redis:6379
      - APP_RD_AUTH=password
      - APP_RD_DBNAME=0
      - APP_SETTINGS=project.config.DevelopmentConfig
      - DATABASE_URL=postgres://postgres:postgres@users-service-
db:5432/users_prod?sslmode=disable
      - DATABASE_DEV_URL=postgres://postgres:postgres@users-service-
db:5432/users_dev?sslmode=disable
      - DATABASE_TEST_URL=postgres://postgres:postgres@users-service-
db:5432/users_test?sslmode=disable
    depends_on:
      users-service-db:
        condition: service_healthy
      redis:
        condition: service_healthy
    ports:
      - 8080:3000
    links:
      - users-service-db
      - redis
```

We still have to make some changes in our application to use our containers perfectly.

Previously, in our `main.go` file, we were composing the connection string with the database, as follows:

```
connectionString := fmt.Sprintf(
  "user=%s password=%s dbname=%s sslmode=disable",
  os.Getenv("POSTGRES_USER"),
  os.Getenv("POSTGRES_PASSWORD"),
  os.Getenv("POSTGRES_DB"),
)
```

As we declare an environment variable for the connection string of the database in our container, this type of composition of the connection string does not make the most sense. Let's change that to a simple call to the environment variable:

```
connectionString := os.Getenv("DATABASE_DEV_URL")
```

In this case, we will be using the database. Another point that we have to change in this file is the port where the application server is running:

```
a.Run(":3000")
```

Now, yes, everything is ready for us to use our microservices with insulated containers.

Using the containers

We already have our containers declared; the time has come to use them. For this, it is necessary to have installed Docker, the `docker-machine`, and the `docker-compose`.

With Docker running as a service, we will use the `docker-machine` to create our host:

```
$ docker-machine create dev
```

With our host created, let's map the `docker-machine` URL host generated:

```
$ eval "$(docker-machine env dev)"
```

Now, let's use the `docker-compose` to create the containers and initialize them:

```
$ docker-compose up -d -build
```

After a few minutes, all containers will be ready for use. We need to know only when the Docker is running our application. For this, we will execute the following command:

```
$ docker-machine ip dev
```

With the IP passed, simply add the port `8080` to the end and start using the microservice with the awareness that all dependencies are properly installed to be more flexible and that it allows us to handle our application much better.

Storage distribution

Saving data is always something very important in any kind of an application; microservices are no different. The main point is that with a distributed application, there is more flexibility to distribute our data.

There are good practices for treating storage in microservices. Obviously, patterns as CQRS are very useful, but are not always sufficient when it comes to performance. The regionalization and depreciation of data are very useful for the health of the application.

Observing the process run for the creation of containers, we can see that not only for the container of the application itself, in the case of `UsersService`, that there are also specific containers for the data storage layer for both, as a cache for the database itself.

Depreciating data

In the era of scientific computing, where data analysis is so important, deleting data is something that sounds absurd. Yes, it's absurd. Similarly, a database with 1 million data rows generates increasingly slow queries.

The question is: if we cannot delete the data from the database, what should we do so that the queries are not compromised? The answer to that question is depreciating data.

The depreciation of data consists of dividing the active data and inactive data, and moving inactive data to storage that has no relevance to the real-time application layer.

Imagine the situation of an application that sells tickets for events. Every day, events are created and carried out, and purchases of tickets for events are completed. This is the routine of this application.

After a period of time, the data about events that have happened is audited, or it serves only for data analysis. There's no sense in keeping data from recent events or still active ones, along with event data that has already been completed for over a year.

However, over time, keeping all the data in a single storage facility generates slower queries and bigger problems for migration or modifications in the structure of the data. Depreciation is a good practice, especially when automated.

Regionalizing data

The common practice, when taken to an application, is to deploy to a server and provide an access point for the application. If the application wins global proportions, the process is repeated; however, it usually performs deployment on servers geographically closest to the new market where the product wants to be established. There's nothing wrong with that; the problem arises with regard to the location of database servers.

It is relatively common to see applications that are strategically distributed geographically, but fetch data from a server many kilometers away. This practice represents a different experience in each part of the world because, for example, if the database servers are in the United States, the experience for the end user will be much better in the United States than in Australia. This is due to physical distance, latency, and possible loss of packets. The solution to this problem is regionalization of the data. If we think of our news portal, people in Europe are more interested in information about Europe than about South America. This means that when my editorial publishing system publishes a new word, you must store the data first by region and let the data be subsequently standardized in a process similar to the CQRS. In a few moments, the data does not need to be standardized due to the specificity of the subject.

Data distribution strategies by geographical location may be the most diverse. However, something that cannot be passed over is the regionalization of data, because it influences directly on the performance of the application.

Bulkheads – using the ecosystem against failures

Throughout this chapter, we've talked about the prevention of failures and how we can develop an application with high availability and resilience. In this section, we will see how our structure can protect us.

Designing for redundancy

By the time our application has performed in only one instance and is very flexible due to the distribution of components in containers, we are still very susceptible to systemic failure.

The use of redundancy is an interesting approach to solving this problem. With redundancy, even if a node of the application is lost, the others can continue responding.

A good example of redundancy for microservices consists of a load balancer with a usage policy to redirect the request. Many nodes can be created, and if one of these nodes fails, there's still another available to respond.

The following diagram seeks to show exactly that. A request is sent to the load balancer, which, according to some rule chosen by the development team and operations, is directed to the implementation of the business layer.

It is very difficult to have a complete breakdown between all nodes of the application. And, if any instability is presented, we will have time to climb a new version, a correction, or simply identify and fix the error encountered:

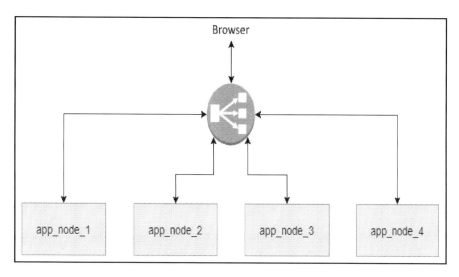

Now, we will apply a load balancer to our application. The most suitable one for a large application is to use a HAProxy, but, in our case, we'll make Nginx assume this responsibility.

In the main directory of our application, we will create another directory with the name nginx, just to be clear on what it is. Within this directory, we will create two new files— Dockerfile and nginx. These files will be enough for our application.

First, we go to the Dockerfile statement. In this file, we are telling Docker which image we will use and what we'll do with a copy of the nginx file, which we still have to create in the /etc/nginx directory of the operating system where Nginx is installed:

```
FROM nginx
COPY nginx.conf /etc/nginx/nginx.conf
```

After the declaration of the Dockerfile, we will create the Nginx configuration file. The nginx.conf file consists of the number of workers that the wrath server handles:

```
worker_processes 4;
```

After this, we apply the configuration of events, in this case, 1024 clients per second:

```
events { worker_connections 1024; }
```

After the initial settings, we will go to the server itself. We will open with the HTTP policy and, at this point, the most important thing is the upstream policy that we are setting up our application nodes in. What is declared in the upstream is what will run on Nginx proxy_pass. Notice that we are passing the name of the container after it is initialized by Docker, and the port where the container is running:

```
upstream user_servers {
    server userservice_userservice_1:3000;
    server userservice_userservice_2:3000;
    server userservice_userservice_3:3000;
    server userservice_userservice_4:3000;
}
```

Finally, our nginx.conf file is as follows:

```
worker_processes 4;

events { worker_connections 1024; }

http {
    sendfile on;

    upstream user_servers {
        server userservice_userservice_1:3000;
        server userservice_userservice_2:3000;
        server userservice_userservice_3:3000;
```

```
        server userservice_userservice_4:3000;
    }

    server {
        listen 80;

        location / {
            proxy_pass http://user_servers;
            proxy_redirect off;
            proxy_set_header Host $host;
            proxy_set_header X-Real-IP $remote_addr;
            proxy_set_header X-Forwarded-For $proxy_add_x_forwarded_for;
            proxy_set_header X-Forwarded-Host $server_name;
        }
    }
}
```

Now, we need to change our `docker-compose.yml` file to create the container of the load balancer. First, modify the `userservice` declaration by removing the `container_name` statement and the ports statement. Remove `container_name` because, with this instruction, Docker does not create names dynamically for each instance of the container. Next, remove ports because now we want access to be performed only by the microservice Nginx server. The port of the microservice is already exposed in the `Dockerfile`. It is only to inform you that the port should stick to Nginx, something we've done in the declaration of the `nginx.conf` file:

```
userservice:
    image: userservice
    build: ./UsersService
    environment:
      - APP_RD_ADDRESS=redis:6379
      - APP_RD_AUTH=password
      - APP_RD_DBNAME=0
      - APP_SETTINGS=project.config.DevelopmentConfig
      - DATABASE_URL=postgres://postgres:postgres@users-service-
db:5432/users_prod?sslmode=disable
      - DATABASE_DEV_URL=postgres://postgres:postgres@users-service-
db:5432/users_dev?sslmode=disable
      - DATABASE_TEST_URL=postgres://postgres:postgres@users-service-
db:5432/users_test?sslmode=disable
    depends_on:
      users-service-db:
        condition: service_healthy
      redis:
        condition: service_healthy
    links:
```

```
    - users-service-db
    - redis
```

Now, let's declare the services of Nginx within the `docker-compose.yml` file. The process is very similar to the declaration of the other services of Docker. Create a name for the container, say where the `Dockerfile` for the build is, in which port we access Nginx, and what is the link for the container:

```
proxy:
    container_name: userservice_loadbalance
    build: ./nginx
    ports:
      - "80:80"
    links:
      - userservice
```

Finally, our `docker-composer.yml` file has the following form:

```
version: '2.1'

services:
  redis:
    container_name: redis
    image: redis
    ports:
      - "6379:6379"
    healthcheck:
      test: exit 0

  users-service-db:
    container_name: users-service-db
    build: ./db
    ports:
      - 5435:5432 # expose ports - HOST:CONTAINER
    environment:
      - POSTGRES_USER=postgres
      - POSTGRES_PASSWORD=postgres
    healthcheck:
      test: exit 0

  userservice:
    image: userservice
    build: ./UsersService
    environment:
      - APP_RD_ADDRESS=redis:6379
      - APP_RD_AUTH=password
      - APP_RD_DBNAME=0
```

```
        - APP_SETTINGS=project.config.DevelopmentConfig
        - DATABASE_URL=postgres://postgres:postgres@users-service-
  db:5432/users_prod?sslmode=disable
        - DATABASE_DEV_URL=postgres://postgres:postgres@users-service-
  db:5432/users_dev?sslmode=disable
        - DATABASE_TEST_URL=postgres://postgres:postgres@users-service-
  db:5432/users_test?sslmode=disable
    depends_on:
      users-service-db:
        condition: service_healthy
      redis:
        condition: service_healthy
    links:
      - users-service-db
      - redis

  proxy:
    container_name: userservice_loadbalance
    build: ./nginx
    ports:
      - "80:80"
    links:
      - userservice
```

This kind of approach is very simple, but it gives our microservice some level of redundancy. The idea is to use tools such as Apache Mesos, Swarm, and Kubernetes; therefore, they possess politics focusing on resilience.

Partitioning by criticality

Knowing the application we're working on, it is very important to know what the most accessed points of the application are, and we end up discovering them the hard way.

Imagine that we are now working with a system of online sales. There are many kinds of components in this type of application, but, obviously, the most important component is what allows the completion of the sale of a product. However, the entire flow of the sale is coupled with business logic. This couples from the window of the store until the moment of payment.

The online store seems to work very well. All times of stress to the system are solved with horizontal scalability by simply adding more machines to the server farm. The problem is that horizontal scalability for this type of application is not an absolute truth. Many resources are shared and immediately available; a delay in this procedure will represent a very high cost for unsatisfactory results or even insignificant ones. Again, the word "success" is a big problem for this application. So is the success that an online store will face on their first Black Friday.

Chaos happens. In a few minutes, we can observe an extremely high number of hits, but with almost no sales. This is definitely not normal. A few more minutes and we will identify the problem. The purchase flow coupling is the major villain in this case. Access to the online shop windows was so high that it blocked the continued purchase; that is, users who were only searching for prices blocked the actual buyers of the products advertised. The prejudice is high and some measures should be taken.

This type of failure in applications with real-time interactivity is very common. Clearly, the amount of hits will be greater than the number of users who will complete the entire flow of interactivity. This type of scenario applies to every type of application that uses real time, whether it is an online store, a game, or a tax declaration system for the government. All these applications have the same feature: high seasonal access with low conversion; however, the conversion to the product, even if less than the amount of hits, can never be affected.

Microservices architecture is very efficient at solving this kind of problem. Using DDD to set the bounded context of each domain and in view of the critical assessment, each part of the application can choose a more intelligent architecture.

As can be seen in the following diagram, adopting the concept of dividing by criticality can climb the application segments that are most required separately. With that, other parts of the software are protected from a stress hit that doesn't belong to them:

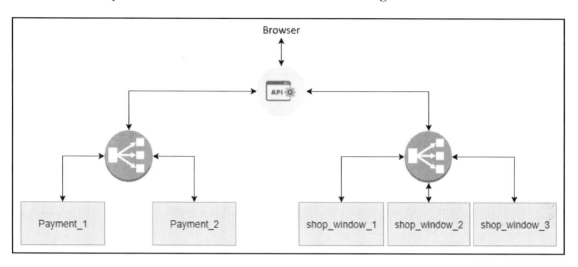

Designing with isolation

We have seen that segregating the application by criticality is something very positive. However, a common misconception is the reuse of components. A classic example of bad resource sharing is the reuse of a database. No matter how optimized your load balancer is, the threading level of criticality to your own application, or how well they have divided their domains, if all or most of your application depends on a single physical component, the collapse is imminent.

The following diagram is a great example of a sloppy design. All components of the application, regardless of the domain, depend on the same physical component, in this case, the database. This type of mistake is also common when it comes to the cache and message broker:

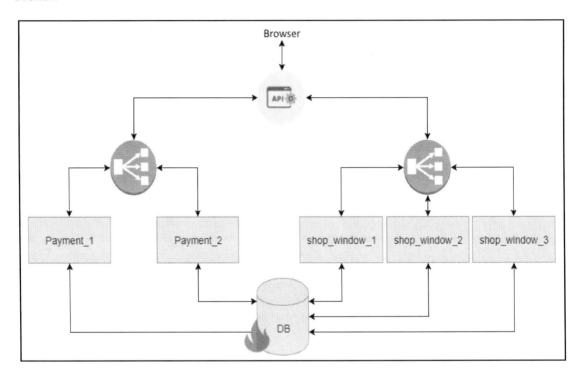

It is important to remember that data, cached or not, is also a part of the domain of microservices. As far as possible, the physical components, such as the database, should also be independent, as shown in the following diagram:

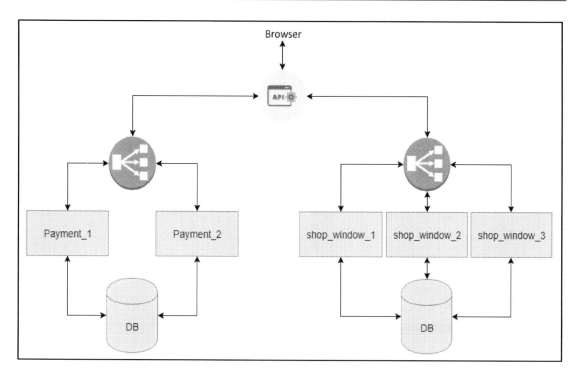

This kind of approach to physical components is more common, allowing more convenience in migrations and database sharding.

Fail fast

We will use an online store as an example. We have seen that dividing the application by criticality, always respecting the boundaries of DDD, is very positive with respect to availability. We also saw that having the software to depend on is a really physical component that represents a big risk point. However, much of this may protect us from glitches or risks in the system architecture. There are times that it does not depend on our part. Sometimes, the external service will use microservices in our ecosystem.

In the case of the payment process in an online store, the microservice is the final step of the purchase, being responsible for completing the payment of the product requested by the client. Payment must be communicated using credit card gateways. If one of these gateways presents any outages, our microservices can start to fail due to dependency on external services.

The following diagram shows an example where our microservice payment is trying to establish a connection with a billing system, but there are problems:

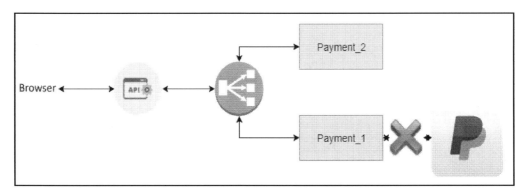

We can't just wait for the connection to be restored; we must fail fast and take a decision on what to do. For this type of problem, the circuit breaker approach can be very interesting. We could set up a timeout or connection failure policy to offer some other form of payment, or submit a friendly message of failure. This avoids a possible widespread system failure due to exhaustion of resources.

Circuit breaker

The circuit breaker is an automatic operating switch that turns itself off when there is an overload or short circuit. As well as the electric fuse, the purpose of the circuit breaker is failing quickly and protecting electrical installations. In the case of a microservice, it protects the general integrity of the application.

Imagine the situation where a microservice presents slowness. The requests keep coming, and it begins to be queued. At some point, collateral damage happens. Especially in the case of a microservice that has a dependency on communication with other microservices, we need to apply the circuit breaker.

The concept of the circuit breaker is relatively simple, possessed by only two states:

- **On**: Releasing the call to the external dependency
- **Off**: Failing the call immediately and taking a previously configured action

In practice, instead of microservices directly accessing the external dependency, the circuit breaker will put itself in the middle of the call. In case of any failure according to predetermined parameters, which, for example, may be a timeout, the circuit breaker interrupts the communication with the dependency that is failing. Of course, something can be taken by the microservice side. The behavior of the circuit breaker can be seen in the following diagram:

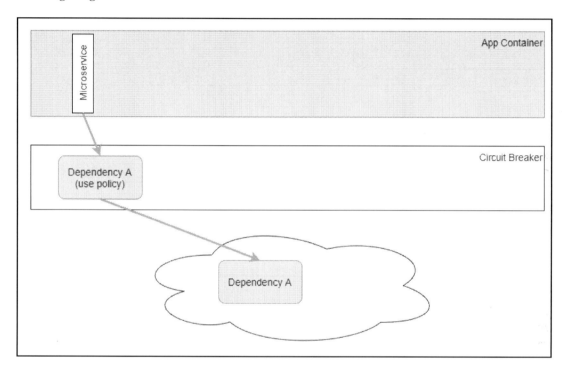

There are some frameworks that assist in the implementation of the circuit breaker. Currently, the framework with greater prominence is Hystrix, which was created by the Netflix development team. Hystrix was originally developed in Java, but there are already implementations of this algorithm in other programming languages, including Go.

Summary

Throughout this chapter, we saw good practices that can make our microservices more resilient and fault tolerant, as well as applying containers in our application and developing a `UsersService` cluster using Nginx.

Towards the end, we understood patterns that can be applied to any technology, which make many microservices safer. Our next step is to go on with our project and get our news portal up and running.

5
Shared Data Microservice Design Pattern

In this chapter, much is said about microservices architecture; several cases of success are demonstrated, and a lot of patterns are taught. In addition, you are introduced to crucial concepts that developers face almost every day. All new concepts are instructive and aim to give more convenience, security, and speed to development using microservices architecture.

However, most concepts and techniques focus on new projects and use the microservice architecture. There are a few cases where something that is thought to be a legacy project is departing from another architectural pattern. There are also even rarer cases of transition of architecture.

Often, migration to microservices is painful due to a lack of documentation and the ultimate goal of achieving high standards. This chapter aims to show you exactly how to make a transition from legacy to the world of microservices.

In this chapter, we'll look at the following:

- Breaking a monolithic application
- Developing new microservices
- Data orchestration
- Response consolidation
- Microservice communication
- Anti-pattern
- Best practices

Understanding the pattern

New designs with any kind of legacy are called **green projects** or **greenfield applications**. The part of the project that already exists is commonly called **brown projects**. It is, obviously, simpler to apply **Domain-Driven Design (DDD)** and patterns on green projects than to legacy projects.

The **shared data pattern** is a controversial pattern when we talk about microservices. It would certainly be considered an anti-pattern if we applied it to a green project. However, it is a pattern that should be considered as a temporary pattern for legacy applications that are in a transitional phase.

The great concept behind this pattern is to use the same physical structure for data storage. This pattern can be used when there is some doubt about the structure of the data, or when the communication layer between the microservices is not well-defined.

The following diagram is quite interesting, as it illustrates how the pattern works:

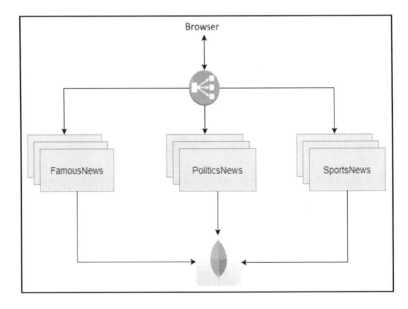

Breaking a monolithic application into microservices

It is very important to know that in the beginning of the transition period, the impression is that we're in a maze without an end, and that it was a big mistake to start the migration process for microservices.

Working with frustrations and pressures is fundamental to successful migration. It is essential to have a plan from the beginning of the project, with clear targets and deadlines.

Obviously, respecting the deadline is the biggest challenge, especially when you walk through unknown terrain. However, it is very important that the deadlines are clearly outlined. This is very useful, as it helps us to know what stage the project is at.

There are some steps that may seem somewhat unnecessary or irrelevant. However, without these steps, any migration project for microservices fails badly. All the steps are described next, in the sequence in which they are to be carried out. These steps are as follows:

1. Defining priorities
2. Setting deadlines
3. Defining the domains of the application
4. Making experiments
5. Defining standards
6. Creating a prototype
7. Sending to production

Defining priorities

Many companies want the best development ecosystem or great speed of implementation of features, but do not understand that this requires investment. In the case of migration of software architecture, the investment is not only financial, but also time-related.

If the development of microservices cannot be defined as a priority for the whole company, it is better not to start the project. Migrations are neither simple nor easy, and may, at first, seem catastrophic. If this migration is not very well-defined as a priority, the project will stop midway, and the company will face something much worse than keeping a monolith. The worst-case scenario is when you are left with a hybrid application, where a part is in the monolith and a part in microservices. Over time, ambiguities may arise where the application represents the business, and maintaining this application would become even harder.

Setting deadlines

It is essential to set deadlines for the migration process. Deadlines serve as metrics for the health and progress of the project. Obviously, the deadlines may be revised as new complexities are aggregated.

These deadlines need to be related to the microservices and may include deadlines for stack definitions, definitions of domains, dates of the early development, and a forecast of when performance tests can be run, for example.

Defining the domain

In Chapter 1, *Understanding the Microservices Concepts*, we talked a lot about DDD, definitions, and the limits of the business layer. It is exactly at this point that all our knowledge about DDD is applied.

Without well-defined domains, the migration process becomes too time-consuming and prone to mistakes, and this leads to the laborious steps of a redesign.

Making experiments

Perform experiments before applying any technology or pattern again. In some cases, there is documentation with performance in simulated scenarios, but these scenarios can be simulated too much or may simply not reflect reality.

All technology developments should be adopted only after good experiments, keeping in mind sequential asynchronous scenarios, with the load in progress and with a lot of immediate loading. The experiments must be played, and preferably, submit deterministic results.

Defining standards

After the experiment, it is very important to define standards. The defaults should not be thought of as comment or code architecture, but as patterns of communication between teams, documentation, language, and processes. When the standards are not clear, the teams become the *Tower of Babel* within a short period of time.

Creating a prototype

A lot can be thought, written, and defined, but, without a practical test, nothing can be taken as real. Of course, venturing into a new ecosystem is a big risk, so, it is best to create a prototype to verify if all concepts, experiments, and patterns chosen can be applied efficiently.

A good tip for creating a prototype is to choose the smallest and least complex field possible; a field which, effectively, does not represent a risk to the application as a whole.

Sending to production

Although many tests may be performed and the prototypes may have obtained success, nothing is equal to validation in production. It seems desperate or insane, but this is really a great advantage when it comes to microservices architecture.

Sending microservices to production can be gradual and controlled. The idea is to send something immature for production and let the customers validate this. In fact, it helps to control the release and take actual metrics.

Developing new microservices

So far, we have been developing `UsersService`, which is our microservice responsible for user data. Now, let's start the development of microservices responsible for manipulating the data. They are as follows:

- `FamousNewsService`
- `PoliticsNewsService`
- `SportsNewsService`

Our domains have been defined in previous chapters. Now, let us write the code of these microservices in practice. Let us start with `FamousNewsService`.

Writing the microservice configuration file

The `config.py` file is where the settings for each development environment exist. The file is divided into classes that have the definition of each environment.

The first class is `BaseConfig`. This class is used only as an inheritance for the other classes:

```python
class BaseConfig:
    """Base configuration"""
    DEBUG = False
    TESTING = False
    MONGODB_SETTINGS = {}
```

After the declaration of `BaseConfig`, we will declare the other classes that manipulate the configuration of each environment. In this case, the environments are Development, Test, and Production, representing each of the environments that we have—`DevelopmentConfig`, `TestingConfig`, and `ProductionConfig` classes respectively.

The classes have identical structures, the only modification being the connection string with the database:

```python
class DevelopmentConfig(BaseConfig):
    """Development configuration"""
    DEBUG = True
    MONGODB_SETTINGS = {
        'db': 'famous_dev',
        'host': '{}{}'.format(
            os.environ.get('DATABASE_HOST'),
            'famous_dev',
        ),
    }
class TestingConfig(BaseConfig):
    """Testing configuration"""
    DEBUG = True
    TESTING = True
    MONGODB_SETTINGS = {
        'db': 'famous_test',
        'host': '{}{}'.format(
            os.environ.get('DATABASE_HOST'),
            'famous_test',
        ),
```

```
    }

class ProductionConfig(BaseConfig):
    """Production configuration"""
    DEBUG = False
    MONGODB_SETTINGS = {
        'db': 'famous',
        'host': '{}{}'.format(
            os.environ.get('DATABASE_HOST'),
            'famous',
        ),
    }
```

Creating our model

At first, our `models.py` has only one entity in the database. This entity is `News`. The structure is very simple and can, clearly, be incremented. This is a good tip: start simple, make tests, and write code that will really be used. The `News` class is the one that represents the central point of the domain of our application.

First, we declare the imports, as follows:

```
import datetime
from flask_mongoengine import MongoEngine
```

After that, we declare an instance of `MongoEngine`, which is the tool that we use to give structure to the data coming from MongoDB:

```
db = MongoEngine()
```

Now, we will declare the class `News` itself with the fields that match the representation of the entity. The class is very simple and the fields are completely self-explanatory:

```
class News(db.Document):
    title = db.StringField(required=True, max_length=200)
    content = db.StringField(required=True)
    author = db.StringField(required=True, max_length=50)
    created_at = db.DateTimeField(default=datetime.datetime.now)
    published_at = db.DateTimeField()
    news_type = db.StringField(default="famous")
    tags = db.ListField(db.StringField(max_length=50))
```

Exposing the microservice data

With the model declared, let's implement the `views.py` file. As mentioned in a previous chapter, let us use `flask` as the framework of microservices for `News`.

First, we declare the imports necessary for the operation of the `views.py` file:

```
import datetime
import mongoengine
from flask import Blueprint, jsonify, request
from models import News
```

Now, we will instantiate the class from the `flask` called `Blueprint`. This tool will need a few decorators to declare the access routes for the application:

```
famous_news = Blueprint('famous_news', __name__)
```

The first route that will be declared is responsible for providing a `News` by ID—a simple process. First, we use the variable `famous_news` with the `Blueprint` as a decorator for prescribing the route of access. Note that we indicate in the decorator that only requests using the HTTP GET verb will be accepted. Another interesting point is that we specify the type of ID that will be allowed, in this case, a string. This is precisely because MongoDB IDs are unique hashes:

```
@famous_news.route('/famous/news/<string:news_id>', methods=['GET'])
```

After this, we declare the function name that will be our view. Inside the function, there is a `dict` as a template to create the response that will be sent by our view:

```
def get_single_news(news_id):
    """Get single user details"""
    response_object = {
        'status': 'fail',
        'message': 'User does not exist'
    }
```

So, we need to search by ID in the database itself with a success response template. This process is wrapped in a `try...except` block. If an invalid or non-existent ID is passed, MongoEngine sends us the `DoesNotExist` exception. In the end, we JSONify to format the output in JSON with the appropriate HTTP code. Take a look at the following example:

```
try:
    news = News.objects.get(id=news_id)
    response_object = {
        'status': 'success',
        'data': news,
```

```
    }
    return jsonify(response_object), 200
except mongoengine.DoesNotExist:
    return jsonify(response_object), 404
```

The first function of our view is in the following format:

```
@famous_news.route('/famous/news/<string:news_id>', methods=['GET'])
def get_single_news(news_id):
    """Get single user details"""
    response_object = {
        'status': 'fail',
        'message': 'User does not exist'
    }
    try:
        news = News.objects.get(id=news_id)
        response_object = {
            'status': 'success',
            'data': news,
        }
        return jsonify(response_object), 200
    except mongoengine.DoesNotExist:
        return jsonify(response_object), 404
```

All views have very similar structures; we change only the internal code of each function to allow for what the view must do.

The next view is responsible for bringing all the news in paged form. Again, the view creation process is the same. First, access the route, then search for the composition of the template of a reply in the database, and then the reply itself using the JSONify:

```
@famous_news.route('/famous/news/<int:num_page>/<int:limit>',
methods=['GET'])
def get_all_news(num_page, limit):
    """Get all users"""
    news = News.objects.paginate(page=num_page, per_page=limit)
    response_object = {
        'status': 'success',
        'data': news.items,
    }
    return jsonify(response_object), 200
```

The next function, `views.py`, is similar in structure, but slightly different internally, since this is the view of the creation of `News`.

This function also has the access route and a name, but what is peculiar is that we capture the request and translate JSON received for `dict`. If the information is invalid, an error is returned with the proper HTTP code:

```
if not post_data:
    response_object = {
        'status': 'fail',
        'message': 'Invalid payload.'
    }
    return jsonify(response_object), 400
```

After validation, we instantiate and save `News` with the data from the request:

```
news = News(
    title=post_data['title'],
    content=post_data['content'],
    author=post_data['author'],
    tags=post_data['tags'],
).save()
```

In the end, our view has the following form with all the persistence layers and with the appropriate HTTP responses:

```
@famous_news.route('/famous/news', methods=['POST'])
def add_news():
    post_data = request.get_json()
    if not post_data:
        response_object = {
            'status': 'fail',
            'message': 'Invalid payload.'
        }
        return jsonify(response_object), 400
    news = News(
        title=post_data['title'],
        content=post_data['content'],
        author=post_data['author'],
        tags=post_data['tags'],
    ).save()
    response_object = {
        'status': 'success',
        'news': news,
    }
    return jsonify(response_object), 201
```

In our domain, we create `News`, but do not publish immediately. For this task, we have another function in the `views.py` file.

This endpoint receives in your route the ID of the `News` that we publish, performs the same search in the database, performs an update on the date of the publication of `News`, and returns the appropriate HTTP response. The only difference that we've done so far is update the related `News`:

```
@famous_news.route('/famous/news/<string:news_id>/publish/',
methods=['GET'])
def publish_news(news_id):
    try:
        news = News.objects.get(id=news_id)
        news.update(published_at=datetime.datetime.now)
        news.reload()
        response_object = {
            'status': 'success',
            'news': news,
        }
        return jsonify(response_object), 200
    except mongoengine.DoesNotExist:
        return jsonify(response_object), 404
```

Obviously, the only update we do in `News` is not related to the date of publication. Misconceptions about the contents of `News` can happen, and we need to allow edits. The process is strictly equal to the update of the date of publication, with only some fields that have the information changed:

```
@famous_news.route('/famous/news', methods=['PUT'])
def update_news():
    try:
        post_data = request.get_json()
        news = News.objects.get(id=post_data['news_id'])
        news.update(
            title=post_data.get('title', news.title),
            content=post_data.get('content', news.content),
            author=post_data.get('author', news.author),
            tags=post_data.get('tags', news.tags),
        )
        news.reload()
        response_object = {
            'status': 'success',
            'news': news,
        }
        return jsonify(response_object), 200
    except mongoengine.DoesNotExist:
        return jsonify(response_object), 404
```

The last function of our view so far is that it allows the deletion of News. The process is identical to the other views, the only difference being in the execution of the deletion in the database:

```python
@famous_news.route('/famous/news/<string:news_id>', methods=['DELETE'])
def delete_news(news_id):
    News.objects(id=news_id).delete()
    response_object = {
        'status': 'success',
        'news_id': news_id,
    }
    return jsonify(response_object), 200
```

Finally, our complete views.py file has the following formatting:

```python
import datetime
import mongoengine

from flask import Blueprint, jsonify, request
from models import News
famous_news = Blueprint('famous_news', __name__)
@famous_news.route('/famous/news/<string:news_id>', methods=['GET'])
def get_single_news(news_id):
    """Get single user details"""
    response_object = {
        'status': 'fail',
        'message': 'User does not exist'
    }
    try:
        news = News.objects.get(id=news_id)
        response_object = {
            'status': 'success',
            'data': news,
        }
        return jsonify(response_object), 200
    except mongoengine.DoesNotExist:
        return jsonify(response_object), 404
@famous_news.route('/famous/news/<int:num_page>/<int:limit>',
methods=['GET'])
def get_all_news(num_page, limit):
    """Get all users"""
    news = News.objects.paginate(page=num_page, per_page=limit)
    response_object = {
        'status': 'success',
        'data': news.items,
    }
    return jsonify(response_object), 200
```

```python
@famous_news.route('/famous/news', methods=['POST'])
def add_news():
    post_data = request.get_json()
    if not post_data:
        response_object = {
            'status': 'fail',
            'message': 'Invalid payload.'
        }
        return jsonify(response_object), 400
    news = News(
        title=post_data['title'],
        content=post_data['content'],
        author=post_data['author'],
        tags=post_data['tags'],
    ).save()
    response_object = {
        'status': 'success',
        'news': news,
    }
    return jsonify(response_object), 201


@famous_news.route('/famous/news/<string:news_id>/publish/',
methods=['GET'])
def publish_news(news_id):
    try:
        news = News.objects.get(id=news_id)
        news.update(published_at=datetime.datetime.now)
        news.reload()
        response_object = {
            'status': 'success',
            'news': news,
        }
        return jsonify(response_object), 200
    except mongoengine.DoesNotExist:
        return jsonify(response_object), 404


@famous_news.route('/famous/news', methods=['PUT'])
def update_news():
    try:
        post_data = request.get_json()
        news = News.objects.get(id=post_data['news_id'])
        news.update(
            title=post_data.get('title', news.title),
            content=post_data.get('content', news.content),
            author=post_data.get('author', news.author),
            tags=post_data.get('tags', news.tags),
```

```
        )
        news.reload()
        response_object = {
            'status': 'success',
            'news': news,
        }
        return jsonify(response_object), 200
    except mongoengine.DoesNotExist:
        return jsonify(response_object), 404


@famous_news.route('/famous/news/<string:news_id>', methods=['DELETE'])
def delete_news(news_id):
    News.objects(id=news_id).delete()
    response_object = {
        'status': 'success',
        'news_id': news_id,
    }
    return jsonify(response_object), 200
```

Preparing the app to run

The app.py file has the responsibility to run any application. For this file, let's start declaring the imports necessary. Note that, in addition to Flask, we import the Blueprint with all our routes and the MongoEngine instance containing the declaration of our entity:

```
import os
from flask import Flask
from views import famous_newsfrom models import db
```

Now, we go on to instantiate Flask and pass the settings of the environments, the database instance, and the instance of the view routes, as follows:

```
# instantiate the app
app = Flask(__name__)

# set config
app_settings = os.getenv('APP_SETTINGS')
app.config.from_object(app_settings)

db.init_app(app)

# register blueprints
app.register_blueprint(famous_news)
```

At the end of the file, we have a simple statement to perform `Flask` on port 5000:

```
if __name__ == '__main__':
    app.run(host='0.0.0.0', port=5000)
```

The file `app.py` consists of the following formatting:

```
import os
from flask import Flask

from views import famous_news
from models import db

# instantiate the app
app = Flask(__name__)

# set config
app_settings = os.getenv('APP_SETTINGS')
app.config.from_object(app_settings)

db.init_app(app)

# register blueprints
app.register_blueprint(famous_news)

if __name__ == '__main__':
    app.run(host='0.0.0.0', port=5000)
```

Creating the Dockerfile

Our application is being developed on all containers and this case is no different. Let us declare our microservice `Dockerfile`. In this case, we will use a Python container, since it is the programming language used in microservices.

In this file, there are two points of attention. The first is the file `requirements.txt`, which contains all the dependencies of the project. The second point of attention is the exhibition of port 5000, because the application server runs there:

```
FROM python:3.6.1
COPY . /app
WORKDIR /app
RUN pip install -r requirements.txt
ENTRYPOINT ["python"]
CMD ["app.py"]
EXPOSE 5000
```

Dependencies with requirements.txt

This is the file with the project dependencies. Don't worry about understanding all the dependencies that are in this file—many of them are dependencies of dependencies. The important thing here is that before using the application, the installation of these libraries is required:

```
appnope==0.1.0
blinker==1.4
click==6.7
decorator==4.1.2
Flask==0.12.2
flask-mongoengine==0.9.3
Flask-Script==2.0.6
Flask-WTF==0.14.2
ipdb==0.10.3
ipython==6.2.1
ipython-genutils==0.2.0
itsdangerous==0.24
jedi==0.11.0
Jinja2==2.9.6
MarkupSafe==1.0
mongoengine==0.14.3
parso==0.1.0
pexpect==4.2.1
pickleshare==0.7.4
prompt-toolkit==1.0.15
ptyprocess==0.5.2
Pygments==2.2.0
pymongo==3.5.1
simplegeneric==0.8.1
six==1.11.0
traitlets==4.3.2
wcwidth==0.1.7
Werkzeug==0.12.2
WTForms==2.1
Flask-Testing==0.6.2
```

Regarding the code, the three `News` microservices are strictly equal, the only changes being some internal declarations, as in routes and settings.

Consider the following routes:

```
@famous_news.route('/famous/news/<string:news_id>', methods=['GET'])
@politics_news.route('/politics/news/<string:news_id>', methods=['GET'])
@sports_news.route('/sports/news/<string:news_id>', methods=['GET'])
```

Consider the following configuration:

```
MONGODB_SETTINGS = {
        'db': 'famous_test',
...

MONGODB_SETTINGS = {
        'db': 'politics_test',
...

MONGODB_SETTINGS = {
        'db': 'sports_test',
...
```

In fact, the microservices arise with the same structure. However, the evolution and the development of each of these microservices is completely independent.

Data orchestration

In shared data patterns, there is no need for the orchestration of data, because the microservices will use the same physical component for storage of the data. In the case of our related microservice, `News`, this can be seen in the `docker-compose.yml` file of our application.

In our archive, we add that MongoDB is our database. The declaration is done very simply by giving a name to the container, specifying the door where MongoDB will be exposed, and giving the command that should be executed for the functioning of Mongo:

```
mongo:
    image: mongo:latest
    container_name: "mongodb"
    ports:
        - 27017:27017
    command: mongod --smallfiles --logpath=/dev/null # --quiet
```

Now, we add the microservices that we created earlier. The three offices have the same pattern. The highlight is the environment variables. The `APP_SETTINGS` variable indicates which setting we adopt in the microservice according to what is contained in the `config.py` file of the application. The `DATABASE_HOST` variable shows us the route of access to the database. Consider the following code:

Note that the three microservices point to the same database, because they use the same container.

```
famous_news_service:
    image: famous_news_service
    build: ./FamousNewsService
    volumes:
      - '.:/usr/src/app'
    environment:
      - APP_SETTINGS=config.DevelopmentConfig
  - DATABASE_HOST=mongodb://mongo:27017/
      depends_on:
        - mongo
      links:
        - mongo

politics_news_service:
    image: politics_news_service
    build: ./PoliticsNewsService
    volumes:
      - '.:/usr/src/app'
    environment:
      - APP_SETTINGS=config.DevelopmentConfig
  - DATABASE_HOST=mongodb://mongo:27017/
      depends_on:
        - mongo
      links:
        - mongo

sports_news_service:
    image: sports_news_service
    build: ./SportsNewsService
    volumes:
      - '.:/usr/src/app'
    environment:
      - APP_SETTINGS=config.DevelopmentConfig
  - DATABASE_HOST=mongodb://mongo:27017/
      depends_on:
        - mongo
      links:
        - mongo
```

However, the internal control patterns of data is highly recommended. **Command Query Responsibility Segregation** (**CQRS**) and caching first can be applied normally. CQRS is a little more complicated than just the amount of physical data storage components, but caching fits nicely into this pattern.

The alert point is exactly about the cache. The shared data pattern is not just about sharing the storage of the database, but also of other physical storage resources such as cache. So, removal of items from the cache should be treated very thoroughly.

Consolidating responses

The shared data pattern does not address any kind of consolidation of reply, because this is a pattern with the focus on storage. However, we need to access our microservices. To do that, we'll modify some of our Nginx configurations.

We'll totally modify the instances of upstream configuration. As you can see, we modified the upstream name and added more server instances to the direction of our microservices. In this setting, each microservice has four instances:

```
upstream proxy_servers {
        server bookproject_userservice_1:3000;
        server bookproject_userservice_2:3000;
        server bookproject_userservice_3:3000;
        server bookproject_userservice_4:3000;
        server bookproject_famous_news_service_1:5000;
        server bookproject_famous_news_service_2:5000;
        server bookproject_famous_news_service_3:5000;
        server bookproject_famous_news_service_4:5000;
        server bookproject_politics_news_service_1:5000;
        server bookproject_politics_news_service_2:5000;
        server bookproject_politics_news_service_3:5000;
        server bookproject_politics_news_service_4:5000;
        server bookproject_sports_news_service_1:5000;
        server bookproject_sports_news_service_2:5000;
        server bookproject_sports_news_service_3:5000;
        server bookproject_sports_news_service_4:5000;
    }
```

After you modify the configuration of the upstream method, change the proxy_pass update so that upstream is used:

```
location / {
            proxy_pass              http://proxy_servers;
```

Microservice communication

So far, all our microservices are accessed directly using the HTTP protocol. With the shared data pattern, that will not be modified. All the necessary communication for our microservices is declared in the configuration file of our Nginx so far.

We are in the process of the gradual evolution of our application and, in later chapters, you'll start learning about microservices communication itself.

Storage sharing anti-pattern

The shared data pattern is definitely an anti-pattern for green projects and, as such, should not be seen as a final solution, even if it is for legacy projects. In the previous chapter, we saw the consequences of depositing too much responsibility on a physical component.

The ideal situation is to always seek an elegant solution for data sharing. Improvements in communication between microservices, specialization of endpoints to receive all necessary information for business, and system message queues are only a few options with regards to the sharing of information.

Best practices

Hardly any application has no storage, and it is always very inviting to use it indiscriminately. However, improper use of storage can be a problem for any type of application, including microservices.

When we think of the use of a pattern such as shared data, we have to adopt some good practices, which are listed as follows:

- **Databases are for storing data, not for business rules**: Storing business rules in the database is a mistake, because it makes the application dependent on a structure, the implementation of caches, and hinders the process of data migration and distribution.
- **Databases are for storing data, not to communicate events**: Some development teams adopt the process of triggers with their own database resources or workers observing changes to the information stored. The problem is that these triggers are difficult to monitor and debug, and are also a way to get business rules for storage.

- **Do not create entities with cyclic dependency**: Without a doubt, this is one of the biggest problems that can happen in storage. Migration to a standalone database is practically impossible without the restructuring of domains.

When you don't pay attention to the aforementioned basic good practices, the development of your application using other patterns becomes very difficult.

Testing

As the shared data pattern focuses on the storage layer, we will have layers of extremely simple tests, where unit tests and functional tests are enough. Let's look at a brief example.

In the file `FamousNewsService tests.py`, there's a bunch of interesting tests to run. First, let's declare our `import` statements. The highlight is `flask_testing`, which will be the basis of all our tests. This tool provides a couple of interesting functionalities—including how to access the settings of the Flask and HTTP clients:

```
import json
import unittest
from app import app
from flask_testing import TestCase
```

Now, we write the base class for our functional tests. We use the `TestingConfig` setting for this task:

```
class BaseTestCase(TestCase):

    def create_app(self):
        app.config.from_object('config.TestingConfig')
        return app
```

We then declare the unit tests of our configuration layer:

```
class TestDevelopmentConfig(TestCase):
    def create_app(self):
        app.config.from_object('config.DevelopmentConfig')
        return app
    def test_app_is_development(self):
        self.assertTrue(app.config['DEBUG'] is True)
class TestTestingConfig(TestCase):
    def create_app(self):
        app.config.from_object('config.TestingConfig')
        return app
```

```python
    def test_app_is_testing(self):
        self.assertTrue(app.config['DEBUG'])
        self.assertTrue(app.config['TESTING'])

class TestProductionConfig(TestCase):
    def create_app(self):
        app.config.from_object('config.ProductionConfig')
        return app

    def test_app_is_production(self):
        self.assertFalse(app.config['DEBUG'])
        self.assertFalse(app.config['TESTING'])
```

Now, let us write a test of our routes as an example. In this case, we're trying to create a News microservice. This is a functional test, since we access the application via the endpoint and check the result received. Note that the client that performs the POST is in the instance, which, by using inheritance, comes from flask_testing:

```python
class TestNewsService(BaseTestCase):
    def test_add_news(self):
        """Ensure a new user can be added to the database."""
        with self.client:
            response = self.client.post(
                '/famous/news',
                data=json.dumps(dict(
                    title='My Test',
                    content='Just a service test',
                    author='unittest',
                    tags=['Test', 'Functional_test'],
                )),
                content_type='application/json',
            )
            data = json.loads(response.data.decode())
            self.assertEqual(response.status_code, 201)
            self.assertIn('success', data['status'])
            self.assertIn('My Test', data['news']['title'])
```

At the end, we write the code responsible for performing tests in a call from Python:

```python
if __name__ == '__main__':
    unittest.main()
```

As the tests show no pattern again, I won't go into the details. In later chapters, we will see some very interesting patterns. It is worth remembering that we are evolving our application.

Pros and cons of the shared data pattern

The shared data pattern is liked by many as an anti-pattern, but seen by others as an old concept that should no longer be applied. However, there is considerable distance between the ideal world and the real world.

In the ideal world, all projects are greenfields and nobody needs to work on legacy code or change the architecture of a monolithic application. However, the reality is not that. Legacy projects are now serving users. These applications are online stores, financial applications, social networks, and a myriad of businesses that require upgrading to achieve automation, scalability, and resilience.

The shared data pattern search just speeds up the process of change for these legacy applications. It has the positive benefit of giving the development team time to segregate the information from the database and evaluate the consistency of the data.

Definitely, the shared data pattern helps many companies to reset architecture projects.

A negative point is the fact that the pattern creates at least one point of systemic risk because all the microservices are deposited on storage.

Yes, the shared data pattern can be considered an anti-pattern, which cannot be used. In the end, it is up to the development team to understand the capability and the need for the software in which they are working.

Summary

In this chapter, we created our `News` microservice and connected it to the database. We have looked at an extremely useful pattern for migration from monolithic to microservices.

If the problem revolves around scaling an application, the shared data pattern is a good option on a temporary basis. The problem may also involve the storage layer; we'll see how to solve this in the next chapter.

6
Aggregator Microservice Design Pattern

In the previous chapter, we saw the operation and applicability of the shared data pattern design. We know that the pattern mentioned here is temporary; that is, it is a pattern for some transition scenarios from monolithic to microservices because of the risk over some components. In this chapter, we will move on from the shared data design pattern to apply a more consistent pattern with good development practices to microservices.

It will be presented and applied to the **aggregator design pattern**. Precisely, with the new pattern, we will apply **Command Query Responsibility Segregation (CQRS)** and **event sourcing** to our News microservices. Another interesting point is that we will restructure our storage distribution. There is no doubt that this will be a chapter full of new concepts and a lot of practice.

In this chapter, we'll see the following:

- Database segregation
- Microservice refactoring
- Microservice communication
- Functional tests
- Integration tests

Understanding the pattern

The aggregator design pattern is a pattern with a simple concept, but the applicability can be complex, depending on the scenario to which it applies. If we look at the real world, we will see that the aggregator design pattern is one of the most applicable and scalable patterns.

Obviously, there must be a need for the use of the aggregator design pattern. Let's look at our current microservices. We built a microservice to manipulate data from the `UsersService` and three other microservices to manipulate the data from the `News` microservice.

When we deal with our `UsersService`, we can say that, so far, this microservice is sufficient in itself. The business of a microservice is very simple and consists of registering and exposing user data; there is no business requirement that makes us think of modifying this microservice currently.

We can't say the same when it comes to the `News` microservices. One of the clients of our microservices is the portal main screen, and, for this client, it is interesting to show a mix of news together. To meet this requirement, we will use the aggregator design pattern.

The following diagram demonstrates exactly how our application should behave after applying the aggregator design pattern. The microservice responsible for the `Users` data follows with direct access through the load balancer/proxy, but microservices responsible for the `News` data have a new layer of interaction before the load balancer. The news layer works as an orchestrator:

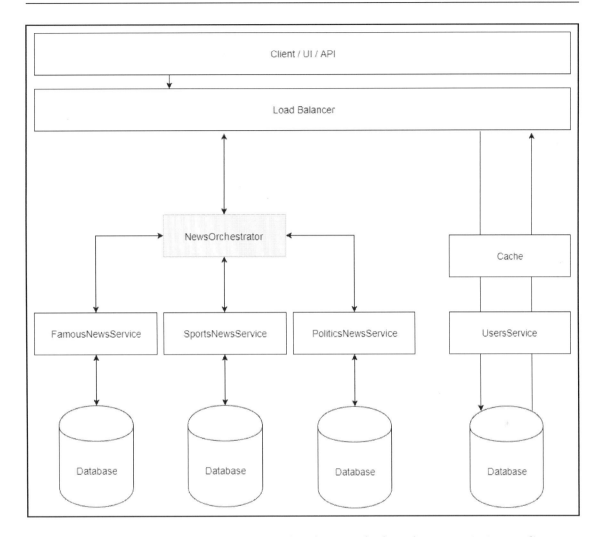

Let's reflect a little more on our client's needs. The UI, which in this scenario is our client, needs information from three different types of news. To accomplish this task, the UI should know each route for each type of news, identify the best way to gather the data received, and obviously make at least three different requests for the backend. This is definitely a lot of responsibility for the web client. We will simply be creating an application that does not meet the real need of who is consuming our microservices.

To fix this type of problem, we will apply the aggregator design pattern. With this pattern, we created a microservice responsible for orchestrating the data for the client and provided a single access point for the information. Consequently, the number of requests by the UI can be reduced from at least three to only one request.

In this way, we are also applying a new concept where we have the **Internal Services**, which are the microservices that generate and provide data, and **Public Facing Services**, which are the microservices responsible for orchestrating the multiple data, Internal Services, and have more direct contact with the client layer.

To properly apply the aggregator design pattern, we have to follow certain steps:

1. Segregate the shared database
2. Modify the communication layer
3. Create the microservice data orchestrator

After these steps, we will be applying our new pattern. However, let's not just segregate data and create an orchestrator. We will do this by applying CQRS and event sourcing.

These two internal patterns are very pertinent to `News` applications. Remember that a renowned journalism portal needs a good reputation with readers, and event sourcing is perfect for auditing news content to avoid errata and possible public retractions.

CQRS is also very applicable in these microservices, precisely because the core of our business is to provide content in the same way while always preparing the latest content. This means that we have to be efficient at recording new data as well as showing the data recorded. With CQRS, we will provide just that by optimizing the writing layer separately from the reading data.

Applying CQRS and event sourcing

Currently, we have three microservices responsible for the provision of news in our application: `famous_news_service`, `sports_news_service`, and `politics_news_service`. Each have the same technical structure, but are separated by having different domains. As the domain of each of these microservices is set, it can receive completely different technical developments; however, in this case, we will modify the three, in the same way, to apply the aggregator design pattern. The first modification will be in the storage tier.

Separating the database

Inside of each microservice directory, we will create two more directories. In each of these new directories will be a `Dockerfile` with configurations for the database. We will use two different databases for each microservice to use CQRS. One database is for CommandStack and one for QueryStack.

With these changes, the directory structure for the `News` microservices looks like this:

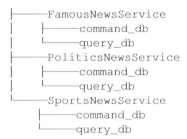

```
├──────FamousNewsService
│     ├──────command_db
│     └──────query_db
├──────PoliticsNewsService
│     ├──────command_db
│     └──────query_db
└──────SportsNewsService
      ├──────command_db
      └──────query_db
```

I'll show the code changes only in the `famous_news_service` microservice, but such changes should be applied in the other two `News` microservices.

Inside the `command_db` directory, we have two files—a `Dockerfile` and `create.sql`.

Writing the CommandStack container

Inside the `command_db` directory, we'll define the `Dockerfile` for the CommandStack container. The `Dockerfile` has environment variables, and the initial file responsible for creating the databases. Look at the following file content:

```
FROM postgres

ENV POSTGRES_USER=postgres
ENV POSTGRES_PASSWORD=postgres

# run create.sql on init
ADD create.sql /docker-entrypoint-initdb.d
```

Creating the news databases

In the `command_db/create.sql` file, we will define the production, development, and test databases. Consider the following example:

```
CREATE DATABASE news_prod;
CREATE DATABASE news_dev;
CREATE DATABASE news_test;
```

Writing the QueryStack container

After we create the files from CommandStack, it's time to create the files in QueryStack.

In the `query_db` directory, we have only one `Dockerfile`. In this file, we have configured a MongoDB as the database. Look at the following file:

```
FROM mongo:latest
CMD [ "mongod", "--smallfiles", "--logpath=/dev/null" ]
```

At the end of the database configuration settings, we have a PostgreSQL for the CommandStack segment and a MongoDB for the QueryStack segment. This choice is due to the characteristics of the two technologies in front of the business. Postgres addresses an area where consistency is paramount, and Mongo addresses an area where non-impedance is most important.

Refactoring the microservices

What we will start now is a giant change in our application. In the first chapters, we say that microservices do not have a long life, which can and should be modified whenever a business requirement arises. It is precisely this kind of moment that we have reached now.

Due to a business need, we will apply a new pattern that will have a direct impact on our stack and microservices. It is important to understand that the `News` microservices do not have external communication, they are Internal Services, and good practice is not to use HTTP in the communication between internal microservices.

Our `News` microservices were built on the Flask framework and had an API that spoke directly to the client. Now, this will be totally modified. We will use a new messaging system, with a message broker being responsible for communication. Our main framework in the composition of microservices will be another—the Nameko.

Selecting our requirements

We will begin by defining the microservice dependencies. In the `requirements.txt` file, set Nameko as a framework, SQLAlchemy as an ORM, MongoEngine for MongoDB access, Postgres driver, and PyTest for testing. See the following file content:

```
nameko
nameko-sqlalchemy
mongoengine
sqlalchemy
psycopg2
pytest
```

Configuring the framework

The `config.yaml` file has the configuration for the fully functioning Nameko. First, we inform Nameko of the access route to the message broker, in this case, the RabbitMQ:

AMQP_URI: `'amqp://guest:guest@rabbitmq'`

Then, we pass the route to access the database, thus allowing the dependency injection by Nameko:

```
DB_URIS:
    "command_famous:Base": ${COMMANDDB_DEV_HOST}
```

The next setting refers to the logging level that should be used by our application:

```
LOGGING:
    version: 1
    handlers:
        console:
            class: logging.StreamHandler
    root:
        level: DEBUG
        handlers: [console]
```

The complete `config.yaml` file has the following configuration:

```
AMQP_URI: 'amqp://guest:guest@rabbitmq'

DB_URIS:
    "command_famous:Base": ${COMMANDDB_DEV_HOST}

LOGGING:
```

```
version: 1
handlers:
    console:
        class: logging.StreamHandler
root:
    level: DEBUG
    handlers: [console]
```

Configuring the container

With `config.yaml` and `requirements.txt` ready, let's modify `Dockerfile`. While the execution of the `requirements.txt file` is all the same as before, the difference is due to `ENTRYPOINT` and `CMD`, because now they will use the Nameko framework. See also that, in `CMD`, we are passing the `config.yaml` file that we just created:

```
FROM python:3.6.1
COPY . /app
WORKDIR /app
RUN pip install -r requirements.txt
ENTRYPOINT ["nameko"]
CMD ["run", "--config",  "config.yaml", "service"]
EXPOSE 8000
```

Writing the models

To implement CQRS, we have two representations of entities for the database—a representation serving the CommandStack and another representation to service the QueryStack. We'll create the `models.py` file.

As usual in Python files, we start with importing the dependencies. First, we should import the native library dependencies and MongoEngine, such as types of fields and the `connect` function that is responsible for connecting the model with an instance of MongoDB:

```
import os
from datetime import datetime
from mongoengine import (
    connect,
    Document,
    DateTimeField,
    ListField,
    IntField,
    StringField,
)
```

Then, we add the imports to SQLAlchemy. These imports are for field definition and to indicate what type of SQLAlchemy database to use:

```
from sqlalchemy import (
    Column,
    String,
    BigInteger,
    DateTime,
    Index,
)
from sqlalchemy.dialects import postgresql
from sqlalchemy.ext.declarative import declarative_base
```

Let's CommandStack the entity's definition using SQLAlchemy with Postgres. Here, we start preparing our application for the use of event sourcing. Note that, in addition to a unique ID, they also own a *version* field. This ID and version field will be the composite key of our database. With this, we will never do an update on an article, but include a new version of the same news:

```
Base = declarative_base()

class CommandNewsModel(Base):
    __tablename__ = 'news'

    id = Column(BigInteger, primary_key=True)
    version = Column(BigInteger, primary_key=True)
    title = Column(String(length=200))
    content = Column(String)
    author = Column(String(length=50))
    created_at = Column(DateTime, default=datetime.utcnow)
    published_at = Column(DateTime)
    news_type = Column(String, default='famous')
    tags = Column(postgresql.ARRAY(String))

    __table_args__ = Index('index', 'id', 'version')
```

The next step is to define the QueryStack entity. Note that the connect function establishes database access by using an environment variable. As the CommandStack entity, we also have to version information on QueryStack. However, in this case, we will do an update on the data and we will always keep the latest version:

```
connect('famous', host=os.environ.get('QUERYBD_HOST'))

class QueryNewsModel(Document):
    id = IntField(primary_key=True)
    version = IntField(required=True)
    title = StringField(required=True, max_length=200)
```

```
    content = StringField(required=True)
    author = StringField(required=True, max_length=50)
    created_at = DateTimeField(default=datetime.utcnow)
    published_at = DateTimeField()
    news_type = StringField(default="famous")
    tags = ListField(StringField(max_length=50))
```

At the end, the complete file is as follows:

```python
import os
from datetime import datetime
from mongoengine import (
    connect,
    Document,
    DateTimeField,
    ListField,
    IntField,
    StringField,
)

from sqlalchemy import (
    Column,
    String,
    BigInteger,
    DateTime,
    Index,
)
from sqlalchemy.dialects import postgresql
from sqlalchemy.ext.declarative import declarative_base


Base = declarative_base()

class CommandNewsModel(Base):
    __tablename__ = 'news'

    id = Column(BigInteger, primary_key=True)
    version = Column(BigInteger, primary_key=True)
    title = Column(String(length=200))
    content = Column(String)
    author = Column(String(length=50))
    created_at = Column(DateTime, default=datetime.utcnow)
    published_at = Column(DateTime)
    news_type = Column(String, default='famous')
    tags = Column(postgresql.ARRAY(String))

    __table_args__ = Index('index', 'id', 'version'),
```

```
connect('famous', host=os.environ.get('QUERYBD_HOST'))

class QueryNewsModel(Document):
    id = IntField(primary_key=True)
    version = IntField(required=True)
    title = StringField(required=True, max_length=200)
    content = StringField(required=True)
    author = StringField(required=True, max_length=50)
    created_at = DateTimeField(default=datetime.utcnow)
    published_at = DateTimeField()
    news_type = StringField(default="famous")
    tags = ListField(StringField(max_length=50))
```

Creating the service

Previously, the file where the communication layer of our News microservices was located was called views.py. However, the HTTP communication layer does not exist in our application and, consequently, the views.py file doesn't either. Instead, we have a new file called services.py, which is responsible for establishing communication with the message broker. The service.py file is exactly where we will declare the CommandStack and QueryStack.

As always, we will first declare our dependencies. In this part of the following piece of code, we will declare our models and everything necessary for the use of Nameko:

```
import mongoengine

from models import (
    CommandNewsModel,
    Base,
    QueryNewsModel,
)

from sqlalchemy import Sequence

from nameko.events import EventDispatcher
from nameko.rpc import rpc
from nameko.events import event_handler
from nameko_sqlalchemy import DatabaseSession
```

With the declared imports, we will write the class responsible for the command. The first three are the class attributes that define the command name and instantiate the event dispatcher and dependency injection database respectively:

```
class Command:
    name = 'command_famous'
    dispatch = EventDispatcher()
    db = DatabaseSession(Base)
```

Then, we have a method with the `rpc` decorator. The decorator comes from the Nameko framework and establishes the RPC communication model. As we are using the internal event sourcing pattern together with CQRS, we must pay attention to some peculiarities.

The `add_news` method will be part of the RPC call within the orchestration microservice. This method is imperative and represents a command for creating news. If we think of a typical CRUD process, it means that the writing operations are executed by the same command. This is due to the fact that, in reality, we no longer have the update operation. When the client requests the update operation, in fact, this creates a historical event on the desired data and not an existing data update on the DB:

```
@rpc
def add_news(self, data):
```

We will now handle the ID and version of our news addition event. This control flow verifies whether it is something new or a new version of the existing `News article`. With this practice, we are just generating event sourcing on `add_news`:

```
try:
    version = 1
    if data.get('version'):
        version = (data.get('version') + 1)
    if data.get('id'):
        id = data.get('id')
    else:
        id = self.db.execute(Sequence('news_id_seq'))
```

After the identification control of the `add_news` events, we will instantiate the entity responsible for registering `News` in the database:

```
news = CommandNewsModel(
    id=id,
    version=version,
    title=data['title'],
    content=data['content'],
```

```
        author=data['author'],
        published_at=data.get('published_at'),
        tags=data['tags'],
    )
    self.db.add(news)
    self.db.commit()
```

With the registration process in the normalized database defined, we will work on dispatching an event to register in the database non-normalized, that is, the QueryStack database. The `dispatch` instance stated in the beginning of the class is now used to send data from our domain for non-normalized DB. Parallel to sending the event to QueryStack, we generate a new event using the RPC call to inform what happened to the `add_news` command:

```
        data['id'] = news.id
        data['version'] = news.version
        self.dispatch('replicate_db_event', data)
        return data
```

If we have any problems in our process, we will execute a rollback in the standard base. More deferentially, we will understand why we do not perform the same procedure in the non-standardized database:

```
    except Exception as e:
        self.db.rollback()
        return e
```

After you create the CommandStack layer, go to the development of QueryStack. First, we will go with the class declaration and the reference name for the Nameko framework, as shown here:

```
class Query:
    name = 'query_famous'
```

So, we wrote the handler responsible for listening to the event that was dispatched by CommandStack:

```
    @event_handler('command_famous', 'replicate_db_event')
    def normalize_db(self, data):
```

Our QueryStack database will have a very peculiar feature. This base will not be a complete mirror of the CommandStack database, but, rather, a specialized database, with only the latest data on a respective news article. This is a summary table and provides faster searches for data due to the practicality of indexing.

To make this a specialized database, we will first look for data on a news article. If there is no event generated with the news data we have searched for, we have created a new news record. This is the main reason why we do not roll back to the base of QueryStack when an error occurs in our layer of CommandStack. The point is that we are always specializing the data, and, if any problem occurs, the eventual inconsistency is not a considerable problem, especially if we think of our business:

```python
try:
    news = QueryNewsModel.objects.get(
        id=data['id']
    )
    news.update(
        version=data.get('version', news.version),
        title=data.get('title', news.title),
        content=data.get('content', news.content),
        author=data.get('author', news.author),
        published_at=data.get('published_at', news.published_at),
        tags=data.get('tags', news.tags),
    )
    news.reload()
except mongoengine.DoesNotExist:
    QueryNewsModel(
        id=data['id'],
        version=data['version'],
        title=data.get('title'),
        content=data.get('content'),
        author=data.get('author'),
        tags=data.get('tags'),
    ).save()
except Exception as e:
    return e
```

The next step is to create the access points for the QueryStack data. First, create the ID search. Let's write a get_news method that has an RPC decorator from Nameko. Within the get_news method, there is no complexity; we will simply use MongoEngine to search News using the unique ID as a reference:

```python
@rpc
def get_news(self, id):
    try:
        news = QueryNewsModel.objects.get(id=id)
        return news.to_json()
    except mongoengine.DoesNotExist as e:
        return e
    except Exception as e:
        return e
```

Then, we will create another RPC request that will be a paged search for all news registered in our database:

```
@rpc
def get_all_news(self, num_page, limit):
    try:
        if not num_page:
            num_page = 1
        offset = (num_page - 1) * limit
        news = QueryNewsModel.objects.skip(offset).limit(limit)
        return news.to_json()
    except Exception as e:
        return e
```

In the end, our complete `service.py` file has the following formatting:

```
import mongoengine

from models import (
    CommandNewsModel,
    Base,
    QueryNewsModel,
)

from sqlalchemy import Sequence

from nameko.events import EventDispatcher
from nameko.rpc import rpc
from nameko.events import event_handler
from nameko_sqlalchemy import DatabaseSession


class Command:
    name = 'command_famous'
    dispatch = EventDispatcher()
    db = DatabaseSession(Base)

    @rpc
    def add_news(self, data):
        try:
            version = 1
            if data.get('version'):
                version = (data.get('version') + 1)
            if data.get('id'):
                id = data.get('id')
            else:
                id = self.db.execute(Sequence('news_id_seq'))
```

```python
            news = CommandNewsModel(
                id=id,
                version=version,
                title=data['title'],
                content=data['content'],
                author=data['author'],
                published_at=data.get('published_at'),
                tags=data['tags'],
            )
            self.db.add(news)
            self.db.commit()
            data['id'] = news.id
            data['version'] = news.version
            self.dispatch('replicate_db_event', data)
            return data
        except Exception as e:
            self.db.rollback()
            return e


class Query:
    name = 'query_famous'

    @event_handler('command_famous', 'replicate_db_event')
    def normalize_db(self, data):
        try:
            news = QueryNewsModel.objects.get(
                id=data['id']
            )
            news.update(
                version=data.get('version', news.version),
                title=data.get('title', news.title),
                content=data.get('content', news.content),
                author=data.get('author', news.author),
                published_at=data.get('published_at', news.published_at),
                tags=data.get('tags', news.tags),
            )
            news.reload()
        except mongoengine.DoesNotExist:
            QueryNewsModel(
                id=data['id'],
                version=data['version'],
                title=data.get('title'),
                content=data.get('content'),
                author=data.get('author'),
                tags=data.get('tags'),
            ).save()
        except Exception as e:
```

```
            return e

    @rpc
    def get_news(self, id):
        try:
            news = QueryNewsModel.objects.get(id=id)
            return news.to_json()
        except mongoengine.DoesNotExist as e:
            return e
        except Exception as e:
            return e

    @rpc
    def get_all_news(self, num_page, limit):
        try:
            if not num_page:
                num_page = 1
            offset = (num_page - 1) * limit
            news = QueryNewsModel.objects.skip(offset).limit(limit)
            return news.to_json()
        except Exception as e:
            return e
```

When we finish the `service.py` file, we have our functional microservice again. The changes we made to `famous_news_service` should be replicated in the other `News` microservices. The next step is to create the data orchestrator.

Preparing the database containers to work together

For our project to run as a Docker container and apply the new databases that meet CQRS, we have to make some changes to the `docker-compose.yml` news of our projects. Again, I'll apply the changes only to `famous_news_service`. However, the changes must be applied to all `News` microservices.

First, let's create the containers for the database. We know that every database in each news container has a `Dockerfile`, and that's exactly what we'll use. The first container we will create is to service the application's QueryStack. Notice that we will do the build pointing to the internal `Dockerfile` of the `famous_news_service` microservice:

```
querydb_famous:
    image: querydb_famous
    build: ./FamousNewsService/query_db/
    ports:
        - "5433:5432"
    restart: always
```

The second container that we will create is for the CommandStack. Similar to what we did with the QueryStack database container, we pointed the build to the internal microservice directory, as shown here:

```
commanddb_famous:
  image: commanddb_famous
  build: ./FamousNewsService/command_db/
  ports:
    - "27017:27017"
  restart: always
  healthcheck:
    test: exit 0
```

Now is the time to reconfigure the microservice to use the containers in the databases. Regarding the build process, nothing is modified. The point of change is due to the new environment variables pointing to the databases that are in the containers that we just created. Another point of attention are the dependencies that we apply to the microservices:

```
famous_news_service:
  image: famous_news_service
  build: ./FamousNewsService
  volumes:
    - './FamousNewsService:/app'
  environment:
    - QUERYBD_HOST=mongodb://querydb_famous:27017/
    - QUEUE_HOST=amqp://guest:guest@rabbitmq
    - COMMANDDB_HOST=postgresql://postgres:postgres@commanddb_famous:
5432/news_prod?sslmode=disable
    - COMMANDDB_DEV_HOST=postgresql://postgres:postgres@commanddb_famous:
5432/news_dev?sslmode=disable
    -
COMMANDDB_TEST_HOST=postgresql://postgres:postgres@commanddb_famous:
5432/news_test?sslmode=disable
  depends_on:
    - querydb_famous
    - commanddb_famous
    - rabbitmq
  links:
    - querydb_famous
    - commanddb_famous
    - rabbitmq
```

Microservice communication

The subject of this book talks about communication between microservices. The best way to address this is in a practical way, and we will understand this communication as we develop our `orchestrator_news_service` microservice.

First, let's understand how we will apply the communication flow. To do this, let's observe the following diagram. The **UI** makes a request that passes through the **Load Balancer** and arrives at the **NewOrchestrator**, which is our microservice responsible for orchestrating the news data. After that, the orchestrator writes in the **Message Broker** (in our case, a RabbitMQ), a message saying what data types the **UI** has requested to be orchestrated.

Each `News` microservice knows exactly what kind of message it is; it is up to you to respond to it. The response process of microservices is very similar to that of the orchestrator, as it also writes a response message to the orchestrator who knows exactly where to read.

This process of exchanging messages is what the `News` microservices will communicate. At times, the communication will be via RPC, and, at other times, it is creating totally asynchronous and non-blocking events.

This communication behavior is already being used in our `famous_news_service` microservice. We will work with this type of communication when we use CQRS internally in the microservice, where we have both RPC to talk to other microservices directly and events when we are posting something new in the CommandStack database. The only difference is that now, we will take this communication model to the systemic level.

Take a look at the following illustration:

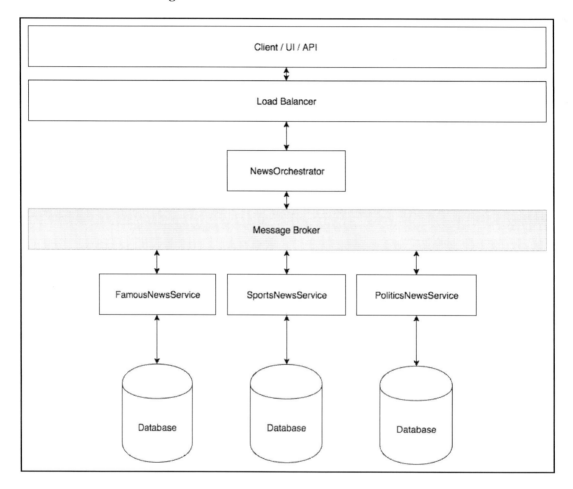

Building the orchestrator

The `orcherstrator_news_service` will have a format very similar to what we had in our `famous_news_service` previously. The orchestrator will be an application using Flask as a framework, but it will not have any database communication layer. The data that this microservice orchestrator uses does not come from its own database, but from other microservices that are consumed by the message broker.

Preparing the microservice container

First, we are going to create the `Dockerfile` and we will declare the container of the orchestrator to apply the same standard of scalability already established for our microservices:

```
FROM python:3.6.1

COPY . /app

WORKDIR /app

RUN pip install -r requirements.txt

ENTRYPOINT ["python"]

CMD ["app.py"]

EXPOSE 5000
```

Writing the dependencies

As can be seen, the dependencies in the `requirements.txt` file are very simple. This is mainly due to not using our own database:

```
Flask
Flask-Testing
nameko
```

Writing the configuration file

Just as we did in our microservices with Flask before, this microservice also has a settings file, `config.py`. The point of attention is because we do not have configurations for access to the database. Let's take a look at the following example:

```
class BaseConfig:
    """Base configuration"""
    DEBUG = False
    TESTING = False


class DevelopmentConfig(BaseConfig):
    """Development configuration"""
    DEBUG = True
```

```
class TestingConfig(BaseConfig):
    """Testing configuration"""
    DEBUG = True
    TESTING = True


class ProductionConfig(BaseConfig):
    """Production configuration"""
    DEBUG = False
```

Writing the server access

The `app.py` file is responsible for an instance of `Flask`. Just like any Python file, we will start by importing the dependencies. Soon after, we have the declaration of the instance of `Flask`, the access settings, the statement of routes, and the command to run the server:

```
import os
from flask import Flask

from views import news

# instantiate the app
app = Flask(__name__)

# set config
app_settings = os.getenv('APP_SETTINGS')
app.config.from_object(app_settings)

# register blueprints
app.register_blueprint(news)

if __name__ == '__main__':
    app.run(host='0.0.0.0', port=5000)
```

Creating the orchestration controller

In import `views.py`, the highlight dependencies file is due to the import of `ClusterRpcProxy`. This dependency comes from the Nameko framework and will provide us with a connection to the other microservices:

```
import os
import json
import itertools
```

```
from flask import Blueprint, jsonify, request
from nameko.standalone.rpc import ClusterRpcProxy
```

After the imports, we will write the instance of `Blueprint` to determine the routes and also the message broker access URI using **Advanced Message Queuing Protocol (AMPQ)**:

```
news = Blueprint('news', __name__)
CONFIG_RPC = {'AMQP_URI': os.environ.get('QUEUE_HOST')}
```

The first route is the one that searches the data by ID. Note that, two parameters should be passed to the route—the first is the type of news and the second is the ID. Within `get_single_news`, there is a function that handles the call to other microservices. We will see this function in detail a little later:

```
@news.route('/<string:news_type>/<int:news_id>', methods=['GET'])
def get_single_news(news_type, news_id):
    """Get single user details"""
    try:
        response_object = rpc_get_news(news_type, news_id)
        return jsonify(response_object), 200
    except Exception as e:
        error_response(e, 500)
```

The second route is the real reason for the existence of `news_service_orchestrator`. This route is used when the consumer of our microservices wants information from all the routes at the same time. This route is a paged search on all the news we have; the highlight is to perform an RPC call for each of the microservices and then organize the data to return it in one response:

```
@news.route(
    '/all/<int:num_page>/<int:limit>',
    methods=['GET'])
def get_all_news(num_page, limit):
    try:
        response_famous = rpc_get_all_news(
            'famous',
            num_page,
            limit
        )
        response_politics = rpc_get_all_news(
            'politics',
            num_page,
            limit
        )
        response_sports = rpc_get_all_news(
            'sports',
```

```
            num_page,
            limit
        )
    # Summarizing the microservices responses in just one
        all_news = itertools.chain(
            response_famous.get('news', []),
            response_politics.get('news', []),
            response_sports.get('news', []),
        )
        response_object = {
            'status': 'success',
            'news': list(all_news),
        }
        return jsonify(response_object), 200
    except Exception as e:
        return erro_response(e, 500)
```

The third route is also a paged search, but for each type of `News`:

```
@news.route(
    '/<string:news_type>/<int:num_page>/<int:limit>',
    methods=['GET'])
def get_all_news_per_type(news_type, num_page, limit):
    """Get all users"""
    try:
        response_object = rpc_get_all_news(
            news_type,
            num_page,
            limit
        )
        return jsonify(response_object), 200
    except Exception as e:
        return erro_response(e, 500)
```

The fourth route receives a `POST` or `PUT` to perform sending new news articles of the corresponding microservice. The interpretation of the payload process is similar to Flask for any application:

```
@news.route('/<string:news_type>', methods=['POST', 'PUT'])
def add_news(news_type):
    post_data = request.get_json()
    if not post_data:
        return erro_response('Invalid payload', 400)
    try:
        response_object = rpc_command(news_type, post_data)
        return jsonify(response_object), 201
    except Exception as e:
```

```
        return erro_response(e, 500)
```

Now, we have some auxiliary functions to the "view" work. The first is `error_response`; this function optimizes a repetitive code to return a friendly error message:

```python
def error_response(e, code):
    response_object = {
        'status': 'fail',
        'message': str(e),
    }
    return jsonify(response_object), code
```

The other three auxiliary functions are used to decide which one performs the RPC call. `rpc_get_news`, `rpc_get_all_news`, and `rpc_command` all have very similar logic, and are used to call `ClusterRpcProxy` to establish the connection with the deep services:

```python
def rpc_get_news(news_type, news_id):
    with ClusterRpcProxy(CONFIG_RPC) as rpc:
        if news_type == 'famous':
            news = rpc.query_famous.get_news(news_id)
        elif news_type == 'sports':
            news = rpc.query_sports.get_news(news_id)
        elif news_type == 'politics':
            news = rpc.query_politics.get_news(news_id)
        else:
            return erro_response('Invalid News type', 400)
        return {
            'status': 'success',
            'news': json.loads(news)
        }


def rpc_get_all_news(news_type, num_page, limit):
    with ClusterRpcProxy(CONFIG_RPC) as rpc:
        if news_type == 'famous':
            news = rpc.query_famous.get_all_news(num_page, limit)
        elif news_type == 'sports':
            news = rpc.query_sports.get_all_news(num_page, limit)
        elif news_type == 'politics':
            news = rpc.query_politics.get_all_news(num_page, limit)
        else:
            return erro_response('Invalid News type', 400)
        return {
            'status': 'success',
            'news': json.loads(news)
        }
```

```
def rpc_command(news_type, data):
    with ClusterRpcProxy(CONFIG_RPC) as rpc:
        if news_type == 'famous':
            news = rpc.command_famous.add_news(data)
        elif news_type == 'sports':
            news = rpc.command_sports.add_news(data)
        elif news_type == 'politics':
            news = rpc.command_politics.add_news(data)
        else:
            return erro_response('Invalid News type', 400)
        return {
            'status': 'success',
            'news': news,
        }
```

Applying the message broker

We have the `orchestrator_news_service` microservice sending messages to the Internal Services that are after the message broker. On behalf of the Internal Services, we are to return messages running from our public facing service, which, in this case, is `orchestrator_news_service`. However, in fact, nothing is happening, and that's because we do not yet have containers of our fully prepared microservices. We will edit our `docker-compose.yml` file to have the necessary instances.

Making the containers work together

First, we have to delete the old instance of MongoDB in the `docker-compose.yml` file that was being shared in the Shared design pattern. This instance will have no more use for us because each of the `News` microservices will have their own database. Let's remove the old code:

```
mongo:
image: mongo:latest
container_name: "mongodb"
ports:
- 27017:27017
command: mongod --smallfiles --logpath=/dev/null # --quiet
```

After we remove the common container Mongo, we will create our RabbitMQ container, which served as the message broker to our microservices.

In the root directory of our project, we will create a new directory called `queue`. Inside the queue directory, let's create a `Dockerfile` with the following configuration:

```
FROM rabbitmq:3-management
ENV RABBITMQ_ERLANG_COOKIE: "random string"
ENV RABBITMQ_DEFAULT_USER: "guest"
ENV RABBITMQ_DEFAULT_PASS: "guest"
ENV RABBITMQ_DEFAULT_VHOST: "/"
```

After the creation of the `Dockerfile`, we will go back to the `docker-compose.yml` file and write the configuration container. RabbitMQ for the container exposes two ports—the `5672` port, used by the tool for the job of communicating, and the `15672` port, used to access the administrative tool in RabbitMQ:

```
rabbitmq:
    image: rabbitmq
    build: ./queue
    ports:
        - "15672:15672"
        - "5672:5672"
    restart: Always
```

It is time we set the instance of our orchestrator. The highlight of this configuration is due to the dependency declaration with microservices of `News` and the message broker:

```
orchestrator_news_service:
    image: orchestrator_news_service
    build: ./NewsOrchestrator
    volumes:
      - './NewsOrchestrator:/app'
    environment:
      - APP_SETTINGS=config.DevelopmentConfig
      - QUEUE_HOST=amqp://guest:guest@rabbitmq
    depends_on:
      - famous_news_service
      - politics_news_service
      - sports_news_service
      - rabbitmq
    links:
      - famous_news_service
      - politics_news_service
      - sports_news_service
      - rabbitmq
```

Updating the proxy/load balancer

Now is the time to make a tremendous change to the application. When we talk about a big change, we are not talking so much at the code level, but rather at the level of impact it has for the application business and for the health of the system.

First, let's remove the upstream we had before. The configuration of the server had some problems, such as route collision and wrong routing:

```
upstream proxy_servers {
        server bookproject_userservice_1:3000;
        server bookproject_userservice_2:3000;
        server bookproject_userservice_3:3000;
        server bookproject_userservice_4:3000;
        server bookproject_famous_news_service_1:5000;
        server bookproject_famous_news_service_2:5000;
        server bookproject_famous_news_service_3:5000;
        server bookproject_famous_news_service_4:5000;
        server bookproject_politics_news_service_1:5000;
        server bookproject_politics_news_service_2:5000;
        server bookproject_politics_news_service_3:5000;
        server bookproject_politics_news_service_4:5000;
        server bookproject_sports_news_service_1:5000;
        server bookproject_sports_news_service_2:5000;
        server bookproject_sports_news_service_3:5000;
        server bookproject_sports_news_service_4:5000;
}
```

After we remove the old upstream, we will create two different upstreams—one for `users_service` and another one for `orchestrator_news_service`. In this way, we are creating entirely separate routes. Note that before we recorded each microservice upstream, we now no longer need to work this way, because we have the orchestrator microservice that handles the data intelligently. Only the orchestrator is exposed to consumers of our microservices:

```
upstream users_servers {
    server bookproject_usersservice_1:3000;
    server bookproject_usersservice_2:3000;
    server bookproject_usersservice_3:3000;
    server bookproject_usersservice_4:3000;
}

upstream orchestrator_servers {
    server bookproject_orchestrator_news_service_1:5000;
    server bookproject_orchestrator_news_service_2:5000;
```

```
        server bookproject_orchestrator_news_service_3:5000;
        server bookproject_orchestrator_news_service_4:5000;
    }
```

Just as we have different upstreams, we will create different locations. This gives us more configuration flexibility and solves the problem of routes collision. Now, we have a location that redirects requests to the `users_servers` upstream, and a location that redirects requests to the `orchestrator_servers` upstream:

```
location / {
    proxy_pass          http://users_servers/;
    proxy_redirect      off;
    proxy_set_header    Host $host;
    proxy_set_header    X-Real-IP $remote_addr;
    proxy_set_header    X-Forwarded-For $proxy_add_x_forwarded_for;
    proxy_set_header    X-Forwarded-Host $server_name;
}

location /news/ {
    proxy_pass          http://orchestrator_servers/;
    proxy_redirect      off;
    proxy_set_header    Host $host;
    proxy_set_header    X-Real-IP $remote_addr;
    proxy_set_header    X-Forwarded-For $proxy_add_x_forwarded_for;
    proxy_set_header    X-Forwarded-Host $server_name;
}
```

At the end of our full `nginx.conf`, it has the following format:

```
worker_processes 4;

events { worker_connections 1024; }

http {
    sendfile on;

    upstream users_servers {
        server bookproject_usersservice_1:3000;
    }

    upstream orchestrator_servers {
        server bookproject_orchestrator_news_service_1:5000;
    }

    server {
        listen 80;
```

```
location / {
    proxy_pass              http://users_servers/;
    proxy_redirect          off;
    proxy_set_header        Host $host;
    proxy_set_header        X-Real-IP $remote_addr;
    proxy_set_header        X-Forwarded-For $proxy_add_x_forwarded_for;
    proxy_set_header        X-Forwarded-Host $server_name;
}

location /news/ {
    proxy_pass              http://orchestrator_servers/;
    proxy_redirect          off;
    proxy_set_header        Host $host;
    proxy_set_header        X-Real-IP $remote_addr;
    proxy_set_header        X-Forwarded-For $proxy_add_x_forwarded_for;
    proxy_set_header        X-Forwarded-Host $server_name;
}
}
}
```

Pattern scalability

The aggregator design pattern provides high capacity scalability for the application, mainly because each component can be scaled individually. When we talk about scalability as the application component, it means that we could create a different number of instances for each microservice independently. Take a look at the following diagram; as you can see, it reflects exactly what we call the ability to scale. The aggregator design pattern allows us to scale just one segment of the application:

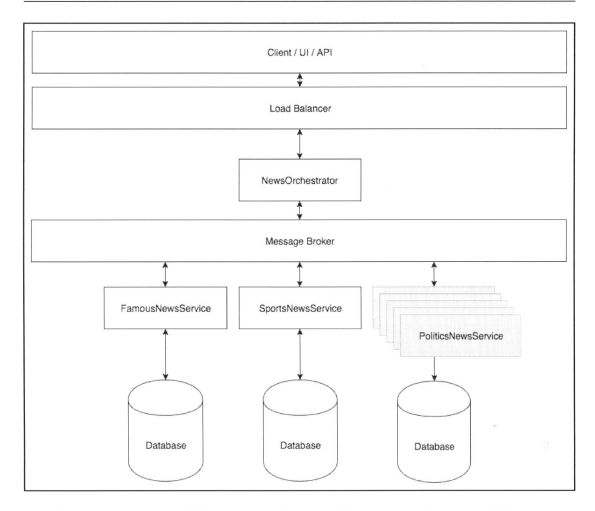

Another interesting point of this pattern is that it enables x-axis and z-axis scalability independently. Remember that the orchestrator is also a microservice, and as such, we can apply caching and other resources to leave the Internal Services further isolated.

Bottleneck anti-pattern

The aggregator design pattern is very efficient for scalability, as we have seen throughout the chapter. However, this pattern can provide us with an anti-pattern if we aren't very careful with what we're doing. The anti-pattern that we can create is called a **bottleneck**. Let's understand how this anti-pattern can be created.

Our application that was a part of the `News` microservice was divided into Public Facing Services and Internal Services. With this design, to access the Internal Services, it is necessary to go through Public Facing Services, and it is here that the problem can occur.

The bottleneck happens whenever engineers misunderstand where the stress point of the application is and where it needs to be scaled. Consider the following scenario—it's the World Series and people want news on this end. Obviously, `sports_news_service` will receive a larger load access. The natural procedure is to create more instances of `sports_news_service`. However, even with a greater amount of resources for `sport_news_service`, the application does not scale. The following diagram shows exactly what is happening with the application:

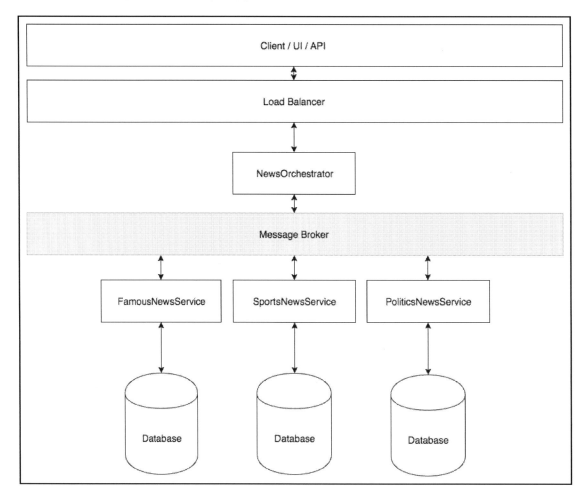

The problem is just happening because we increased the resources of the Internal Service, but not the Public Facing Service. This means that `sport_news_service` does not respond properly because the path that needs to be taken to the microservice is blocked or does not have adequate performance. The problem can be even more serious, because, as the Public Facing Service is serving more than one microservice, other parts of the application are also going through the same problem of slowness. What has been created with this scale of disaster using the aggregator design patterns was a bottleneck.

As a solution to this problem, we must scale the application proportionally, as shown in the following diagram:

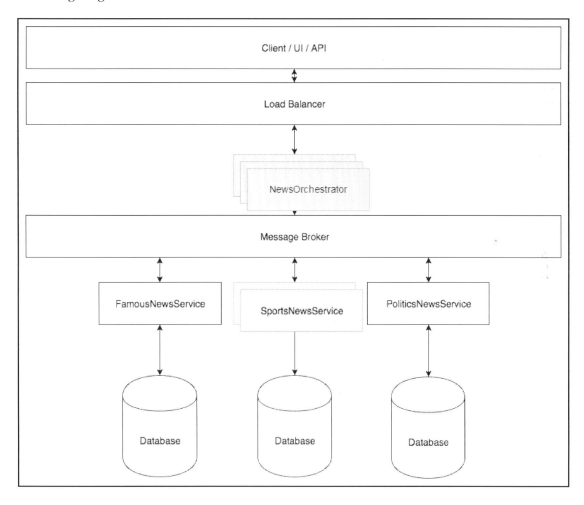

Best practices

In this chapter, we have tried to apply the following best practices of microservices, but it's always good to enumerate what we did:

- **Segregated database**: This allows us to better scale our application, especially in the data storage layer.
- **Microservice encapsulation**: This divides the microservices into two layers—Public Facing Services and Internal Services. Such a division allows for greater flexibility with respect to the signature microservices, as Internal Services can be modified more easily.
- **Applied CQRS**: With CQRS, unnecessary stress points on the application were removed.
- **Applied event sourcing**: With event sourcing, we are conducting a stream of information from a news article. This gives us a real vision of the history of each news article.
- **Applied pattern very scalable**: With a strong pattern and understanding of how to scale the aggregator pattern, we have a clear vision of how to avoid anti-patterns.

The best practices cited earlier form just a basic set of improvements that apply to the design in a fluid and dynamic way. A simple application of patterns that are already well-structured leads to these best practices.

Applying tests

The test process at this time receives new element integration. We need to validate that the minimum functionalities for the full operation of the business are being met. For this, we have two basic approaches—functional testing of each microservice and integrated testing of microservices.

Functional test

The functional test will prove whether a microservice performs its function perfectly. Again, let's take the microservice `famous_news_service` as an example, where we will write the tests of the command layer.

Writing the functional test

First, we will declare imports in the `tests.py` file. Nameko has good support testing and provides the `worker_factory` function, which causes the elements identified by Nameko to be performed without using a real server:

```
import os
import pytest
from .service import Command
from nameko.testing.services import worker_factory
from sqlalchemy import create_engine
from sqlalchemy.orm import sessionmaker
```

After the imports declaration, we'll create a fixture to connect to the test database. For this, we are using PyTest. With this fixture, Nameko injects this connection to the desired element:

```
@pytest.fixture
def session():
    db_engine = create_engine(os.environ.get('COMMANDDB_TEST_HOST'))
    Session = sessionmaker(db_engine)
    return Session()
```

After we define our connection, we will write the test. Note that in this test, we will run the command layer twice. We do this to validate a part of CQRS as if the stream of event sourcing is working:

```
def test_command(session):
    data = {
        "title": "title test",
        "author": "author test",
        "content": "content test",
        "tags": [
            "test tag1",
            "test tag2",
        ],
    }
    command = worker_factory(Command, db=session)
    result = command.add_news(data)
    assert result['title'] == "title test"
    assert result['version'] == 1

    data['id'] = result['id']
    data['version'] = result['version']
    command = worker_factory(Command, db=session)
    result = command.add_news(data)
```

```
assert result['version'] == 2
```

This simple test is validating nearly 50% of this business microservice.

Integration test

I think it is clear to everyone at this point that the `orchestrator_news_service` microservice is a hollow component, which serves us only to orchestrate the data. Thus, there is no great advantage in performing individual tests to find points of failure.

The test that we perform is about the actual behavior of a consumer of our microservices. We have created tests with microservices written in Flask earlier in this chapter.

Writing the integration tests

Right now, we have the declared test class. In this class, we will create two tests. In the first test, using `test_add_news`, we will see if we can add a news article starting from our orchestrator; in the second test, using `get_all_news`, we will check if we can get a news article starting from our orchestrator:

```
class TestNewsService(BaseTestCase):

    def test_add_news(self):
        """Test to insert a News to the database."""
        with self.client:
            response = self.client.post(
                '/famous',
                data=json.dumps(dict(
                    title='My Test',
                    content='Just a service test',
                    author='unittest',
                    tags=['Test', 'Functional_test'],
                )),
                content_type='application/json',
            )
            data = json.loads(response.data.decode())
            self.assertEqual(response.status_code, 201)
            self.assertIn('success', data['status'])
            self.assertIn('My Test', data['news']['title'])

    def test_get_all_news(self):
        """Test to get all News paginated from the database."""
```

```
with self.client:
    test_cases = [
        {'page': 1, 'num_per_page': 10, 'loop_couter': 0},
        {'page': 2, 'num_per_page': 10, 'loop_couter': 10},
        {'page': 1, 'num_per_page': 20, 'loop_couter': 0},
    ]
    for tc in test_cases:
        response = self.client.get(
            '/famous/{}/{}'.format(
                tc['page'], tc['num_per_page'])
        )
        data = json.loads(response.data.decode())
        self.assertEqual(response.status_code, 200)
        self.assertIn('success', data['status'])
        self.assertEqual(len(data['news']) > 0)
        for d in data['news']:
            self.assertEqual(
                d['title'],
                'Title test-{}'.format(tc['loop_couter'])
            )
            self.assertEqual(
                d['content'],
                'Content test-{}'.format(tc['loop_couter'])
            )
            self.assertEqual(
                d['author'],
                'Author test-{}'.format(tc['loop_couter'])
            )
            tc['loop_couter'] += 1
```

Also, there are various other test scenarios that can be applied, and we will see much more in the course of the forthcoming chapters.

Pros and cons of aggregator design pattern

The aggregator design pattern clearly has many more points in favor of it than against it. It is a very elegant scalable pattern and can be applied to almost all scenarios where there are microservices.

Pros of aggregator design pattern

The pros of using the aggregator design pattern are as follows:

- Scalability of both the x-axis and z-axis
- Tunneling microservices
- Microservices signature flexibility to Internal Services
- Providing a single access point for microservices

Cons of aggregator design pattern

Certain cons faced while using the aggregator design pattern are as follows:

- Complexity to orchestrate data
- Bottleneck anti-pattern
- Latency in communication between microservices

Summary

This was a big chapter, where we fixed errors, created new microservices, separated containers, and saw a lot of scalability. We also understood and applied the aggregator design pattern.

In the next chapter, we will continue with our process of learning the design patterns for microservices. Let's next study the proxy design pattern.

7
Proxy Microservice Design Pattern

In the previous chapter, we saw the functioning and applicability of the aggregator design pattern, which is one of the most commonly used patterns in the world of microservices. In this chapter, you will learn about a pattern that is widely used, even though a lot of software engineers are not fully aware of it. We have made use of the **proxy design pattern** for some time, but haven't realized it yet.

This is a more conceptual chapter than the previous chapter, but also very instructive. Let's understand how the proxy design pattern works, and where and when it should be used. In this process, we will see the best practices and the positive and negative sides of this pattern.

In this chapter, we'll look at the following:

- Proxy strategy
- Microservice communication
- Pattern scalability

The proxy approach

The proxy design pattern is a variation of the aggregator design pattern and is used when we want to combine or encapsulate access to microservices, and when no value needs to be aggregated. Basically, it allows direct access to the business, but isolates the technical layer. Just like the aggregator design pattern, the proxy design pattern allows independent scalability, both in the x-axis and the z-axis.

The proxy design pattern can be seen as a more purist pattern because it allows a single point of access to microservices, but there is generally no need for communication between microservices. Another strong feature relative to the proxy design pattern is the flexibility to apply other patterns while the proxy is applied.

Typically, the proxy design pattern does not have the influence of the business layer to apply it, being a fully technical decision. The only exception is in the convenience for the consumer of the application fetching the data from a single reference—the proxy.

As you can see in the following diagram, the **Proxy** is responsible for redirecting the requests. A request is accomplished for a given route. The consumer of the application doesn't know the location of the microservice for the information sought on a certain route; the Proxy, which is responsible for understanding the request and passing it to the microservice, knows to correctly return the desired information or perform some task:

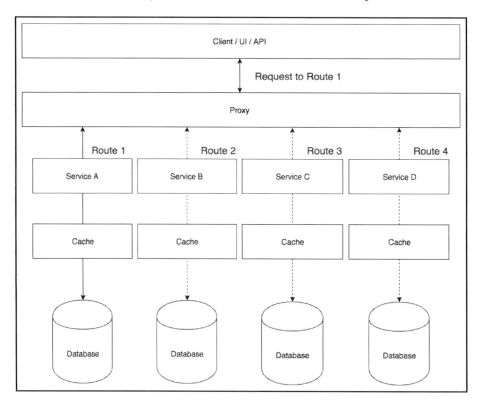

The proxy design pattern basically has two models of approach—dumb proxy and smart proxy. Both models of applicability of the proxy are valid and very usual. What you must have in mind is which model best applies to your business.

Dumb proxy

The dumb proxy, as its name suggests, is a model without any kind of intelligence, where the only goal is to provide a single endpoint to facilitate the application clients and encapsulate direct access to the routes of microservices.

Therefore, in this strategy, we are delegating the requests to the correct places and providing the possibility of scalability and availability of microservices that are over the proxy.

Smart proxy

The smart proxy receives this name precisely by doing more tasks than delegating requisitions to their microservices. There is a range of simple tasks that can be executed using the Smart proxy strategy. The most commonly seen task being executed by a Smart proxy is the content modification.

Imagine the scenario where part of the response of a microservice answers an application client, but by an extra field in the microservice response, it does not attend another application client. Many would say that the ideal approach would be to create two versions of the same API to meet the two different consumers. Something very common is simply to modify the proxy-level response. In this way, there is no cost of redeploying a new route and the two API consumers are met.

Nginx modules, such as `with-http_sub_module`, are used for content transformation. Something interesting, and what is regarded as a smart proxy approach, is the proxy-level caching application.

Understanding our proxy

In the case of our application, we are using the proxy design pattern for the `Create User` microservices and the `News` microservices. All we need to do is apply this pattern to our microservices and, in addition to creating microservices, we apply the proxy policy in our Nginx.

Let's observe the configuration we currently have in our application. As can be seen in the following configuration, we have two upstreams pointing to distinct microservices, as well as distinct locations, precisely to apply the upstream.

In this configuration, we are clearly using the dumb proxy approach, because the proxy does not perform any data modification or any other task that has minimal intelligence. Take a look at the following code:

```
worker_processes 4;

events { worker_connections 1024; }

http {
    sendfile on;

    upstream users_servers {
        server bookproject_usersservice_1:3000;
        server bookproject_usersservice_2:3000;
        server bookproject_usersservice_3:3000;
        server bookproject_usersservice_4:3000;
    }

    upstream orcherstrator_servers {
        server bookproject_orcherstrator_news_service_1:5000;
        server bookproject_orcherstrator_news_service_2:5000;
        server bookproject_orcherstrator_news_service_3:5000;
        server bookproject_orcherstrator_news_service_4:5000;
    }

    server {
        listen 80;

        location / {
            proxy_pass          http://users_servers/;
            proxy_redirect      off;
            proxy_set_header    Host $host;
            proxy_set_header    X-Real-IP $remote_addr;
            proxy_set_header    X-Forwarded-For $proxy_add_x_forwarded_for;
            proxy_set_header    X-Forwarded-Host $server_name;
        }

        location /news/ {
            proxy_pass          http://orcherstrator_servers/;
            proxy_redirect      off;
            proxy_set_header    Host $host;
            proxy_set_header    X-Real-IP $remote_addr;
            proxy_set_header    X-Forwarded-For $proxy_add_x_forwarded_for;
```

```
        proxy_set_header     X-Forwarded-Host $server_name;
    }
  }
}
```

In our application, we will apply two patterns for now. For the `News` microservices, we will apply the aggregator design pattern. However, for `UsersServices` and `OrchestratorNewsService`, we will apply the proxy design pattern. To better understand how we will use these two patterns at the same time, see the following diagram:

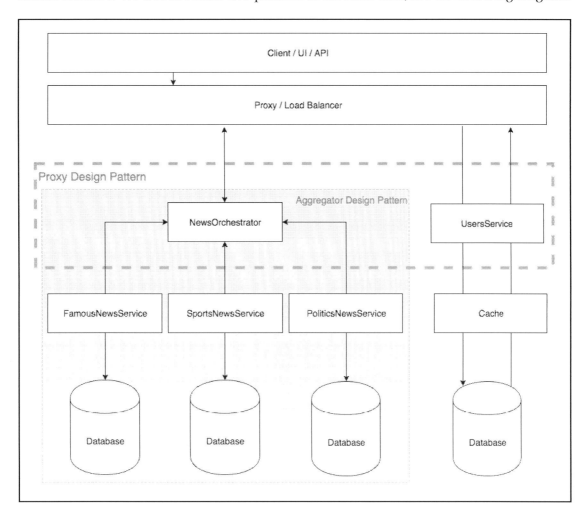

Proxy strategy to orchestrator

The proxy design pattern does not have an elaborated strategy for data orchestration. As already discussed earlier in this chapter, the proxy performs tasks only at the request level. Of course, some information from a request may receive special treatment, but it does not compare to what we saw in the orchestrator design pattern.

When we talk about data orchestration using the proxy design pattern, we are looking directly at the request. The approach using proxy does not preclude the adoption of another pattern for microservices; sometimes, it is of great help to migrate monolithic to microservices.

Imagine that we have a monolithic application that we want to decompose and move its domains to microservices. The initiative is commendable, but we cannot stop developing new features while we are shutting down the monolithic application. Soon, the strategy will be to use the proxy design pattern to keep the application working, while we move the business and apply the new features to microservices. As we stabilize microservices, we go to redirect the requests, using the **Proxy**, for the microservice responsible for responding to the request. The following diagram illustrates exactly the scenario described:

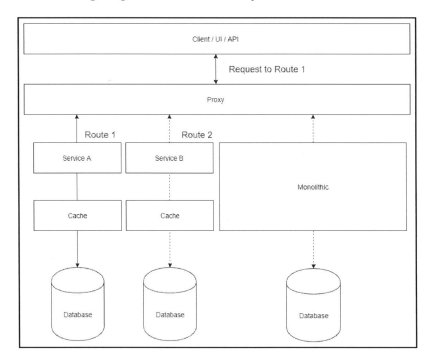

With this strategy, as we move the domains of the monolithic application and create microservices, we redirect the requests to the point where the monolithic application no longer has any reason to exist.

Microservice communication

When we talk about the proxy design pattern, we are practically dealing with communication using only the HTTP protocol. This is because the pattern is typically applied to the Client Facing Services layer.

It is obviously possible to use the proxy design pattern at the level of Internal Services, especially when we are thinking of replacing depreciated microservices with new microservices. However, this application is not very usual, and at some level, it forces the use of the HTTP protocol on the Internal Services layer, which, as we saw earlier, is not the most desirable.

Pattern scalability

The proxy design pattern allows scalability using both the x-axis and the z-axis, and everything is referenced by how many instances of a service are available for proxy access.

According to the configuration of our Nginx, which makes the proxy role for us, we've four instances of each microservice. This can be verified by the number of references to a microservice instance that is in the configuration of our upstream, as shown in the following example:

```
upstream users_servers {
    server bookproject_usersservice_1:3000;
    server bookproject_usersservice_2:3000;
    server bookproject_usersservice_3:3000;
    server bookproject_usersservice_4:3000;
}

upstream orcherstrator_servers {
    server bookproject_orcherstrator_news_service_1:5000;
    server bookproject_orcherstrator_news_service_2:5000;
    server bookproject_orcherstrator_news_service_3:5000;
    server bookproject_orcherstrator_news_service_4:5000;
}
```

In the case of our application, we are treating scalability using the *x*-axis because we are using only horizontal scalability with the proxy design pattern. The following diagram illustrates our scalability strategy:

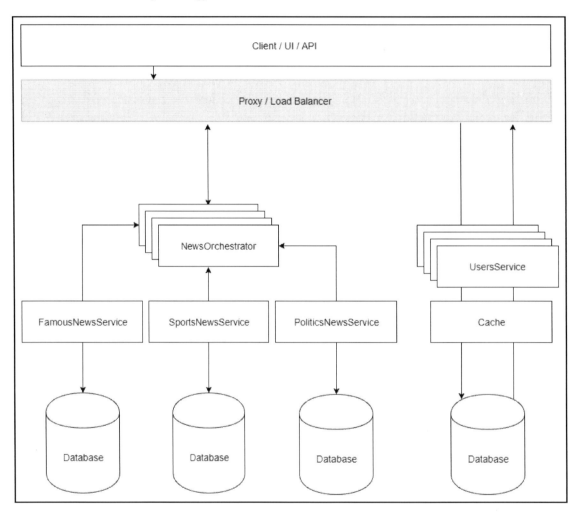

Best practices

The proxy design pattern is relatively simple to maintain and understand when compared to other patterns, whether they are architectural patterns or not. Although it is a simple pattern, there are some points requiring attention, which may not be well-observed, implying possible critical points of failure.

It's always good to emphasize that seeing errors in microservices, primarily under an architectural vision, is not something simple. There are some points that deserve greater emphasis on good practice.

Purest pattern

So far, we used two patterns in our news portal and nothing is preventing us from applying more patterns as needed. However, in some cases, it may not be necessary to apply more than one pattern, and the proxy design pattern is sufficient for the application context.

With the scenario described earlier, the most desirable approach is to keep, or try to keep, as many pure microservices as possible, which means microservices that are sufficient in themselves. When microservices need to communicate using a synchronous protocol with another microservice, primarily in the Internal Service layer, we say that this is not pure.

The non-purism of microservices can generate scalability issues and even availability issues because of overhead in the internal communication between microservices. At first glance, it will seem logical to try to increase the number of instances that are close to the proxy, but the problem may not be there.

Creating microservices that are self-sufficient in themselves is a good practice when dealing with the proxy design pattern; that is, they perform a task without needing to consult another or other microservices.

Looking at the bottleneck

The tasks performed by proxy tools are relatively straightforward and, typically, this type of tool is extremely performant. However, like any software, resources are not infinite.

Sometimes, we see some slowness in microservices that are behind a proxy, and we think the problem is in the microservice. Therefore, we try to improve performance by increasing the number of instances for a microservice that is behind a proxy. This type of behavior seems logical, but it is worth remembering that the load of all microservices is on the proxy, which may be the bottleneck for the microservices.

It is very important to verify that the machine resources, where the proxy tool is installed, are sufficient for the expected load. At this point, performance tests and monitoring of microservices and proxy are crucial to understanding what is generating the bad performance of a microservice.

Caching in the proxy

Some proxy tools have a proxy-level caching capability. This is a good strategy to reduce stress on an application. Obviously, the cache at the proxy level may not be the easiest to control, but, using it carefully, it can be of great use.

Simple response

Many proxy tools could change the HTTP response from an HTTP request. This type of data change can be very seductive, but it is not a good practice.

Some development teams have rigidly defined organizational structures. In this type of scenario, the proxy is something that belongs to Ops or DevOps. Therefore, proxy level changes can be bureaucratic and any modification to the response in an inappropriate way will generate collateral damage that is difficult to detect and alter.

The best practice is to always control the content of the response at the application level, not delegate that task to the proxy.

Pros and cons of proxy design pattern

It may sound repetitive, but the proxy design pattern is one of the simplest and most useful patterns we can apply in the microservices architecture. As positive points, we can point out the following:

- Practical data consumption by the application clients
- Ease of implementation
- Possibility of good programming techniques at proxy level, such as caching
- Encapsulation of access to microservices
- Control and diversion of requests

However, the proxy design pattern can lead to some problems, especially when we are not aware of good practices. The following are the problems related to the proxy design pattern:

- Bottleneck
- Inappropriate change of response
- Obstruction in the identification of overload

Like all other design patterns, the proxy design pattern has both positives and negatives. The most important part is to understand the applicability and focus on good practices, so that this pattern works for the application properly.

Summary

This chapter was a bit shorter than the previous ones, but no less instructive. We have seen how the proxy design pattern works, its benefits, and possible risks.

In the next chapter, we will continue with our project, and we will see another extremely useful pattern for our application.

8
Chained Microservice Design Pattern

In the previous chapter, we saw the functioning and applicability of the proxy design pattern, which is a very widely used pattern, even though it is used unconsciously by some developers. We also understand the flexibility that the proxy provides for migrations from monolithic applications to microservices. In this chapter, you will learn about the **chained design pattern**, a very useful pattern, the use of which may become necessary for large applications that use the architecture of microservices.

During the course of this chapter, you will understand how the pattern functions and when and where it applies. You will also learn about the negative and positive points of the chained design pattern.

In this chapter, we'll look at:

- Microservice communication
- Pattern scalability
- Anti-pattern
- Best practices

Understanding the pattern

Often, a microservice in your business is not able to provide a complete solution to the application, and compiling information with other domains may be necessary. The chained design pattern was developed to respond to and supply this demand by providing a single response to the request made for the application.

This behavior is relatively similar to that of the aggregator design pattern because it aims to provide a single access point for information. However, the way the response to the request is composed has very different characteristics.

First, let's remember how the aggregator design pattern works, so we can clarify the differences between the patterns.

The aggregator has only one access point for the load balancer, which is an orchestrator, which is responsible for aggregating and organizing data in response to a particular request.

After receiving the request, the orchestrator evaluates and triggers concurrent processes for the microservices responsible for composing the response to the request. Each microservice performs the necessary operation to send a response to the orchestrator.

The orchestrator organizes the data, serializes it into a single response, and sends it to the consumer of the application. The following diagram depicts the process described earlier:

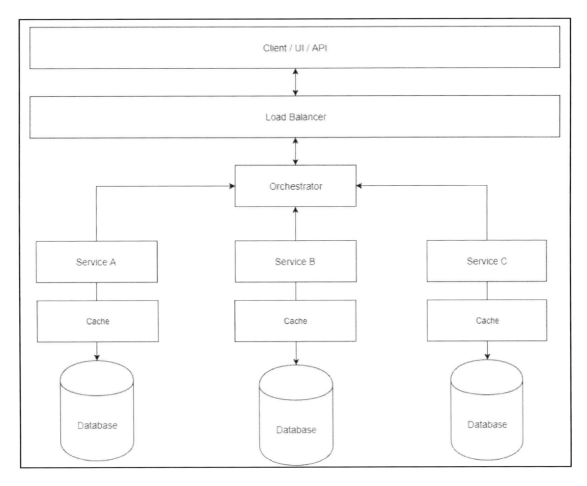

At this point, we recall the process we studied in `Chapter 6`, *Aggregator Microservice Design Pattern*, but our goal in this chapter is the chained design pattern.

Due to the data orchestration design model adopted by the chained design pattern, software engineers often say that it is not an orchestration pattern, but rather a pattern that composes data. In my view, the two interpretations are correct.

Let's understand the flow of the chained design pattern. The goal is to compose a response to the request that was sent through the load balancer. Unlike the aggregator, the chained pattern does not have a specific microservice for data orchestration, so any microservice within the application can assume the role of orchestrating the composition of the data for responses.

Imagine the following situation. **Service A** is called by the **Load Balancer** to respond to the application's consumer. However, **Service A** understands that it does not have all the information it needs for a complete response. In their business, **Service A** knows that some of the information is in **Service B**, so it executes a request for **Service B**, requesting the data that is needed. **Service B**, in turn, knows that it does not have all the required data and asks **Service C**. **Service C** is able to fully respond to **Service B**'s requests and returns the response. After receiving the **Service C** response, **Service B** composes the data and sends it to **Service A**. **Service A** then receives the **Service B** response and also performs a composition. In the end, the **Service A** response is a composition of information from **Service A** itself, **Service B**, and **Service C**. After all the data is properly composed in a single response, **Service A** returns the values expected by the application's consumer.

This flow of data composition can be verified in the following diagram:

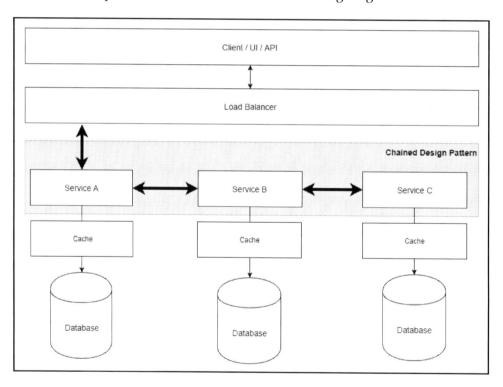

The flow of the example shown in the preceding diagram is sequential, but in reality, no sequence for the composition of data in the **Chained Design Pattern** is mandatory. The request from the **Load Balancer** could be addressed directly to **Service B** by running a stream such as *B-> A-> C* or *B-> C-> A*.

In our application, so far, we do not have a chained design pattern, but we will apply it appropriately in the near future. In fact, we could have used it in our news services instead of applying the aggregator. Both patterns address the need to provide a common, unified response to the get_all_news endpoint. If we had adopted a chained pattern for our news microservices, we would not have OrchestratorNewsService, and we would have to pass the get_all_news endpoint to another part of the application, which, due to the characteristics of our domains, does not seem very semantic. So, the aggregator is more functional for the kind of business we have in our news microservices.

This is what our application diagram would look like if we opted for the chained design pattern instead of the aggregator:

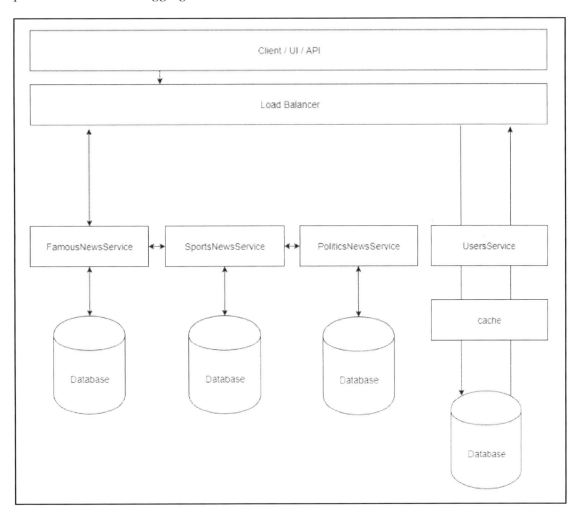

Data orchestration and response consolidation

Data orchestration and response consolidation using the chained design pattern has a certain level of complexity, both in the composition process itself and in the debugging process.

The process of consolidating data using a chained pattern does not occur at a single point, as we are usually accustomed to using an aggregator. With the chained design pattern, data consolidation is gradual and occurs partially at each call stage of the requests chain. The result will be finally completed at the end of all the request processing.

The longer the internal chain of calls to microservices, the longer the data consolidation process will take.

When using the chained design pattern, the **Domain-Driven Design (DDD)** process is necessary to reduce the number of chain calls performed internally by microservices. In order not to have a negative impact on the consumer of our application, it is essential not to have a long chain of communication between microservices. It is worth remembering that because it is a direct communication pattern between microservices, we are passing on to the consumer of the application, not only the processing time of each microservice, but also the latency of communication between each microservice. A long chain of communication, besides generating some level of slowness, also impacts the complexity of debugging the origin and the responsibility of maintaining the data.

Microservice communication

We know that there are two communication models in the architecture of microservices—synchronous and asynchronous. When applying the chained design pattern, we preferentially use synchronous communication because the consumer of the application is waiting for a complete response that will be composed of data from one or more microservices. If the communication model is not synchronous, the response composition control could have a callback system, which grows in complexity and compromises scalability.

It is important to understand that, with the synchronous communication model, we are creating a blocking communication model. We say that the synchronous communication model is blocking because the consumer of the application is waiting for a response that is being composed in a communication chain between microservices. The longer the communication chain between microservices, the longer the consumer's wait for the application will be.

With the synchronous communication model, the simplest implementation is using **HTTP (Hypertext Transfer Protocol)**. Some developers prefer the adoption of another type of synchronous communication, for example, using binary communication protocol or simply some kind of compressor from the packet sent. As alternatives to the HTTP protocol, tools like Thrift, Avro, and gRPC exist, all of which have a binary serializer and the one synchronous sender of information. Two examples of tools that perform only packet serialization are MessagePack and Protocol buffer.

All of the tools we have covered so far have their own set of pros and cons. To decide which tool to adopt, it is always valid to conduct performance tests to understand the scalability pattern and behavior of each one.

Pattern scalability

The chained design pattern allows scalability in the *y*-axis, *x*-axis, and *z*-axis models, all of which are related to how many instances of a service are available for access through a proxy to redirect requests.

It is very common to use the proxy design pattern with the chained design pattern. This approach is adopted so that the proxy is responsible for indicating the microservice through which the chained pattern will begin the possible communication between microservices to compose a response.

Another common practice is that each microservice, using the chained design pattern, has its own server, such as Nginx. It is a slightly different approach than we have adopted so far, since we have an application server, and we manipulate the instances.

A common scalability model is shown in the following diagram, where, after identifying which microservice in the communication chain is slow, new instances of the identified microservice are created to improve performance. In the case of the following diagram, we chose to create more **Service B** instances by applying an *x*-axis or horizontal scalability model:

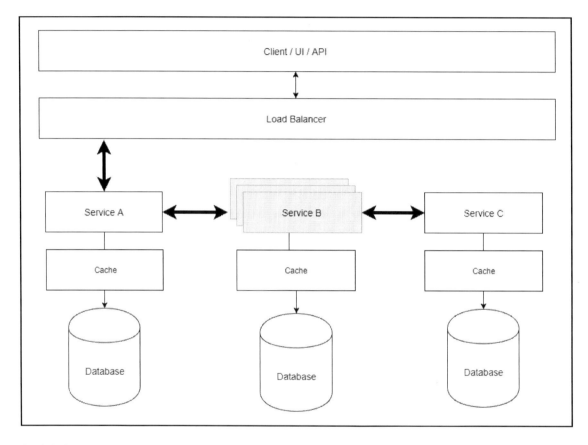

Scalability strategies can be applied to various parts of the application using the chained design pattern, but there is one point of this pattern scalability that can be compromised. This point is the layer of direct communication between microservices. In this case, the best option is to try to minimize any direct communication between microservices. Techniques such as DDD and asynchrony can be very useful in helping to reduce calls.

Big Ball of Mud anti-pattern

All sci-fi fans know or have heard of the **Death Star**. In the architecture of microservices, the name Death Star is used to describe the image created by the *Big Ball of Mud* anti-pattern, especially when we are using patterns like the chained design pattern.

The *Big Ball of Mud* anti-pattern occurs when developing microservices that we do not define well in the domains, which makes microservices dependent on one another to complete trivial tasks. This type of error generates a series of unnecessary calls between the microservices, creating complex problems of being corrected, such as latency and, in the worst cases, cyclic-deployed dependency.

The following diagram exemplifies the working of the *Big Ball of Mud* anti-pattern. Observe that the communication in the diagram looks like the Death Star:

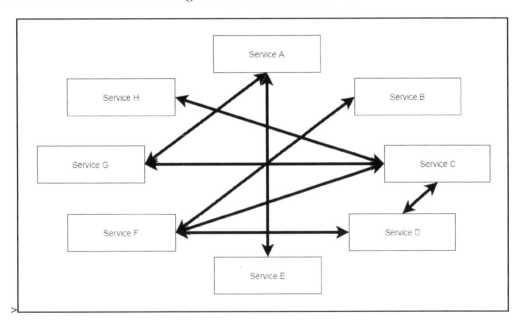

When it comes to a few microservices, free communication seems interesting, but this is a sign that the definitions of domains are not adequate. The direct cyclic communication indicates that the microservices have a strong coupling, forcing one intervention in the releases so as not to generate unavailability.

The following are the main characteristics of a *Big Ball of Mud* so you will be able to identify them:

- **Poorly defined domain**: The domain is badly defined, forcing a direct connection with other microservices. Access points to the microservice do not require enough data to process a task, which forces the inference of data, searching in other microservices.
- **Mandatory direct communication**: When direct communication between microservices is mandatory for most tasks or for all tasks, there is a problem. This indicates that the microservice is anemic or that the application as a whole is poorly developed.
- **Deploy clustered**: When a microservice cannot be sent for production because it needs another microservice all together, or when the change of internal signatures of a microservice causes others to collapse, there is a Death Star anti-pattern issue. Creating business dependencies between microservices means that processes are not automated and fluid.

If your application fits into one of the preceding features, your application is heading for a Death Star. If your application fits into more than one of the characteristics, then you are practically Emperor Palpatine.

Best practices

The chained design pattern is simple to implement, especially to deal with tools that we are already accustomed to, such as the HTTP protocol. However, it is very complex to maintain, since the indiscriminate use of direct communication between microservices can generate problems that are difficult to solve.

In patterns that use complex communication, as in the case of the chained design pattern, consistent logs are helpful for identifying anomalies. However, this can be difficult in distributed communication applications.

To help us identify possible errors within a communication flow between distinct microservices, we can make use of the correlation ID.

Correlation ID helps us get an overview of a task distributed across multiple microservices. A simple way to implement correlation ID using HTTP would be to send a UUID in the header of the requests and use this UUID as an identifier to write the logs.

From the patterns we have studied so far, this is the one that has the most attention points; the slightest slip leads the development, using the chained pattern, down a path where the adjustments are very complicated. The adoption of best practices helps reduce a number of problems that we may have when adopting chained as a pattern.

Purest microservices

The microservices in your business design should be pure. This means that a microservice must be extremely small in its domain and fully capable of performing its function without outside interference from other microservices.

Requesting consistent data

With the desire to not create friction for consumers of microservices, developers often come up with strategies to infer data. Do not be afraid to create friction. A microservice, at its endpoint, must receive all the necessary information for the complete execution of the task for which it was created.

Trying to work with microservices using inconsistent or poor data is the same as getting into a taxi and telling the driver to guess where he should take you.

Understanding chain in depth

We know that sometimes, direct communication between microservices is inevitable. For the moment, the chained design pattern works very well. However, a long chain of communication represents a great complexity of maintenance.

When necessary, maintain direct communication only on one level, for example, Service *A*-> Service *B*. When direct communication has two or more levels, for example, Service *A*-> Service *B*-> Service *C*, the risk of system failures, the complexity of deployment, and scalability increase.

Whenever there is direct communication between microservices as more than one level is implemented, a systemic point of failure is created, particularly if direct communication is performed to collect data for the end user.

Direct communication between microservices is not prohibited, but it should be avoided.

Paying attention to the communication layer

Since the chained design pattern uses direct communication, it is important to try to reduce the latency generated by this type of communication as much as possible. It is noteworthy that while the communication chain and the microservices are being processed, the application consumer is waiting for the response to the request.

To reduce the amount of latency with respect to direct communication between microservices, it is recommended you use binary protocol tools or execute tunings in the protocol being used.

Understanding the pros and cons of chained design pattern

The chained design pattern has both positive and negative aspects, just like any other pattern. However, if it is not very well implemented, chained patterns can create complex problems.

Some examples of the good points that the pattern offers us are as follows:

- Practical implementation
- Dynamism for business
- Independent scalability
- Encapsulation of access to microservices

However, we must also understand some of the negative points of the pattern, such as:

- The possibility of latency points
- The difficulty in understanding data ownership
- The difficulty of debugging

Working with microservices is not easy, since many aspects, besides the technician, influence the final result. In the future, we will apply the chained design pattern properly in our application, and we will understand the scenario in which it best applies in a practical way.

Summary

In this chapter, we gained an understanding of the operation of the chained design pattern. We have seen how we can use it and how it can help us to solve some communication problems.

In the next chapter, we will continue working on our project and learn a new design pattern.

9
Branch Microservice Design Pattern

In the previous chapters, we worked with the aggregator design pattern and the chained design pattern. In this chapter, we will understand the operation of the **branch design pattern**, which is a variation between the aggregator pattern and the chained pattern.

The branch design pattern emerges as an evolutionary attempt by the aggregator and chained design patterns to better serve the business layer of the application.

At the end of this chapter, we will be able to identify, classify, and understand the characteristics of this pattern. We will find the best applicability for the branch design pattern as well as the conceptual rules for applying it.

In this chapter, we'll look at:

- Data orchestration
- Microservice communication
- Pattern scalability
- Best practices

Understanding the pattern

In the previous chapters, we saw how to apply some very interesting patterns, and we could observe that each of these patterns has a very specific utility. In this sense, there are patterns that enable technical functionality, such as scalability, availability, and resilience. We also saw that there are other patterns that focus on enabling the business layer.

This is the case that occurs when we compare the aggregator design pattern and the chained design pattern. The two patterns bring improvements to the business, but it is very clear that the aggregator design pattern is aimed more at the technical part, and the chained design pattern looks for a solution to serve the business, where, in some cases, the solution may not be the healthiest option for the application.

The branch design pattern is an extension of the aggregator design pattern that enables simultaneous processing of responses from two chains of microservices. The branch seeks to be an intermediate solution for the cases where some friction begins to be generated between the technical part and the business layer, being a pattern that aims to combine the positive aspects of the aggregator design pattern and chained design pattern in a single pattern.

We know that the shortcoming of the chained design pattern is that calls are in a long chain for data composition or task execution. The branch design pattern works by using an aggregator to reduce the size of the chain and create a kind of concurrency in the microservices calling.

The concept seems a bit confusing at first, but let's better understand each part of the problem to idealize the solution together.

When using the chained design pattern, it is common for very long chains of synchronous communication to be created, making the application's consumer wait for the execution of each of the microservices that make up the decision chain, as shown in the following diagram:

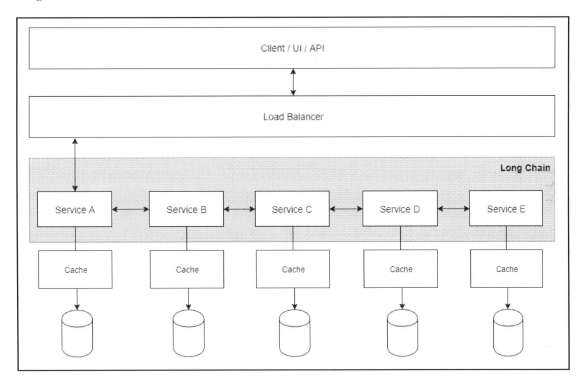

It may seem easy to avoid this long chain type in the call of microservices, but this is not true. Unfortunately, it is normal to create synchronous calls indiscriminately. When it comes to a diagram, it is easy to see the long chain, but when we come across the reality where we have tens, hundreds, or thousands of endpoints, the *long chains* may not be clear.

Here, we have a diagram that shows three requests that are sent to the application. Each of the requests has its own execution chain. As shown in the following diagram, identifying each synchronous call chain as well as its size is a task that gains more and more complexity:

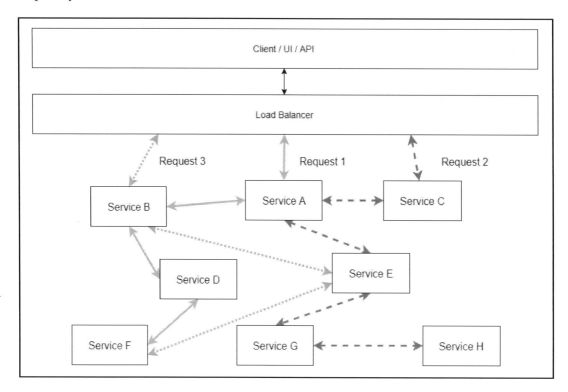

To reduce the complexity of understanding, maintenance, and adding value to the business and the technical part, we will use the branch design pattern.

The branch design pattern has some rules:

- The composition of the response using direct call chains cannot extend one direct call to another microservice
- If more values are required for the response, an aggregation logic is created that will trigger concurrent requests for as many chains as needed

Let's understand this process a little better. From a technical point of view, there is a microservice responsible for orchestrating data that is positioned ahead of all other microservices in the application, as well as the aggregator design pattern. The difference arises from the behavior of microservices that are beneath the orchestrator.

While in the aggregator, the orchestrater propagates messages to microservices; in the branched design pattern, the orchestrator sends messages both to microservices and chains of microservices, where these chains are limited in one synchronous call.

The basic idea of the branch design pattern is to allow direct synchronous communication between microservices, but reduce the cost of long request chains that may occur internally in the application. Again, the domain of each microservice is critical to maintaining proper call structure.

The following diagram exemplifies the behavior of the branch design pattern. In this diagram, the frontend makes requests that pass through the load balancer, and the requests are distributed according to the endpoint responsible for orchestrating the data. Each orchestrator consults the microservice that is needed to compose the information, and these microservices can be either individual or a chain of microservices. With requests for the internal layer, microservices in concurrency and shorter synchronous direct call chains; the response time of the application as a whole is considerably reduced:

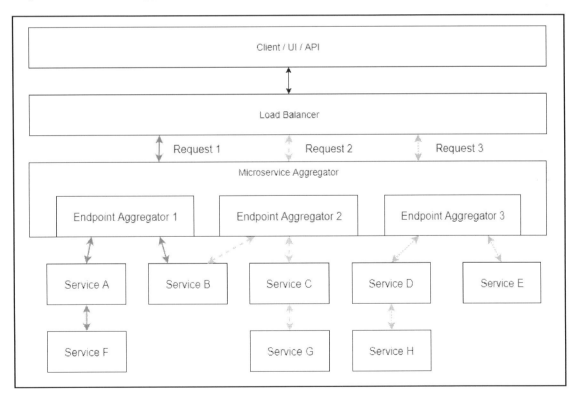

Data orchestration and response consolidation

The level of complexity in the data composition of the branch design pattern can be considered one of the highest. The high complexity is due to the fact that, when using the branch, we are using both the composition of data and the orchestration of data, either in alternation or simultaneously.

Using the branch as the design pattern, the most common scenario is that the composition of the data occurs in the internal layer of microservices, and, obviously, the data orchestration in the public facing layer. It is worth remembering that a more complex data search implies more time and machine resources to create a response with total integrity.

In the following diagram, we have a process where data composition is being performed in the internal layer, and the orchestration of data in the public facing layer:

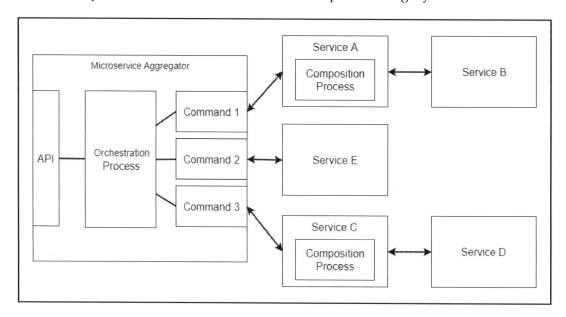

Let's understand the flow of the diagram we just observed:

1. First, the **Microservice Aggregator** receives a request from the **API** and needs to consolidate a response to the application's consumer.
2. The second step is performed by the **Orchestration Process**, where it identifies which commands should be executed for the data search.
3. Next, three commands are triggered, and these commands know which microservices the data can be found in.
4. Now, the internal layer microservices start working to send the information that the commands requested.
5. Some microservices, such as **Service A** and **Service C**, identify that they do not have the capacity to fulfil the task for which they were requested, and call **Service B** and **Service D** respectively.
6. **Service B** and **Service D** return the data in a synchronous process for **Service A** and **Service C**, respectively.
7. With the data coming from **Service B** and **Service D**, **Service A** and **Service C** begin the process of composing the data to return a single response to the commands that initiated the communication.
8. Commands return the received data to the **Orchestration Process**. This, in turn, processes the information and consolidates the data.
9. The last step is the return of consolidated data to the consumer of the application.

This flow is extensive and relatively complex, but this does not mean that it is slow. Obviously, themes such as latency and performance surround the heads of those who develop applications using the microservices architecture. A pattern of microservices in itself does not make an application slow. There are other choices that influence slowness, such as the communication layer, the definition of domains, and bad scalability practices.

Microservice communication

Like in the chained design pattern, the branch design pattern uses the synchronous communication model between microservices. However, some ways to perform synchronous communication can be exploited.

The first of these is synchronous communication using some protocol or direct message. This is the simplest way to apply synchronous communication between microservices. As an example of protocol, there is the famous HTTP, and as a direct message, we can use **Remote Procedure Call** (**RPC**). However, the branch design pattern has a peculiarity—the pattern works with both orchestration and data composition.

In terms of data composition, the use of protocols is quite simple and acceptable. Differently, when we speak of orchestration, we cannot treat it in the same way because the orchestration of data occurs within the same microservice. Having said that, internal communication within a microservice can be worked on in the following three ways:

- **Sequential**: No concurrency or parallelism. This means that when we have to send messages from the commands to the microservices, the entire process will be a sequence. If you need to execute four commands to compose the data, all of them will be executed in a sequence.
- **Threads**: In this case, both **POSIX threads** (**pthreads**) and green threads can be used. Controlling threads is often not simple for developers, and if a thread fails, data orchestration could be compromised. However, it is the most practical way because there is no need for any external components of the programming language to be used for creating some level of competition or parallelism in the execution of the commands.
- **Message Broker**: The use of a transactional message broker for transmitting sensitive data within a microservice is quite usual. The disadvantage is the addition of a physical component within a microservice. However, the advantage is the ability to execute strategies that offer more resiliency in data transmission. The simple fact of working with transactions is already a great resource.

The following diagram exemplifies the operation of a **Message Broker** in a microservice internally. As we can see here, the **Message Broker** creates the bridge between orchestration processing and the commands responsible for calling each microservice or microservice chain, in order to create a unique response for the application consumer:

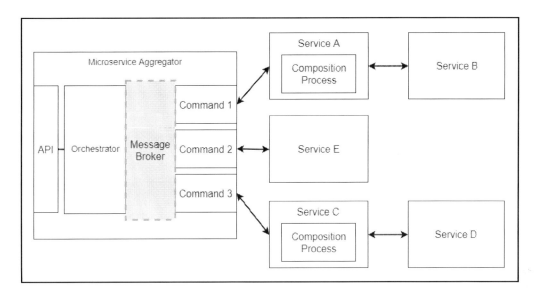

Just as a **Message Broker** is used internally in a microservice, we can apply a very similar strategy of communication between the orchestrating microservice and the other microservices.

By adopting a **Message Broker** as a communication layer, even the microservices that communicate in the form of a chain begin to use this physical component. The following diagram illustrates the concept described previously:

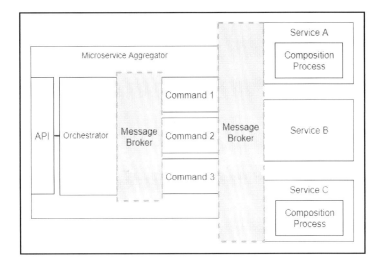

Pattern scalability

The branch design pattern is a combination of the chained pattern and the aggregator pattern. Therefore, all scalability and availability models that apply to each of them can be used by the branch design pattern. Obviously, there are some caveats.

Following the scalability cube model, we can apply the x-axis, y-axis, and z-axis. However, the axis is used differently for each part of the pattern.

In the case of orchestrating microservices, only the y-axis and x-axis can be applied. The reason for this limitation is the fact that the orchestrator does not have any access to data other than that sent by the other microservices with which it is communicating.

When we talk about the microservices responsible for manipulating data, the subject is different. In this case, yes, all axes can be applied to provide scalability for the application.

An important point to note is that if the engineering team made the choice to use a physical component as the communication layer between the microservices instead of a protocol, the physical component must also have scalability, or at least a resilience strategy so that the application does not collapse. Strategies such as physical component clusters or even a simple master/slave can already lead to a drastic reduction in non-availability.

Best practices

The branch design pattern is one of the most complex patterns for implementation, and especially for maintenance. Following good implementation practices for this type of pattern is far from a simple recommendation, but it is indeed mandatory.

In this topic, we will discuss what good practices should be adopted as a checklist to avoid future problems when adopting the branch design pattern.

Domain definition

The chained design pattern is a standard that supports some poorly crafted level of definition for the domain because the need for a long chain of sequential calls indicates this. However, the branch design pattern does not have spaces for this type of a mistake.

Having a short chain of calls, when we think of a branch as an application pattern, is a business option and not an adjustment to lose settings.

Before, during, and after implementing branch design patterns, revisit the domains of the application and thoroughly apply the DDD process to properly limit the scope of each microservice.

Respect the rules

Before deciding to adopt the branch design pattern, understand the pattern operation perfectly. This is one of the most complex patterns we will see in this book and having a complete understanding of the pattern is fundamental.

I am referring to the implementation rules of the pattern. Creating something hybrid or not fully conforming to the pattern implies a loss of performance, the extreme difficulty of maintenance, being difficult to test, and a host of other factors that can be traumatic.

If you come to the conclusion that some pattern rule should be broken because of the domain business, stop and think. There are two possibilities: the domain is poorly defined, or the pattern does not apply to your business.

Attention to physical components

When using the branch design pattern, we have two great concepts—the orchestration of data and the composition of data. Keeping each of these *abstract* concepts in their respective niche is a challenge, and establishing communication between orchestration and composition is even more challenging.

Often, to reduce communication complexity, we use physical components such as message brokers. For these components, we have to pay double attention since all the traffic and data of the application go through these types of components.

Providing scalability, keeping up-to-date, and monitoring these physical components is critical to high application availability.

Keep it simple

The more complex the pattern, the simpler the implementation should be. An overly varied and robust stack further contributes to increasing the cost of maintaining, understanding, and learning about an application.

In a pattern like the branch design pattern, maintaining simplicity is directly related to reducing the cost of implementing new features. Obviously, reducing complexity does not mean making the business of the domain impossible to adopt the pattern. This is about making assertive choices, and not thinking about the possibility that is not properly validated.

Pros and cons of the branch design pattern

The branch design pattern is complex, but at the same time, it is very useful and flexible. Understanding the operation and when to apply this pattern is fundamental for preventing future problems.

Some examples of the good points that the pattern offers us are:

- The flexibility of implementation
- Independent scalability
- Encapsulation of access to microservices
- Compositional ability and orchestration

However, we must also understand some negative points of the pattern:

- The possibility of latency points
- The difficulty in understanding data ownership
- The difficulty of debugging

The initial complexity of the branch design pattern may scare you a bit. However, the range of possibilities from both a technical point of view and a business point of view make the branch a pattern that deserves your full attention.

Summary

In this chapter, we have looked at one of the most complex patterns, the branch design pattern. We have an understanding of how and when to apply the pattern, as well as having learnt some aspects that we should have double focus on when implementing the pattern.

In the next chapter, we will continue our journey of knowledge to learn a new pattern for the microservice architecture.

10

Asynchronous Messaging Microservice

In the previous chapters, we looked at very interesting patterns that mostly work with direct sequential communication between microservices. In this chapter, we will understand and apply the **asynchronous messaging design pattern**. For this, we will create another microservice, `RecommendationService`, which will be responsible for indicating what kind of news each registered user of our application is most interested in.

In the course of this chapter, we will practice all the concepts of the asynchronous messaging design pattern. By the end, we will be able to identify where and when to apply it.

This chapter will cover:

- Domain definition
- Data definition
- Applying the message broker
- Pattern scalability
- Anti-patterns
- Best practices

Understanding the pattern

We know the simplicity and practicality of **REST (Representational State Transfer)**, mainly because this knowledge is already very well-established in the market. The number of tools and frameworks for the REST layer also help with its popularity.

REST calls have a synchronous character, and synchronous calls are blocked due to the request/response model of the technology. This type of call is often necessary for the business of the application, although it is not the most indicated. This shows us there is some level of coupling between the microservices of the application.

A purist microservice must be fully capable of performing the task for which it has been assigned without the need for communication with another microservice. Another feature of a puristic microservice is that it performs a task without the need to return a response by simply receiving the request and doing what needs to be done. In this sense, the asynchronous messaging design pattern is a model that naturally works with purist microservices. Due to the characteristics of the pattern, messages are sent and there is no response or propagation of information to the other microservices. So, we're saying that the request generator does not need to be told what's going on to continue working; it just sends a message and knows that somewhere, some microservice will get a message and execute what is determined.

This pattern is undoubtedly the most scalable of all; due to the asynchronous character of microservices, there is an opportunity to complete the tasks without causing any inconvenience to the final consumer of the application.

The asynchronous messaging design pattern can be used with any other pattern. Also, when it comes to the communication model between microservices, this is the pattern most indicated to be used.

Looking at the following diagram, we can understand the flow of the asynchronous messaging design pattern a bit better. In this diagram, we have **Service A** that establishes synchronous communication with **Service B**, **Service C**, and **Service D**. In turn, **Service B**, **Service C**, and **Service D** identify that there is a task to be performed, but this task is not necessary for the continuity of the workflow of these microservices, so then they send a message to a queue. On the other side are **Service E** and **Service F**, listening to the queue to perform a task using the message that was sent. This communication model, where a message is sent and no type of response is expected, is called an asynchronous model. It is exactly this type of work that the asynchronous messaging design pattern is used for:

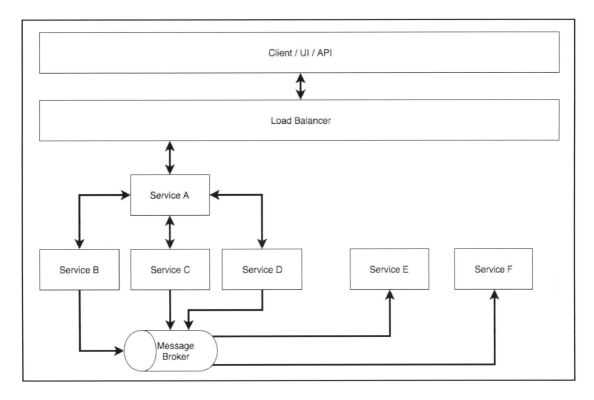

Now that we have seen the behavior and how the asynchronous messaging design pattern works, let's apply this pattern to our application.

To use the asynchronous messaging design pattern in our news portal, we will create a new microservice responsible for storing recommendations for users of the application. This microservice will be the `RecommendationService` microservice and will work in two ways—listening to messages sent to a queue, and with an HTTP API connected directly to the application proxy. In this way, we will store the information about the news preferences of a given user and we will be able to consult the preferences recorded directly by an application API.

In addition to the asynchronous message that the `RecommendationService` microservice will use to create the recommendation, it will also use a synchronous call to complete the recommendation information with the `UsersService` microservice's data.

The following diagram summarizes how the distribution of our microservices will be at the end of this chapter. As you can see here, it is similar to the preceding diagram that we used to understand the operation of the asynchronous messaging design pattern:

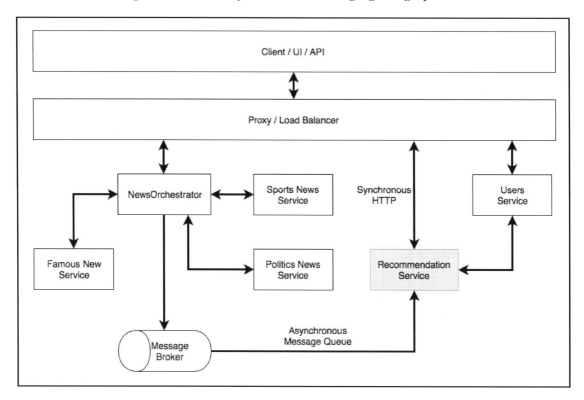

Domain definition
– RecommendationService

We already know that we will apply the asynchronous messaging design pattern in our application using the RecommendationService microservice as an example. This is a very simple service to create and is far from the complexity of microservices of recommendations in production in the real world. Therefore, RecommendationService is a microservice with a didactic purpose for practicing the use of the asynchronous messaging design pattern.

Having made this initial caveat, let's define the business and `RecommendationService` domain. The idea is very simple. Whenever a news portal user searches for any specific news, the labels in that news will be associated with the user ID. By relating the IDs on the labels, we can find out what the favorite subjects of a user are, and we can use it to recommend news and customize web pages.

The microservice will also have an endpoint where you can see the labels that a user has as favorites and another endpoint where we will consult users that are connected to a specific label as a preference.

Data definition – RecommendationService

Let's begin the technical development of our `RecommendationService` microservice by creating a container with the database that will be used. In the case of our microservices, we will use a database based on graphs—the Neo4j. The behavior of this database is very interesting, besides being easy to implement, thus being a perfect example for our application.

In our `docker-compose.yml` file, we make a small change by adding Neo4j to our stack:

```
recommendation_db:
  image: neo4j:latest
  ports:
    - "7474:7474"
    - "7687:7687"
  environment:
    NEO4J_AUTH: "none"
```

With this simple particle of code, we already have an instance of Neo4j inside a Docker container.

Coding the microservice

We have the database of the `RecommendationService` microservice defined and created in our `docker-compose.yml` file. We will now do the same to create a container for the microservice. Again, let's edit the `docker-compose.yml` file.

In this code, we have a dependency, the database, and the message broker, besides some definitions of environmental variables, mainly to connect to the database and queues:

```
recommendation_service:
  image: recommendation_service
  build: ./RecommendationService
    volumes:
      - './RecommendationService:/app'
    environment:
      - QUEUE_HOST=amqp://guest:guest@rabbitmq
      - DATABASE_URL=http://recommendation_db:7474/db/data
      - USER_SERVICE_ROUTE=http://172.17.0.1/user/
    depends_on:
      - recommendation_db
      - rabbitmq
    links:
      - recommendation_db
      - rabbitmq
```

Now, let's create the `RecommendationService` directory and files. At the end, the structure of the microservice will be as follows:

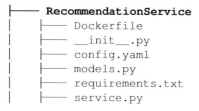

```
├── RecommendationService
│   ├── Dockerfile
│   ├── __init__.py
│   ├── config.yaml
│   ├── models.py
│   ├── requirements.txt
│   ├── service.py
```

Let's write the code of our microservice, `RecommendationService`. We will start by editing `Dockerfile`. The `Dockerfile` code is identical to that of the `News` microservice. This is due to the fact that we are using the same framework, in this case, `nameko`:

```
FROM python:3.6.1
COPY . /app
WORKDIR /app
RUN pip install -r requirements.txt
ENTRYPOINT ["nameko"]
CMD ["run", "--config", "config.yaml", "service"]
EXPOSE 5000
```

The next step is to write `config.yaml`, which is the file responsible for telling `nameko` what type of settings to work with. As we will also use `nameko` for communication using the HTTP protocol, there are definitions such as the number of workers and in which route `nameko` will respond to the requests. Take a look at the following code:

```yaml
AMQP_URI: 'amqp://guest:guest@rabbitmq'
WEB_SERVER_ADDRESS: '0.0.0.0:5000'
max_workers: 10
parent_calls_tracked: 10
LOGGING:
    version: 1
    handlers:
        console:
            class: logging.StreamHandler
    root:
        level: DEBUG
        handlers: [console]
```

Now that we have the files responsible for creating the application instances ready, we will now create the `requirements.txt` file responsible for indicating what our dependencies are. This file has four dependencies. The first is `pytest`, which is our unit testing tool; `nameko`, which is the application framework; and `Py2neo`, which is the driver between the application and the Neo4j database. In addition, we will use `requests`, whose utility we'll cover in the application later. The following is the content present in the `requirements.txt` file:

```
pytest
nameko
py2neo
requests
```

With all the configuration files ready, let's write our `models.py` file. This file is slightly different from the other `models.py` file that we wrote in the application, due to the characteristics of the database driver that we are using. In the end, it will not be a model composed of entities, but a grouping of functions that work with the data in the database.

The first step is to write imports from the `models.py` file. The highlight is the import of the database. Because it is a database that uses graphs, we do not import unidentifiable types into a database, but we are importing types that create relationships in a graph model, as shown in the following code:

```python
import os
from py2neo import (
    Graph,
    Node,
```

```
    Relationship,
)
```

So, we declare constants that structure our business in code. We know that for our business, relationships will be between application users and news labels, where the type of relationship will always be a recommendation:

```
USERS_NODE = 'Users'
LABELS_NODE = 'Labels'
REL_TYPE = 'RECOMMENDATION'
```

Then, we create the connection to the database using an environment variable created in the `docker-compose.yml` file:

```
graph = Graph(os.getenv('DATABASE_URL'))
```

The first function of `models.py` is responsible for fetching the node of a user, passing the `user_id` as a parameter:

```
def get_user_node(user_id):
    return graph.find_one(
        USERS_NODE,
        property_key='id',
        property_value=user_id,
    )
```

The second function is very similar to the first. However, it searches the node using the label parameter:

```
def get_label_node(label):
    return graph.find_one(
        LABELS_NODE,
        property_key='id',
        property_value=label,
    )
```

The third function is responsible for fetching all labels that have a user's relationship. For this search, we use the `user_id` as the parameter. Note that before executing the search of the relationship, we must perform a search for the user node. With the user node, we can search the relationship using the labels. Take a look at the following example:

```
def get_labels_by_user_id(user_id):
    user_node = get_user_node(user_id)
    return graph.match(
        start_node=user_node,
        rel_type=REL_TYPE,
    )
```

The fourth function is very similar to the third one, with the difference that we are now searching for all users related to a label:

```
def get_users_by_label(label):
    label_node = get_label_node(label)
    return graph.match(
        start_node=label_node,
        rel_type=REL_TYPE,
    )
```

After writing all the functions responsible for the created queries, we will write the functions responsible for creating the data in the database.

The first function creates a user node in Neo4j if the node has not already been created in the database previously:

```
def create_user_node(user):
    # get user info from UsersService
    if not get_user_node(user['id']):
        user_node = Node(
            USERS_NODE,
            id=user['id'],
            name=user['name'],
            email=user['email'],
        )
        graph.create(user_node)
```

The second creation function performs the same process as the first, but creates label nodes:

```
def create_label_node(label):
    # get user info from UsersService
    if not get_label_node(label):
        label_node = Node(LABELS_NODE, id=label)
        graph.create(label_node)
```

The third function works by creating the user/label and label/user relationship. By running the relationship process on both sides, we're allowing the search process to run on both sides; otherwise, this would not be possible:

```
def create_recommendation(user_id, label):
    user_node = get_user_node(user_id)
    label_node = get_label_node(label)
    graph.create(Relationship(
        label_node,
        REL_TYPE,
        user_node,
    ))
```

```
graph.create(Relationship(
    user_node,
    REL_TYPE,
    label_node,
))
```

Our next step is to write the `service.py` file code, which works as a kind of microservice controller.

As in all other Python files in our microservice, we begin by declaring the imports. In this case, the biggest highlight is created by importing into the `nameko` handler. This is the first time we will use `nameko` for the HTTP handler:

```
import json
import logging
import os
import requests

from nameko.web.handlers import http
from nameko.events import event_handler

from models import (
    create_user_node,
    create_label_node,
    create_recommendation,
    get_labels_by_user_id,
    get_users_by_label,
)
```

After we have written package imports, we will write the reader of the messages that will be in the message broker. The following code is a normal class with a `receiver` method, a decorator that causes the method to become a handler for the message broker. Read the code comments to understand each step of the process:

```
class Recommendation:

    name = 'recommendation'

    # declaring the receiver method as a handler to message broker
    @event_handler('recommendation_sender', 'receiver')
    def receiver(self, data):
        try:
            # getting the URL to do a sequential HTTP request to
UsersService
            user_service_route = os.getenv('USER_SERVICE_ROUTE')
            # consuming data from UsersService using the requests lib
            user = requests.get(
```

```
            "{}{}".format(
                user_service_route,
                data['user_id'],
            )
        )
        # serializing the UsersService data to JSON
        user = user.json()
        # creating user node on Neo4j
        create_user_node(user)
        # getting all tags read
        for label in data['news']['tags']:
            # creating label node on Neo4j
            create_label_node(label)
            # creating the recommendation on Neo4j
            create_recommendation(
                user['id'],
                label,
            )
    except Exception as e:
        logging.error('RELATIONSHIP_ERROR: {}'.format(e))
```

With the receiver ready, let's write the API code responsible for informing the recommendations registered by `RecommendationService`. Again, it's a Python class as decorators creating the routes for HTTP calls:

```
class RecommendationApi:

    name = 'recommnedation_api'
```

The first method of the `RecommendationApi` class is `get_recommendations_by_user`, which receives `user_id` as a parameter. This method returns the labels that are related to the user:

```
@http('GET', '/user/<int:user_id>')
    def get_recommendations_by_user(self, request, user_id):
        """Get recommendations by user_id"""
        try:
            relationship_response = get_labels_by_user_id(user_id)
            http_response = [
                rel.end_node()
                for rel in relationship_response
            ]
            return 200, json.dumps(http_response)
        except Exception as ex:
            error_response(500, ex)
```

The second method of the `RecommendationApi` class is
`get_users_recommendation_by_label`. In this case, we are receiving the label as a
parameter and we will answer all the IDs of users that are related to this label:

```
@http('GET', '/label/<string:label>')
    def get_users_recomendations_by_label(self, request, label):
        """Get users recommendations by label"""
        try:
            relationship_response = get_users_by_label(label)
            http_response = [
                rel.end_node()
                for rel in relationship_response
            ]
            return 200, json.dumps(http_response)
        except Exception as ex:
            error_response(500, ex)
```

At the end of the file, there is a function that serves to assist the answers with some possible
exceptions. Take a look at the following code:

```
def error_response(code, ex):
    response_object = {
        'status': 'fail',
        'message': str(ex),
    }
    return code, json.dumps(response_object)
```

Microservice communication

The `RecommendationService` microservice is a completely new microservice with
communication features we already know and others that are equally new. This
microservice will consist of an API with HTTP endpoints and a message reader that is going
to read messages sent from `NewsOrchestrator`, which is the microservice responsible for
the orchestration of data.

The messages sent are asynchronous and carried through a dispatcher. In this way, the
microservice that sends messages does not get blocked threads waiting for a response.

A system of messaging and non-blocking communication is the heart of the asynchronous
messaging design pattern. Basically, this pattern has a focus on the communication layer.

Due to the asynchronous character of the microservice that this pattern uses, it is fundamental to use communication tools that are resilient or have an efficient retry mechanism. In our microservice, we are using RabbitMQ because it has a transactional messaging system. Other tools can be used, but it is always good to keep in mind something that offers resilience.

To successfully apply the asynchronous messaging design pattern, more important than the chosen tool, you should fully understand the domain's business to see what can communicate asynchronously and apply the pattern as much as possible.

Obviously, the asynchronous messaging design pattern is not just an available style of communication. It is far beyond that; it is the ability to develop fully independent microservices where the return of a response is irrelevant to the business.

Applying the message broker and queues

Unlike the patterns we have worked on so far, there is effectively no model of data orchestration or response consolidation when we use the asynchronous messaging design pattern. Due to the pattern's asynchronous communication model, there is no type of response, so there is no data orchestration.

In fact, a gauge of whether the microservices work is receiving messages from a queue or receiving messages and properly performing the tasks upon receipt.

In this sense, it is important to keep in mind which type of tool to use for sending messages. If the messages have a high level of criticality, it is interesting to use some tool that is transactional for the processing of messages. ActiveMQ, RabbitMQ, and Kafka in their most current versions are really great asynchronous communication platforms.

In our application, we are already using RabbitMQ, and we will continue with it. However, we should make some changes to the `NewsOrchestrator` code. The changes are made so that upon receiving a request to display a news article, the user ID and the news data that the user has requested are sent to the `RecommendationService` microservice. For this, we will use a pub/sub model.

Preparing the pub/sub structure

In software architecture, publish-subscribe or pub/sub is a messaging pattern where message senders, called *publishers*, do not program messages to be sent directly for specific receivers, called *subscribers*, but categorize messages published in classes without knowledge of which subscribers wish to receive the messages. Likewise, subscribers express interest in one or more classes and only receive messages that are of interest, without knowing which publishers they have submitted.

The pub/sub messaging pattern is one of the best fits, if not the best, for the asynchronous messaging design pattern.

Let's change the `NewOrchestrator` microservice a bit to send the messages to the `RecommendationService` microservice using the pub/sub.

All necessary changes will be made to the `views.py` file. It will not be necessary to use any other new framework, since `nameko`, which we already use to communicate with `News` microservices, will be used in the pub/sub for `RecommendationService`.

The first change will be in the imports. We need to import another `nameko` method, the `event_dispatcher`. At the beginning of the file, type the following line:

```
from nameko.standalone.events import event_dispatcher
```

With this, we are already able to apply the pub/sub. For the sake of semantics, we will change the name and a constant from `CONFIG_RPC` to `BROKER_CONFIG`. In this way, all `views.py` code must have the name of that constant changed; for example, in the following line:

```
BROKER_CONFIG = {'AMQP_URI': os.environ.get('QUEUE_HOST')}
```

The next and last change point to fully enable the pub/sub is the `get_single_news` function. In this method, we will add the dispatcher.

Let's carefully understand the changes made. Structurally, the function does not have major changes; we only add the dispatcher code.

First, we create a dispatcher using the function we import from `nameko`. Then, we pass to this same function the constant `BROKER_CONFIG`. In turn, the `nameko` method will return the `dispatcher` object:

```
dispatcher = event_dispatcher(BROKER_CONFIG)
```

Now, let's get the message ready. The message sent to the
RecommendationService microservice is composed of the ID of the user seeking the news.
This user_id is picked up from a request cookie as if we were simulating a user that was
logged in. The other item that composes the message is JSON with all the news data:

```
dispatcher('recommendation_sender', 'receiver', {
    'user_id': request.cookies.get('user_id'),
    'news': response_object['news'],
})
```

After applying the dispatcher, the formatting of the get_single_news function is as
follows:

```
@news.route('/<string:news_type>/<int:news_id>', methods=['GET'])
def get_single_news(news_type, news_id):
    """Get single user details"""
    try:
        response_object = rpc_get_news(news_type, news_id)
        dispatcher = event_dispatcher(BROKER_CONFIG)
        dispatcher('recommendation_sender', 'receiver', {
            'user_id': request.cookies.get('user_id'),
            'news': response_object['news'],
        })
        return jsonify(response_object), 200
    except Exception as e:
        return erro_response(e, 500)
```

With the help of a simple framework such as nameko and by keeping the application
simple, we have our pub/sub system ready.

Now, whenever we call the get_single_news method of the
NewsOrchestrator microservice, we will send a message to the queue that the
RecommendationService microservice is waiting for. After the data is processed by
RecommendationService, the final result will be something like the following diagram:

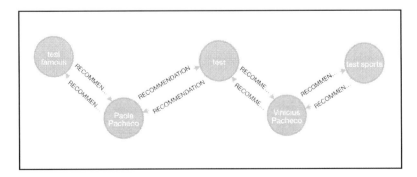

In the preceding image, we see that two users have executed calls to see two news articles each. **Vinicius Pacheco** requested on **test** and **test sports**, while **Paola Pacheco** requested on **test** and **test famous**. Soon, news with the label **test** will be the one that would be more suitable for the two users.

Pattern scalability

The asynchronous messaging design pattern enables scalability across all axes of the scalability cube. Scalability can happen with more instances, more powerful machines for running processes, scaling the distribution of data, and there are still many other ways. However, the asynchronous messaging design pattern has something that no other microservice communication pattern possesses—the ability to perform a lazy process.

A lazy process in microservices can be created whenever we use the asynchronous communication model between microservices. Because of the working character of a lazy process, the number of instances of a lazy microservice typically uses fewer instances than sequential working microservices.

Let's better understand scalability models for the asynchronous messaging design pattern based on the scalability cube:

- The y-axis is the first choice when using the asynchronous messaging design pattern, but processes are slow even for lazy processes, or when processes are heavy.
- The x-axis is usually gaining prominence when the y-axis is no longer enough to offer the design pattern properly. It is common to see the y-axis and x-axis together in this case.
- The z-axis can be used, but its application is totally dependent on the type of microservice business domain.

There is no doubt that the asynchronous messaging design pattern is one of the simplest for scalability.

Process sequence anti-pattern

The process sequence anti-pattern is a microservice version of a known anti-pattern in the OOP ecosystem—sequential coupling. The process sequence occurs whenever a call to a microservice is dependent on the execution of another call.

This type of behavior is sometimes not an anti-pattern for microservices that work with synchronous calls. However, with respect to the microservices of asynchronous characteristics, it is a mistake of drawing in the communication and domains of microservices.

Unlike sequential coupling, where one class depends on the method of another class, in the case of microservices, the process sequence depends on the end of the processing of a microservice to use data already processed previously in another microservice.

We are not talking about the case where a microservice calls another microservice asynchronously. This is where two microservices are listening to layers in separate queues, but one of them needs to know that the other has finished processing to continue.

The following diagram demonstrates exactly the anti-pattern that is generated in the microservices layer of the application:

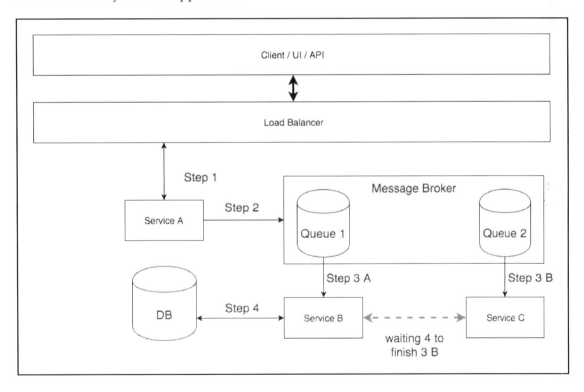

Best practices

The asynchronous messaging design pattern is a pattern with a high level of complexity for understanding, while having great scalability.

For this pattern, it is fundamental to adopt best practices to make it easy for us to understand the structure of asynchronous messages.

Application definition

Applying the asynchronous messaging design pattern is very healthy for applications, but it is necessary to think of the application as a whole to reach as many microservices as possible using the pattern appropriately.

Often, a micro vision is required to work with other microservices, which is why DDD strength is so important. But sometimes, it is fundamentally a macro view of things making it possible to understand all the communication points of the application and where asynchronism is possible, and moreover, where synchronized communication is unnecessary.

Often, we hope to offer a complete response in the interaction of microservices but, in fact, this may not be necessary. If the application is mature and has a high level of resilience, it is not necessary to wait for all the processing of a task to return an OK response. The OK response can be delivered at the beginning of the processing. This OK response changes meaning, from *OK, your data was processed successfully*, to *OK, we accept your data for processing*. This is a major paradigm shift, but it is extremely useful when it comes to scalability.

Don't try to create responses

Attempting to create responses for asynchronous calls is extremely complex to maintain. If the domain always has to return a complete response, it is a signal that its microservices should not work with asynchronous messages.

The attempt to create a request/response template with asynchronous messages breaks the asynchronous messaging design pattern template.

Creating a request/response in asynchronous messaging means that an ID template must be implemented for each message received and that this must compose a queue in another part of the broker, making the pub/sub a two-way path. This makes complexity, which of course if not simple, will grow even more.

Keep it simple

Simplicity in asynchronous communication is critical to maintaining the maintainability of the application as a whole. Just as a *Death Star* can be created when we use synchronous communication between microservices, the same can happen when we use asynchronous communication. However, there is an aggravation; with the asynchronous communication, it is a little more complicated to identify points of failure immediately.

Pros and cons of the asynchronous messaging design pattern

The asynchronous messaging design pattern is complex to understand initially, but it offers extreme scalability. Understanding the pattern, practicing creating proofs of concept, and choosing the tools well, makes your application have scalability and resilience and reduces the complexity of the pattern.

Some examples of the good points that the pattern offers us are:

- Independent scalability
- Extreme scalability
- Lazy processing
- Encapsulation of accesses to microservices

However, we must also understand some negative points of the pattern:

- Complexity in the monitoring of requisitions
- Complexity of the initial understanding of the pattern
- Difficulty of debugging

The complexity of the asynchronous messaging design pattern should not serve as a barrier for using the pattern. A good domain design and choosing the tools to work well with are fundamental to the full operation of the microservices that use the pattern. Any initial problems presented by the asynchronous messaging design pattern will be compensated with the scalability that the pattern offers.

Summary

In this chapter, we have seen a really interesting pattern for high performance. The gains for an application while adopting the asynchronous messaging design pattern are tremendous.

In the next chapter, we will work a little more on our project and we will apply binary communication between microservices.

11
Microservices Working Together

It is now time to evaluate everything that we've done so far. We've covered numerous concepts, looked at various patterns, and have written a lot of code. Now, we'll look at an overview of the project, with all the patterns implemented.

In our project, there are adjustments to make and we will do that in this chapter. By the end of the chapter, you will be able to see how the concepts of microservices patterns merge and evolve. We will solidify all the knowledge acquired so far and review much of what has been studied.

This chapter will cover:

- General tools
- Communication
- Pattern distribution
- Fail strategies
- API integration

Understanding the current application status

Right now, all microservices in our news portal have already been written. With each microservice, we're performing the expected task and are ready to make them work as a single application in a scalable way with resilience and good performance.

For the consumers of our application, there is no real awareness of everything that has been used, but we must be fully aware of how all the links of the software connect and which are the critical points in our application that we need to pay attention to.

In order to have this view, we have to understand each part of the application, with a macro and micro view of the software, almost at the same time. We will divide the application, so that we understand everything that has been developed, into three large blocks:

- The public facing layer
- The internal layer
- General tools

This will cover all the general concepts applied as a solution to the microservices architecture, which is what we are using. The following diagram is a high-level overview of how our news portal is distributed.

In this diagram, we are not considering the demonstration of any pattern that is being applied, be it the communication pattern or the internal pattern of the microservices:

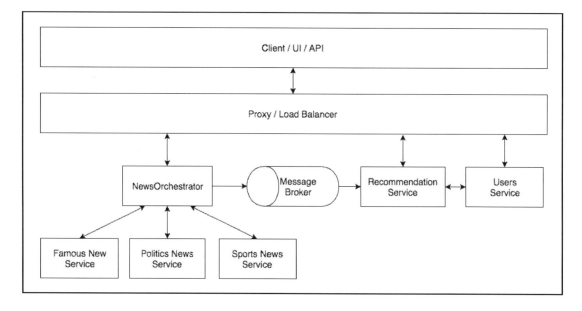

The public facing layer

In the public facing layer, we have three microservices—`OrchestratorService`, `UsersService`, and `RecommendationService`. The last two microservices mentioned are also used in the internal layer at certain times.

This is a great tip. Whenever you are working with microservices, try to first understand the outermost layer. In this way, it becomes easier to understand what kind of response the end user is expecting. Always remember that any software, before an engineering project, should be a solution to a real problem. The following diagram shows the internal composition of the **Orchestrator Service**:

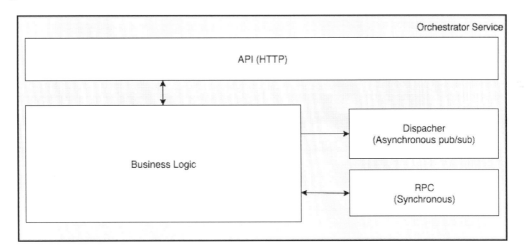

Let's begin our analysis through the `OrchestratorService` microservice. This is a microservice that acts as a data orchestrator for some microservices that are in the internal layer. Its logic consists only of interpreting the calls and redirecting them to the microservices responsible for generating the information. The microservice has an **HTTP API** for communicating with external clients, **RPC** for synchronous communication between microservices, and a pub/sub model for asynchronous communication with other microservices. `OrchestratorService` does not have a storage layer, but could implement a cache. This would cause many requests to have no need to redirect to the internal layer.

The following diagram shows the internal composition of the **Users Service**:

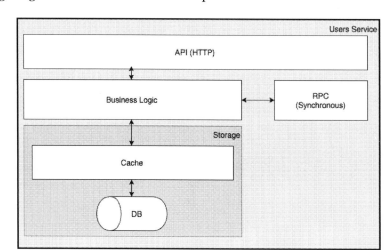

With `UsersService`, the scenario is a bit different. There is a persistence layer and cache, and an internal pattern is applied. The microservice has the internal pattern **Caching First**, causing the data entered for persistence to be stored first in the cache and then in an asynchronous process sent to the database. This microservice uses Redis as a queue tool for internal persistence and it performs resilience control through goroutines.
`UsersService` has two layers of communication, HTTP for the API layer and RPC synchronous communication for the internal layer. The following diagram shows the internal composition of the **Recommendation Service**:

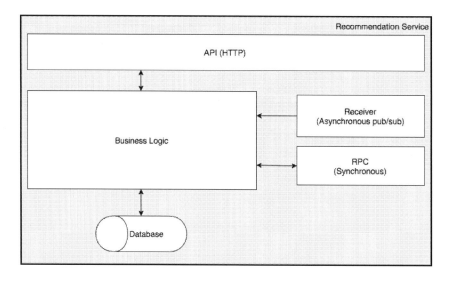

RecommendationService is a microservice with a unique function because all the microservice processing can be considered as an internal layer, but because of the API, RecommendationService is also in the public facing layer, since it receives requests directly from the proxy. The RecommendationService microservice's communication is made through HTTP to the API, using the pub/sub through a message broker acting with an information receiver, and it also has synchronous RPC to establish communication with UsersService. There is a simple storage tier using a NoSQL database. There is no kind of internal pattern.

The internal layer

When we are working on the internal layer, we have two types of microservices: RecommendationService and the microservices responsible for the news.

We have already shown the internal operation of RecommendationService. So, let's take a look at the news microservices in this internal layer session.

There are three news microservices—FamousNewsService, PoliticsNewsService, and SportsNewsService. Even though the main theme of the three microservices is news, they were created separately so that they can evolve, both in business and technically, separately.

However, the architecture of these microservices so far remains the same. All news services have two databases implementing CQRS and event sourcing. For the communication layer, we are using RPC with sequential synchronous messaging.

They do not have any type of API for external access to the application proxy and all connect with the `OrchestratorService` microservice to expose the data:

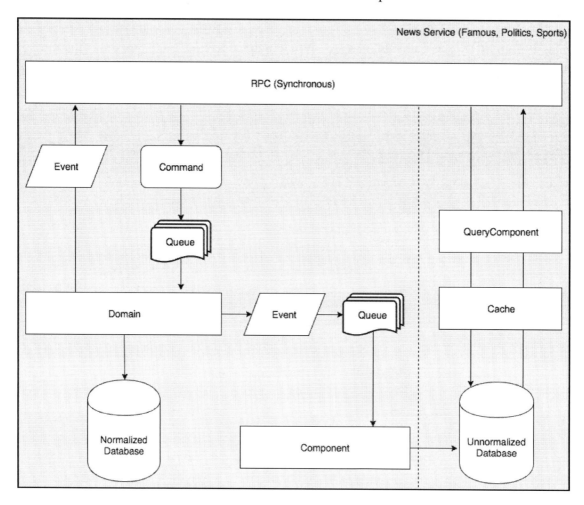

Understanding general tools

We must highlight the general tools because there are some tools that not only help us in the development of the application, but also allow the adoption of some patterns, and in some cases, behave as a type of service.

Two prominent tools in our stack are the message broker and proxy; in this case, RabbitMQ and Nginx, respectively.

The message broker enables synchronous RPC communication between `OrchestratorService` and news microservices. It allows communication using the pub/sub model, of asynchronous messaging, between `OrchestratorService` and `RecommendationService`.

The same proxy tool is what has provisioned the load balancer so far. In this case, this tool is Nginx. With the approach adopted using Nginx, we are using the tool as a real part of our application and not just as a type of server.

Communication layer and accreditation between services

Currently, the communication between microservices has the following model of calls:

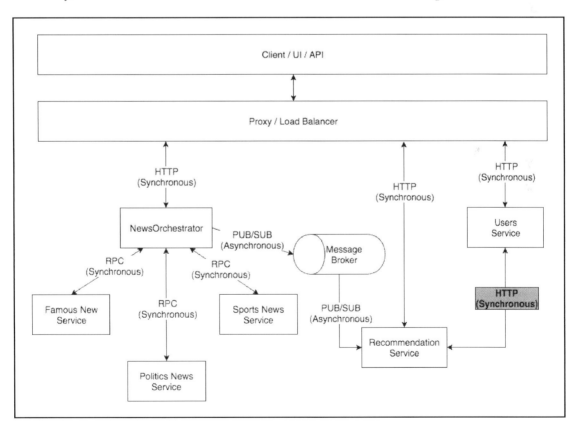

As you can see, we use **RPC** and **PUB/SUB** for the internal layer and **HTTP** calls for calls made in the public-facing layer. At one point in our internal layer, we make use of the HTTP protocol. There is nothing wrong with this, but RPC for calls between microservices is the most efficient, especially if we use some kind of data wrapper, such as binary protocol or some other mechanism for packet reduction.

Let's modify this call to an RPC. However, it will be different from the RPCs we currently have, since we will pass a binary protocol package. For this, we will use the gRPC, creating a server in `UsersService` and a client in `RecommendationService`.

This HTTP call that we want to delete is in `RecommendationService`, in the receiver method of the `Recommendation` class, inside the `service.py` file, as you can see here:

```
    ...
    def receiver(self, data):
        ...
            user = requests.get(
                "{}{}".format(
                    user_service_route,
                    data['user_id'],
                )
            )
        ...
    ...
```

The HTTP call is being executed using `requests`, a Python library.

Understanding the data contract between services

Before we modify the unwanted HTTP call, let's understand the data contract between microservices.

Imagine that we just created an application and that we should call a microservice to complete a task for our business. We read the microservice documentation with which we must communicate and implement a client to make the calls. When we try to integrate with the microservice, we get an error. Something in the microservice signature is not exactly the same as the documentation that was used as the basis for creating our client.

The preceding scenario is much more common than you can imagine. Microservices change all the time, and microservices signature breaks are often more common than they should be. Often, this kind of inconsistency happens within the company itself between different development teams.

Now, imagine if instead of a document being outdated, there was a common file that was used to create the server and client. Imagine if with this file all the server/client boilerplate code were no longer needed. It is exactly in this way that binary protocol traffic tools have been working.

The main advantage of using binary protocol tools for microservices is with regard to the accreditation between microservices. This means a file is created with the attributes, parameters, and methods that must be processed in the communication between two or more microservices, creating a kind of contract between microservices. In this way, the only possibility that one of the microservices does not respect or know the signature of a service is if a wrong accreditation file is used.

For the communication between `RecommendationService` and `UsersService`, let's create this contract file between microservices. We will use gRPC (`https://grpc.io`) for this. In our project, we will create a directory called `ProtoFiles`, where we will create the files that will be used for gRPC, for creation and code.

After creating the `ProtoFiles` directory, we will create the `user_data.proto` file. This file will have all the signatures required for communication.

First, we write in the file the version of protocol buffer that we will use:

```
syntax = "proto3";
```

The `service` is responsible for performing the processing with the method that will be used for communication. Note that the `GetUser` method receives a specific type defined as a request and sends another specific type as a response:

```
service GetUserData {
    rpc GetUser (UserDataRequest) returns (UserDataResponse) {}
}
```

Now, let's create the type of input expected by the `GetUser` method. This type is composed of a 32-bit `int`:

```
message UserDataRequest {
    int32 id = 1;
}
```

Finally, we write the specific type of response:

```
message UserDataResponse {
    int32 id = 1;
    string name = 2;
    string email = 3;
}
```

The complete file has the following formatting:

```
syntax = "proto3";
service GetUserData {
    rpc GetUser (UserDataRequest) returns (UserDataResponse) {}
}

message UserDataRequest {
    int32 id = 1;
}

message UserDataResponse {
    int32 id = 1;
    string name = 2;
    string email = 3;
}
```

Clearly, it's not a very large file, but it's definitely very powerful for what we need.

With the `user_data.proto` file and with the gRPC installed, we will execute the command lines necessary to create our server and our client. Remember that the server will be in Go and the client in Python.

In the same directory where the `.proto` file is, run the command lines on the following terminal:

```
$ protoc --go_out=plugins=grpc:. *.proto
$ python -m grpc_tools.protoc -I. --python_out=. --grpc_python_out=.
user_data.proto
```

These two lines can create all the code necessary for communication between microservices; the first line to generate the files for Go, and the other for Python. The following are the files created after running the command lines:

```
├── user_data.pb.go
├── user_data_pb2.py
└── user_data_pb2_grpc.py
```

The `user_data.pb.go` file must be sent to the `UsersService` directory inside the `user_data` folder. The microservice `UsersService` directory is distributed as follows:

```
├── Dockerfile
├── Godeps
│       ├── Godeps.json
│       └── Readme
├── Makefile
├── app.go
├── cache.go
├── db
│       ├── Dockerfile
│       ├── create.sql
│       └── dbmigrate.go
├── main.go
├── main_test.go
├── models.go
├── user_data
│       └── user_data.pb.go
```

The `user_data_pb2.py` and `user_data_pb2_grpc.py` files must be sent to the `root` directory of `RecommendationService`. The `RecommendationService` directory has the following constitution:

```
├── Dockerfile
├── __init__.py
├── config.yaml
├── models.py
├── requirements.txt
├── service.py
├── tests.py
├── user_client.py
├── user_data_pb2.py
└── user_data_pb2_grpc.py
```

Applying binary communication

With the server/client files created and properly positioned in our project, we will edit the `UsersService` microservice to provide the user data using the gRPC.

Refactoring is a common and constant process in microservices; we will modify the `app.go` file so that the search for users through the cache and database is more reusable. Currently, this search is within the `getUser` method in two large blocks of code.

The first block of code searches directly from the cache:

```
...
if value, err := a.Cache.getValue(id); err == nil && len(value) != 0 {
    log.Println("from cache")
    w.Header().Set("Content-Type", "application/json")
    w.WriteHeader(http.StatusOK)
    w.Write([]byte(value))
    return
}
...
```

The second code block searches the database if no data is found in the cache:

```
...
user := User{ID: id}
if err := user.get(a.DB); err != nil {
  switch err {
    case sql.ErrNoRows:
    respondWithError(w, http.StatusNotFound, "User not found")
    default:
    respondWithError(w, http.StatusInternalServerError,
        err.Error())
  }
return
}
...
```

Let's encapsulate these blocks of code into two methods. The first will be `getUserFromCache`method, where the logic is strictly the same as we had before in the block of code we were modifying:

```
func (a *App) getUserFromCache(id int) (string, error) {
    if value, err := a.Cache.getValue(id); err == nil &&
        len(value) != 0 {
      return value, err
    }
    return "", errors.New("Not Found")
}
```

The second method is `getUserFromDB`, which is responsible for getting data from the database:

```
func (a *App) getUserFromDB(id int) (User, error) {
    user := User{ID: id}
    if err := user.get(a.DB); err != nil {
        switch err {
            case sql.ErrNoRows:
                return user, err
            default:
                return user, err
        }
    }
    return user, nil
}
```

Now, we will apply these two methods to `getUser`. After the modification, the `getUser` method has the following format:

```
func (a *App) getUser(w http.ResponseWriter, r *http.Request) {
    vars := mux.Vars(r)
    id, err := strconv.Atoi(vars["id"])
    if err != nil {
        respondWithError(w, http.StatusBadRequest, "Invalid product ID")
        return
    }
    if value, err := a.getUserFromCache(id); err == nil {
        log.Println("from cache")
        w.Header().Set("Content-Type", "application/json")
        w.WriteHeader(http.StatusOK)
        w.Write([]byte(value))
        return
    }
    user, err := a.getUserFromDB(id)
    if err != nil {
        switch err {
            case sql.ErrNoRows:
                respondWithError(w, http.StatusNotFound, "User not found")
            default:
                respondWithError(w, http.StatusInternalServerError,
                    err.Error())
        }
        return
    }
    response, _ := json.Marshal(user)
    if err := a.Cache.setValue(user.ID, response); err != nil {
        respondWithError(w, http.StatusInternalServerError,
```

```
        err.Error())
      return
    }
    w.Header().Set("Content-Type", "application/json")
    w.WriteHeader(http.StatusOK)
    w.Write(response)
}
```

After code refactoring, we will finally prepare what is needed for the gRPC. For imports, within the app.go file, add the necessary imports to the gRPC:

```
...
pb "github.com/viniciusfeitosa/BookProject/UsersService/user_data"
"google.golang.org/grpc"
"google.golang.org/grpc/reflection"
...
```

We will create a struct that will serve as a logic handler to provide user data:

```
type userDataHandler struct {
    app *App
}
```

Let's write the code responsible for composing the type of response expected by the gRPC:

```
func (handler *userDataHandler) composeUser(user User)
    *pb.UserDataResponse {
    return &pb.UserDataResponse{
      Id:    int32(user.ID),
      Email: user.Email,
      Name:  user.Name,
    }
}
```

As we write the method that prepares the response, we will write the method responsible for receiving the request through the gRPC. The emphasis is on the context and request parameters that are passed by dependency injection. We can see this in the following code:

```
func (handler *userDataHandler) GetUser(ctx context.Context,
    request *pb.UserDataRequest) (*pb.UserDataResponse, error) {
  var user User
  var err error
  if value, err := handler.app.getUserFromCache(int(request.Id));
      err == nil {
    if err = json.Unmarshal([]byte(value), &user); err != nil {
      return nil, err
    }
    return handler.composeUser(user), nil
```

```
        }
        if user, err = handler.app.getUserFromDB(int(request.Id));
            err == nil {
         return handler.composeUser(user), nil
        }
        return nil, err
    }
```

With the request and response prepared, let's write the gRPC server code. First, we declare the name of the method that will execute the server:

```
    func (a *App) runGRPCServer(portAddr string) {
```

Then, we prepare the server listener:

```
    lis, err := net.Listen("tcp", portAddr)
    if err != nil {
      log.Fatalf("failed to listen: %v", err)
    }
```

We create the server instance and register it in the gRPC. If we do not have any type of error, we will have our communication layer using the gRPC running perfectly:

```
    s := grpc.NewServer()
    pb.RegisterGetUserDataServer(s, &userDataHandler{app: a})
    reflection.Register(s)
    if err := s.Serve(lis); err != nil {
      log.Fatalf("failed to serve: %v", err)
    }
    }
```

The entire method responsible for the server gRPC has the following formatting:

```
    func (a *App) runGRPCServer(portAddr string) {
      lis, err := net.Listen("tcp", portAddr)
      if err != nil {
        log.Fatalf("failed to listen: %v", err)
      }
      s := grpc.NewServer()
      pb.RegisterGetUserDataServer(s, &userDataHandler{app: a})
      reflection.Register(s)
      if err := s.Serve(lis); err != nil {
        log.Fatalf("failed to serve: %v", err)
      }
    }
```

With all of the server created, we will have the server activated together with `UsersService` in a transparent way. In the `main.go` file, let's add another constant with the gRPC port:

```
const (
    createUsersQueue = "CREATE_USER"
    updateUsersQueue = "UPDATE_USER"
    deleteUsersQueue = "DELETE_USER"
    portAddr         = ":50051"
)
```

Still in the `main.go` file, we will create a goroutine to have the two servers running at the same time: the API server and the gRPC server:

```
...
a := App{}
a.Initialize(cache, db)
go a.runGRPCServer(portAddr)
a.initializeRoutes()
a.Run(":3000")
...
```

The last step in regards to the server layer is exposing the gRPC port in the Dockerfile. To do this, simply add the port in the Dockerfile of `UsersService`. We already have 3000, and we will expose 50051, as follows:

```
EXPOSE 3000 50051
```

We have the server ready. Let's prepare the client. This client will be in `RecommendationService`. The first step is to create the `user_client.py` file.

In `user_client.py`, we first write the `import` statements:

```
import logging
import os
import grpc

import user_data_pb2
import user_data_pb2_grpc
```

We will create a class that will be like a Python Context Manager. Read the comments in the following code to understand what is running:

```
class UserClient:

    def __init__(self, user_id):
        self.user_id = int(user_id)
```

```
# Open a communication channel with UsersService
self.channel =
   grpc.insecure_channel(os.getenv('USER_SERVICE_HOST'))
# Creating stub to get data
self.stub =
   user_data_pb2_grpc.GetUserDataStub(self.channel)

def __enter__(self):
   # Call common method between both microservices passing
      the request type
   return self.stub.GetUser(
       user_data_pb2.UserDataRequest(id=self.user_id)
   )

def __exit__(self, type, value, traceback):
   # Logging the process
   logging.info('Received info using gRPC', [type, value, traceback])
```

After our client is ready, we will modify our business logic to remove HTTP and use the gRPC as a means of communication. The change in logic must be made in the `service.py` file of `RecommendationService`.

First, we will remove the import of the requests to use the client import we just created:

```
from user_client import UserClient
```

In the receiver method, we will replace the requests with `user_client`. Note that we are no longer translating the data received into JSON, since the response of the gRPC is of a specific type that we declare in our `.proto` file:

```
@event_handler('recommendation_sender', 'receiver')
def receiver(self, data):
  try:
     # consuming data from UsersService using the requests lib
     with UserClient(data['user_id']) as response:
        user = response
     # creating user node on Neo4j
     create_user_node(user)
  ...
```

Due to the type of object returned by gRPC, there is no need to bind JSON, but we will have to change the `create_user_node` function of the `models.py` file to accept this new type. Note that instead of looking for the data as in a dict, we are directly using the attributes of the object, as in a class:

```
def create_user_node(user):
    # get user info from UsersService
    if not get_user_node(user.id):
        user_node = Node(
            USERS_NODE,
            id=user.id,
            name=user.name,
            email=user.email,
        )
    graph.create(user_node)
```

The last step is to create an environment variable in the `docker-compose.yml` file so that `RecommendationService` knows the route to `UsersService`:

```
recommendation_service:
  image: recommendation_service
  build: ./RecommendationService
  volumes:
    - './RecommendationService:/app'
  environment:
    - QUEUE_HOST=amqp://guest:guest@rabbitmq
    - DATABASE_URL=http://recommendation_db:7474/db/data
    - USER_SERVICE_HOST=usersservice:50051
  depends_on:
    - recommendation_db
    - rabbitmq
    - usersservice
  links:
    - recommendation_db
    - rabbitmq
    - usersservice
```

After these changes, we have the gRPC working perfectly and we eliminate any HTTP call in the internal layer. The communication diagram between our microservices has the following structure:

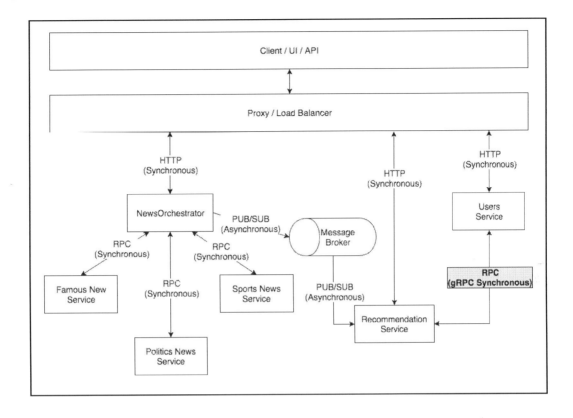

Pattern distribution

Throughout the book, we have worked with various patterns of communication between microservices. We applied almost all the mentioned patterns, and in the course of the development process, we were remodeling our code, modifying and adding patterns in our application.

We are currently applying the following patterns in the application:

- **Proxy microservice design pattern**: This is applied using Nginx in the role of proxy. This pattern refers to the proxy for the `OrchestratorNewsService`, `UsersService`, and `RecommendationService` APIs.
- **Aggregator microservice design pattern**: `OrchestratorNewsService` performs the role of aggregator for the `FamousNewsService`, `SportsNewsService`, and `PoliticsNewsService` microservices.

- **Branch microservice design pattern**: This is the pattern that we have used to establish communication between `UsersService` and `RecommendationService`, because `RecommendationService` needs information synchronously from `UsersService` to finish the task it proposes.
- **Asynchronous messaging microservice design pattern**: This pattern is applied between `OrchestratorNewsService` and `RecommendationService`.

For an overview of the previous bullet points, refer to the following diagram:

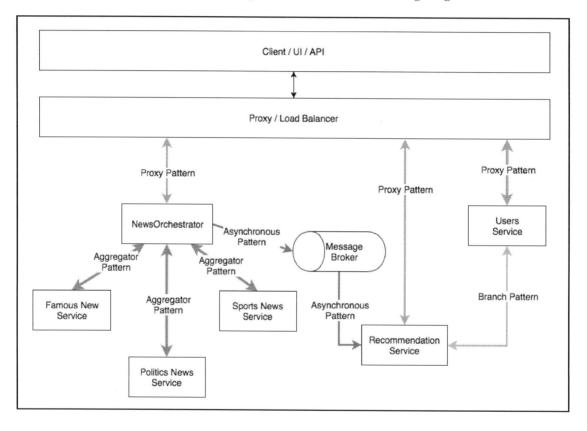

Fail strategies

We saw a number of anti-patterns in the process of developing our application. However, among all the collateral damage that can be generated by anti-patterns, the most harmful for an application that uses the microservices architecture is the cyclic call between microservices.

Cyclic calls prevent continuous integration, independent deployment, and progressive evolution of each microservice and create a false sense of success in tests. A good example of this kind of failure is if we removed `NewsOrchestrator` and passed the orchestration responsibility to one of the internal layer microservices. A microservice would have the domain corrupted, in addition to generating the need to deploy with other parts of the application at the same time.

The proper adoption of the patterns acts to prevent this type of failure in the strategy of microservices.

Obviously, techniques such as circuit breaker and timeout, as explained in `Chapter 4`, *Microsystem Ecosystem*, are welcome whenever we deal with communication between microservices.

API integration

The API of a microservice is the gateway to the business that the microservice must perform. If there is any kind of problem with the microservice API, business is compromised.

Usually, API problems are generated due to the necessary changes in the signature of a microservice not being properly informed. The first approach to avoid this kind of problem is to use a mechanism where there is a common file between the application that serves the data and the application that consumes the data. In our microservices, the gRPC fulfils this function.

Another way to achieve successful integrations of a microservice's APIs is by adopting API versioning. Let's revisit our `nginx.conf` file. Note that the location settings are inconsistent and have no version indication:

```
...
  server {
    listen 80;

    location / {
```

```
      ...
    }

    location /news/ {
    ...
    }

    location /recommendation/ {
    ...
    }
...
```

Let's modify this to have versions of our APIs. Now, for each upstream Nginx instruction, we have a version-defined location:

```
...
upstream users_servers {
  server bookproject_usersservice_1:3000;
}
upstream orcherstrator_servers {
  server bookproject_orcherstrator_news_service_1:5000;
}
upstream recommendation_servers {
  server bookproject_recommendation_service_1:5000;
}
server {
  listen 80;

    location /users/v1/ {
      proxy_pass          http://users_servers/;
      ...
    }

    location /news/v1/ {
      proxy_pass          http://orcherstrator_servers/;
      ...
    }

    location /recommendation/v1/ {
      proxy_pass          http://recommendation_servers/;
      ...
    }
}
```

Suppose that we want to change the `UsersService` microservice to a new version and we will temporarily keep two routes until all API consumers are completely migrated to the new version of the API:

```
upstream users_servers {
  server bookproject_usersservice _1:3000;
}

upstream users_servers_v2 {
  server bookproject_usersservice_v2_1:3000;
}

server {
  listen 80;

  location /users/v1/ {
    proxy_pass          http://users_servers/;
    ...
  }

  location /users/v2/ {
    proxy_pass          http://users_servers_v2/;
    ...
  }
}
```

Summary

In this chapter, we've understood the current status of our microservices and worked on our application to create binary modeling and versioning endpoints.

In the next chapter, we'll look at some of the types of tests that we can apply to microservices. We will apply integration tests, unit tests, and some others that not only help us to find possible errors, but also make our application more maintainable.

12
Testing Microservices

Throughout all the previous chapters, we have done a great job implementing a series of patterns in our application, the news portal. Now, it is time to understand and validate whether the project business flows are working properly.

Even though it is not a very large microservices project, performing manual tests would be complex and we would surely fail in our evaluation or forget some important tasks for the business of the application.

There is no doubt that automated testing is best suited for any type of software. In this chapter, we will cover the following topics:

- Unit tests
- Integration tests
- End-to-end tests
- Pipelines
- Signature tests
- Monkey tests

Unit tests

Unit tests are well-known and are already normative in the software development industry. There are a number of standards and practices for unit tests. However, the best practice for unit tests is to make sure that they are running every software built.

The unit tests are used to prove the smallest testable part of a computer program. In this sense, the great challenge is to write code that is testable; otherwise, it will be impossible to apply the unit tests.

An important feature is that unit tests only prove the code unit segment. Imagine that we are going to test a function that communicates with the database. When we create the unit test, we have to use a mechanism so that the function test does not touch the database. The mechanism is commonly known as a **mock**. When applying a mock to the unit test, we isolate the function we want to test, then any possible changes in the database will not create conflict in the unit test scenarios.

Unit tests that have factors that can change their results, such as databases and floating time variables, corrupt the strongest principle around the unit tests that are to be deterministic and idempotent. A deterministic unit test is one that no matter how many times it is executed, the result will always be the same. A non-deterministic unit test is a big mistake.

A good practice to follow when applying unit tests is to not only prove the success scenarios, but also the potential failures. This practice is very useful for finding possible coding errors for handling exceptions.

In our news portal, we will use the `OrchestratorNewsService` microservice as an example to apply unit tests. This microservice is very interesting due to its complexity.

The `OrchestratorNewsService` microservice has a public API layer, RPC communication with internal services, and it publishes data in a message broker. All these characteristics make the tests more complex.

We saw that, due to the concept of the unit tests, we have to isolate the segment of code that has to be proved. We must keep in mind that our aim is to make deterministic tests that cover both scenarios of success and failure. Now, let's start writing unit tests for our `OrchestratorNewsService` microservice. I will not write all the possible unit tests for this microservice, but I will cover the more complex scenarios, especially the cases that present communication with other microservices.

In the `OrchestratorNewsService` directory, we will create the `tests.py` file. After creating the file, we must make the declaration of the necessary imports to create the unit tests. Note that in addition to importing the `unittest` dependency, we are importing the patch decorator from the `mock` package. This will be very useful for creating deterministic unit tests:

```python
import json
import unittest

from mock import patch

from app import app
from views import error_response
```

```
from flask_testing import TestCase
```

Let's create the `BaseTestCase` class, which is responsible for loading the basic test settings:

```
class BaseTestCase(TestCase):

    def create_app(self):
        app.config.from_object('config.TestingConfig')
        return app
```

Now, we've created the tests that validate the settings of our development environment:

```
class TestDevelopmentConfig(TestCase):

    def create_app(self):
        app.config.from_object('config.DevelopmentConfig')
        return app

    def test_app_is_development(self):
        self.assertTrue(app.config['DEBUG'] is True)
```

Then, the tests that validate the test configuration:

```
class TestTestingConfig(TestCase):

    def create_app(self):
        app.config.from_object('config.TestingConfig')
        return app

    def test_app_is_testing(self):
        self.assertTrue(app.config['DEBUG'])
        self.assertTrue(app.config['TESTING'])
```

To finalize the configuration tests, the cases that validate the configurations for production are as follows:

```
class TestProductionConfig(TestCase)

    def create_app(self):
        app.config.from_object('config.ProductionConfig')
        return app

    def test_app_is_production(self):
        self.assertFalse(app.config['DEBUG'])
        self.assertFalse(app.config['TESTING'])
```

So far, we have explored common unit tests without great difficulty. However, let's consider a very interesting scenario, where we create a unit test for when we search for a news article. First, we declare the test class:

```
class TestGetSingleNews(BaseTestCase):
```

Next, we'll create the method that validates the search success case. Note that we are applying the patch decorator, which allows us to create the mock for the rpc_get_news function and for the event_dispatcher function. The instances of the patches are passed by dependency injection:

```
@patch('views.rpc_get_news')
@patch('nameko.standalone.events.event_dispatcher')
    def test_success(self, event_dispatcher_mock, rpc_get_news_mock):
```

At this point, we will declare the values that must be returned by the mocks. The first mock is the event_dispatcher_mock, where an anonymous function will be passed that takes the values and does nothing. The second mock refers to the return of the RPC:

```
event_dispatcher_mock.return_value = lambda v1, v2, v3: None
rpc_get_news_mock.return_value = {
    "news": [
        {
            "_id": 1,
            "author": "unittest",
            "content": "Just a service test",
            "created_at": {
                "$date": 1514741833010
            },
            "news_type": "famous",
            "tags": [
                "Test",
                "unit_test"
            ],
            "title": "My Test",
            "version": 1
        }
    ],
    "status": "success"
}
```

Now, we'll call the `get_single_news` endpoint by sending a news article ID as a parameter. Then, we interpret the call coming from mocks and validate the response:

```
With self.client:
    response = self.client.get('/famous/1')
    data = json.loads(response.data.decode())
    self.assertEqual(response.status_code, 200)
    self.assertIn('success', data['status'])
    self.assertTrue(len(data['news']) > 0)
    for d in data['news']:
        self.assertEqual(d['title'], 'My Test')
        self.assertEqual(d['content'], 'Just a service test')
        self.assertEqual(d['author'], 'unittest')
```

We will use a very similar process to validate a failure event of the same `get_single_news` endpoint. We also use the patch decorators and pass values to the mocks, but in this case, we are forcing an error. Note that `rpc_get_news_mock` receives `None` as a value; this will generate an error because the function does not know how to work using the `None` value. At the end of the process, we validate if the error message is what we expect:

```
@patch('views.rpc_get_news')
@patch('nameko.standalone.events.event_dispatcher')
def test_fail(self, event_dispatcher_mock, rpc_get_news_mock):
    event_dispatcher_mock.return_value = lambda v1, v2, v3: None
    rpc_get_news_mock.return_value = None
    response = self.client.get('/famous/1')
    data = json.loads(response.data.decode())
    self.assertEqual(response.status_code, 500)
    self.assertEqual('fail', data['status'])
    self.assertEqual("'NoneType' object is not subscriptable",
data['message'])
```

After we test the search for a news article, we will test the creation. Again, we declare a class for the unit test:

```
class TestAddNews(BaseTestCase):
```

Now, our patch will be from the `rpc_command` function. Again, the patch instance is passed as a parameter of the test method via dependency injection:

```
@patch('views.rpc_command')
def test_sucess(self, rpc_command_mock):
    """Test to insert a News."""
```

Let's create a `dict` that will be the input of data and will also be part of the expected response:

```
dict_obj = dict(
    title='My Test',
    content='Just a service test',
    author='unittest',
    tags=['Test', 'unit_test'],
)
rpc_command_mock.return_value = {
    'status': 'success',
    'news': dict_obj,
}
with self.client:
    response = self.client.post(
        '/famous',
        data=json.dumps(dict_obj),
        content_type='application/json',
    )
    data = json.loads(response.data.decode())
    self.assertEqual(response.status_code, 201)
    self.assertEqual('success', data['status'])
    self.assertEqual('My Test', data['news']['title'])
```

Just as we validate the success case, we will validate the case of an error. In this scenario, we are assigning the value None to dict_obj. This will create an error, indicating that the payload received by the add_news function is invalid:

```
def test_fail_by_invalid_input(self):
    dict_obj = None
    with self.client:
        response = self.client.post(
            '/famous',
            data=json.dumps(dict_obj),
            content_type='application/json',
        )
        data = json.loads(response.data.decode())
        self.assertEqual(response.status_code, 400)
        self.assertEqual('fail', data['status'])
        self.assertEqual('Invalid payload', data['message'])
```

It is very important to think about a variety of scenarios for unit tests. We wrote a test that validates what happens when a wrong payload is passed, but what if the problem is in the microservice that registers the payload in a database? It is exactly this test that we are going to write now.

First, we apply the decorator with the patch and then create the `dict` with a valid payload:

```
@patch('views.rpc_command')
def test_fail_to_register(self, rpc_command_mock):
    """Test to insert a News."""
    dict_obj = dict(
        title='My Test',
        content='Just a service test',
        author='unittest',
        tags=['Test', 'unit_test'],
    )
```

However, let's create the mock with a side effect, which will raise an exception. We complete the process of sending information by calling the endpoint of the `add_news` function:

```
rpc_command_mock.side_effect = Exception('Forced test fail')
with self.client:
    response = self.client.post(
        '/famous',
        data=json.dumps(dict_obj),
        content_type='application/json',
    )
    data = json.loads(response.data.decode())
```

At the end, we'll validate whether we get the message sent by the exception from the mock:

```
self.assertEqual(response.status_code, 500)
self.assertEqual('fail', data['status'])
self.assertEqual('Forced test fail', data['message'])
```

The next class will validate the `get_all_news_per_type` function using unit tests. The process is exactly the same as we have applied so far. We make a declaration of the class, then using a decorator for the patch, create the mock, call the endpoint, and validate what is returned. This whole process can be seen in the following code:

```
class TestGetAllNewsPerType(BaseTestCase):

    @patch('views.rpc_get_all_news')
    def test_sucess(self, rpc_get_all_news_mock):
        """Test to get all News paginated."""
        rpc_get_all_news_mock.return_value = {
            "news": [
                {
                    "_id": 1,
                    "author": "unittest",
                    "content": "Just a service test 1",
```

```
            "created_at": {
                "$date": 1514741833010
            },
            "news_type": "famous",
            "tags": [
                "Test",
                "unit_test"
            ],
            "title": "My Test 1",
            "version": 1
        },
        {

            "_id": 2,
            "author": "unittest",
            "content": "Just a service test 2",
            "created_at": {
                "$date": 1514741833010
            },
            "news_type": "famous",
            "tags": [
                "Test",
                "unit_test"
            ],
            "title": "My Test 2",
            "version": 1
        },
    ],
    "status": "success"
}
with self.client:
    response = self.client.get('/famous/1/10')
    data = json.loads(response.data.decode())
    self.assertEqual(response.status_code, 200)
    self.assertIn('success', data['status'])
    self.assertEqual(2, len(data['news']))
    counter = 1
    for d in data['news']:
        self.assertEqual(
            d['title'],
            'My Test {}'.format(counter)
        )
        self.assertEqual(
            d['content'],
            'Just a service test {}'.format(counter)
        )
        self.assertEqual(
            d['author'],
            'unittest'
```

```
        )
        counter += 1
```

In the same way, as we did with the other scenarios, let's create a unit test for the failure case. As in all the other unit tests, the process is the same:

```
@patch('views.rpc_get_all_news')
def test_fail(self, rpc_get_all_news_mock):
    """Test to get all News paginated."""
    rpc_get_all_news_mock.side_effect = Exception('Forced test fail')
    with self.client:
        response = self.client.get('/famous/1/10')
        data = json.loads(response.data.decode())
        self.assertEqual(response.status_code, 500)
        self.assertEqual('fail', data['status'])
        self.assertEqual('Forced test fail', data['message'])
```

Obviously, as we have more complex test scenarios, we can create classes for simpler scenarios, such as tests for auxiliary functions. The following unit test is extremely simple and validates whether the function responsible for encapsulating the logic of the error messages is working correctly:

```
class TestUtilsFunctions(BaseTestCase):
    def test_error_message(self):
        response = error_response('test message error', 500)
        data = json.loads(response[0].data.decode())
        self.assertEqual(response[1], 500)
        self.assertEqual('fail', data['status'])
        self.assertEqual('test message error', data['message'])
```

At the end of the file, we write a condition so that the native Python test tool can be executed:

```
if __name__ == '__main__':
    unittest.main()
```

As can be seen, the unit test process is simple in execution. The complex part is to think about all the possible scenarios for efficient coverage of the tests.

To see the `OrchestratorNewsService` unit tests running, just use the following command lines:

```
$ docker-compose -f docker-compose.yml up --build -d

$ docker exec -it $(shell docker ps -q --filter
"name=orcherstrator_news_service_1") python tests.py
```

Preparing the containers for the integration test

Before we really talk about the integration test, let's prepare our containers for testing. We use `docker-compose` in our development environment, but currently, all of our application settings are in the same `docker-compose.yml` file.

`docker-compose` allows us to override settings by passing `docker-compose.yml` files into jail, as shown in the following example:

```
$ docker-compose -f docker-compose.yml -f docker-compose.test.yml up --
build -d
```

Let's separate the settings and create different `docker-compose` files. Each file will be for a specific environment. We will create a new file, `docker-compose.test.yml`. This file has only the settings that we want to overwrite:

```
version: '3'
services:
  users_service:
    environment:
      -
DATABASE_URL=postgresql://postgres:postgres@users_service_db:5432/users_tes
t?sslmode=disable

  famous_news_service:
    environment:
      - QUERYBD_HOST=mongodb://querydb_famous:27017/news_test
      -
COMMANDDB_HOST=postgresql://postgres:postgres@commanddb_famous:5432/news_te
st?sslmode=disable

  politics_news_service:
    environment:
      - QUERYBD_HOST=mongodb://querydb_politics:27017/news_test
      -
COMMANDDB_HOST=postgresql://postgres:postgres@commanddb_politics:5432/news_
test?sslmode=disable

  sports_news_service:
    environment:
      - QUERYBD_HOST=mongodb://querydb_sports:27017/news_test
      -
COMMANDDB_HOST=postgresql://postgres:postgres@commanddb_sports:5432/news_te
st?sslmode=disable
```

```
recommendation_service:
  environment:
    - DATABASE_URL=http://recommendation_db:7474/db/test_data
```

As shown in the preceding code block, all the changes refer to the database routes. This is to create special databases for the tests, a kind of sandbox.

Just as we created a new file with specific settings, we should remove the unnecessary settings in the `docker-compose.yml` file.

Some microservices use environment variables that must be replaced, such as `UsersServices` in the `main.go` file. Replace the settings, as shown in the following example:

```
...
connectionString := os.Getenv("DATABASE_DEV_URL") // replace this
connectionString := os.Getenv("DATABASE_URL") // by this
...
```

Repeat this process on all microservices.

Integration tests

Integration tests are very similar to unit tests in the process of building tests, but they have a different concept.

Like unit tests, integration tests must also be deterministic, but they do not prove only an isolated segment of the code. Integration tests, in the case of microservices, will validate the entire flow from the starting point of the test to the last interaction; it could be a vendor app or a database, as an example.

In the case of the `OrchestratorNewsService` microservice, which is the microservice that we are using as an example for our tests, when we test an endpoint, we will not create any kind of mock. We will let the process be as real as possible. However, we must ensure that all tests are deterministic. For this, we will use a specific test database, as well as write good integration tests. Let's see this in practice.

First, let's create the `tests_integration.py` file inside the `OrchestratorNewsService` repository. We'll start by writing the imports and declaring the base class for the tests:

```
import json
import unittest
from app import app
```

```
from flask_testing import TestCase


class BaseTestCase(TestCase):

    def create_app(self):
        app.config.from_object('config.TestingConfig')
        return app
```

Then, we'll create a class for the entire integration test:

```
class TestIntegration(BaseTestCase):
```

Now, let's write the setUp method. This method is executed whenever the class is instantiated and before any other method. Note that we are doing an HTTP POST for the microservice, but there is no mock. This means that we are effectively persisting the information in the database. When we run setUp, we are saving the response and the JSON returned in instance variables:

```
def setUp(self):
    dict_obj = dict(
        title='My Test',
        content='Just a service test',
        author='unittest',
        tags=['Test', 'unit_test'],
    )
    with self.client:
        self.response_post = self.client.post(
            '/famous',
            data=json.dumps(dict_obj),
            content_type='application/json',
        )
        self.data_post = json.loads(
            self.response_post.data.decode()
        )
```

Our first integration test only validates if the post information run by setUp is perfect:

```
def test_add_news(self):
    """Test to insert a News."""
    self.assertEqual(self.response_post.status_code, 201)
    self.assertEqual('success', self.data_post['status'])
    self.assertEqual('My Test', self.data_post['news']['title'])
```

Our second integration test makes a call to `get_single_news` and integrates with the `FamousNewsService` microservice. Here's the ID of the news article we just created:

```
def test_get_single_news(self):
    response = self.client.get(
        'famous/{id}'.format(id=self.data_post['news']['id'])
    )
    data = json.loads(response.data.decode())
    self.assertEqual(response.status_code, 200)
    self.assertIn('success', data['status'])
    self.assertTrue(len(data['news']) > 0)
    self.assertEqual(data['news']['title'], 'My Test')
    self.assertEqual(data['news']['content'], 'Just a service test')
    self.assertEqual(data['news']['author'], 'unittest')
```

At the end, we once again have the condition that performs the integration tests:

```
if __name__ == '__main__':
    unittest.main()
```

To see the `OrchestratorNewsService` integration tests running, just use the following command lines:

```
$ docker-compose -f docker-compose.yml -f docker-compose.test.yml up --build -d

$ docker exec -it $(shell docker ps -q --filter "name=orcherstrator_news_service_1") python tests_integration.py
```

Clearly, the integration tests and the unit tests can have identical test suite tools if we discard the mock tools. The tests are similar; it's just the concept that is indeed different.

End-to-end tests

The end-to-end tests are conceptually similar to integration tests, but they validate the entire business flow of the application. The main purpose of this type of test is to check whether any flow stages are corrupted. Many developers get confused about the difference between end-to-end and integration tests.

Let's say the big difference is that the integration tests validate the integration of a part of the application with other microservices, tools, or vendors. However, end-to-end tests validate an application business flow and not the integration with a smaller follow-up.

It is possible to have several end-to-end tests validating several different flows. In the case of our application, the flow that we are going to test is as follows:

1. Create a user.
2. Create a news article for each type of news service (famous, politics, and sports).
3. Search for all news articles created in the test by sending the `user_id` function in the request cookie.
4. Validate the recommendations created for the user.

Let's go to the code. First, at the root of our project, we will create a new directory called `TestRobot`, and inside this directory, a file called `main.go`. This file will be our end-to-end test tool.

First, in the `TestRobot/main.go` file, we will declare the package, imports, constants, and structs that will be used in the test:

```go
package main

import (
        "bytes"
        "encoding/json"
        "errors"
        "fmt"
        "io/ioutil"
        "log"
        "net/http"
        "os"
        "strings"
        "time"
)

const (
        baseURL             string = "http://localhost/"
        newsURL             string = baseURL + "v1/news/"
        usersURL            string = baseURL + "v1/users/"
        recommendationURL   string = baseURL + "v1/recommendation/"
)

type News struct {
        ID          int         `json:"id"`
        Author      string      `json:"author"`
        Content     string      `json:"content"`
        NewsType    string      `json:"news_type"`
        Tags        []string    `json:"tags"`
        Title       string      `json:"title"`
```

```
        Version   int       `json:"version"`
}

type RespNewsBody struct {
        News    News    `json:"news"`
        Status  string  `json:"status"`
}

type Users struct {
        ID        int       `json:"id"`
        Name      string  `json:"name"`
        Email     string  `json:"email"`
        Password  string  `json:"password"`
}

type RecommendationByUser struct {
        ID string  `json:"id"`
}
```

The next step is to write some auxiliary functions to avoid code duplicity. The
newsUnmarshaler function translates the received JSON into the struct
instance, RespNewsBody:

```
func newsUnmarshaler(resp *http.Response) (RespNewsBody, error) {
        defer resp.Body.Close()
        body, _ := ioutil.ReadAll(resp.Body)
        var respBody RespNewsBody
        if err := json.Unmarshal(body, &respBody); err != nil {
                return respBody, err
        }
        return respBody, nil
}
```

The newsIntegrityValidator function validates whether the received data is actually
the expected data:

```
func newsIntegrityValidator(respBody RespNewsBody, newsType string) error {
        if respBody.News.Version < 1 {
                return errors.New("News wasn't created")
        }
        if strings.Title(newsType)+" end-to-end Test" !=
respBody.News.Author {
                return fmt.Errorf("Inconsistent value checking the author:
%s", respBody.News.Author)
        }
        return nil
}
```

The `recommendationUnmarshaler` function translates the received JSON into a list of instances of the `RecommendationByUser` struct:

```
func recommendationUnmarshaler(resp *http.Response)
([]RecommendationByUser, error) {
        defer resp.Body.Close()
        body, _ := ioutil.ReadAll(resp.Body)
        var respBody []RecommendationByUser
        if err := json.Unmarshal(body, &respBody); err != nil {
                return respBody, err
        }
        return respBody, nil
}
```

The `recommendationIntegrityValidator` function validates whether the received data actually is the expected data:

```
func recommendationIntegrityValidator(recommendations
[]RecommendationByUser) error {
        if len(recommendations) < 3 {
                return fmt.Errorf("Fail. The quantity of recommendations was
less then spected. expected: 3 received: %d", len(recommendations))
        }
        return nil
}
```

Let's start writing a function that validates the flow we determined at the beginning of the session. First, we declare the name of the function that will be `StartToEndTestMinimalFlow`:

```
func StartToEndTestMinimalFlow() {
        log.Println("### Starting minimal validation flow ###")
        log.Println("Validating user creation")
```

We created the payload to create the user and executed the POST method. If user validation succeeds, we continue with the process:

```
        reqBody := []byte(`{
                "name": "end-to-end User",
                "email": "end-to-end@test.com",
                "password": "123456"
        }`)
        resp, err := http.Post(usersURL, "Application/json",
bytes.NewBuffer(reqBody))
        if err != nil {
                os.Exit(1)
        }
```

```
        defer resp.Body.Close()
        body, _ := ioutil.ReadAll(resp.Body)
        var respUser Users
        if err := json.Unmarshal(body, &respUser); err != nil {
                log.Fatalln(err)
        }
        if respUser.Email != "end-to-end@test.com" {
                log.Fatalln("Inconsistent value checking the user email: ",
respUser.Email)
        }
        log.Println("User creation validated with success")
```

Now, we will create the payload for the news articles:

```
        mapNews := map[string][]byte{
                "famous": []byte(`{
                        "author": "Famous end-to-end Test",
                        "content": "This content is just a test using the
famous end-to-end test robot",
                        "tags": ["Famous test"],
                        "title": "FamousNews test end-to-end"
                }`),
                "politics": []byte(`{
                        "author": "Politics end-to-end Test",
                        "content": "This content is just a test using the
politics end-to-end test robot",
                        "tags": ["Politics test"],
                        "title": "PoliticsNews test end-to-end"
                }`),
                "sports": []byte(`{
                        "author": "Sports end-to-end Test",
                        "content": "This content is just a test using the
sports end-to-end test robot",
                        "tags": ["Sports test"],
                        "title": "SportsNews test end-to-end"
                }`),
        }
        newsTypeID := make(map[string]int)
```

Next, we will process a loop that will repeat the flow for each payload item:

```
        for newsType, reqBody := range mapNews {
                log.Println("Validating news creation:", newsType)
```

We will use the HTTP POST for the orchestrator:

```
resp, err := http.Post(newsURL+newsType, "Application/json",
bytes.NewBuffer(reqBody))
        if err != nil {
                os.Exit(1)
        }
        respBody, err := newsUnmarshaler(resp)
        if err != nil {
                log.Fatalln(err)
        }
```

For each news article, the content of the returned data will be validated. If the validator does not return an error, the process continues:

```
        if err := newsIntegrityValidator(respBody, newsType); err !=
nil {
                log.Fatalln(err)
        }
        log.Println("News creation validated with success:",
newsType)
```

We will do the search for the news article created, passing `user_id` in the request cookie:

```
        log.Println("Validating news get:", newsType)
        client := &http.Client{}
        req, err := http.NewRequest("GET", fmt.Sprintf("%s%s/%d",
newsURL, newsType, respBody.News.ID), nil)
        if err != nil {
                log.Fatalln(err)
        }
        req.Header.Set("Cookie", fmt.Sprintf("user_id=%d",
respUser.ID))
        resp, err = client.Do(req)
        if err != nil {
                log.Fatalln(err)
        }
        respBody, err = newsUnmarshaler(resp)
        if err != nil {
                log.Fatalln(err)
        }
```

Again, we will validate the integrity of the news article, this time with the result of the search:

```
        if err := newsIntegrityValidator(respBody, newsType); err !=
nil {
                log.Fatalln(err)
```

```
        }
        log.Println("Got news with success:", newsType)
```

At the end of the loop, we will create a key/value reference between the news type and the news article ID created:

```
        newsTypeID[newsType] = respBody.News.ID
    }
```

Next, we will search and validate the recommendations of news labels for a user:

```
        log.Println("Validating recommendations")
        time.Sleep(1 * time.Second)
        resp, err = http.Get(fmt.Sprintf("%s%s/%d", recommendationURL,
    "user", respUser.ID))
        if err != nil {
                log.Fatalln(err)
        }
        recommendationByUser, err := recommendationUnmarshaler(resp)
        if err != nil {
                log.Fatalln(err)
        }
        if err := recommendationIntegrityValidator(recommendationByUser);
    err != nil {
                log.Fatalln(err)
        }
        log.Println("Recommendations validated with success")
        log.Println("### Finished minimal validation flow ###")
    }
```

At the end of the file, we have the `main` function that performs the test:

```
func main() {
        StartToEndTestMininalFlow()
}
```

To see the end-to-end tests running, just use the following command lines:

```
$ docker-compose -f docker-compose.yml -f docker-compose.test.yml up --
build -d

$ go run ${PWD}/TestRobot/main.go
```

Release pipelines

Pipelines are process flows that must be run before the code is released into production or in a particular version control repository.

It is very common to create pipelines in tools such as Jenkins or other **Continuous Integration (CI)** tools. A common pipeline flow for code testing is as follows:

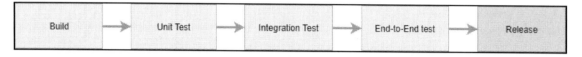

The pipeline concept turns out to be a great test flow controller.

Signature tests

Imagine a scenario where we have several development teams working on different microservices of the same application. These microservices have some communication between them; there is a kind of *contract* between them that is the payload of the microservice, also known as the **Service Signature**. One of the development teams modifies the signature of the microservice causing errors in other parts of the application.

As previously stated, modifying microservices is common, especially if they are part of the internal layer. When a microservice has the signature changed, a task must be generated for the other development teams responsible for microservices that integrate with this signature.

The problem is not the change, but the lack of information. The error was generated because the responsibility of notifying the teams that integrate with the microservice signature was a human responsibility, which is liable to failure and forgetfulness.

The signature tests work for possible alert changes in microservices payloads. There are many ways to do this, from webhooks to version control repositories, or even scripts and CIs.

Take the communication between `RecommendationService` and `UsersService` as an example. There is a common file for creating an RPC client/server communication model between the two microservices. This file is in the `ProtoFiles` repository and is called `user_data.proto`. In this case, the validation is very simple; just check whether this file has been modified.

To validate any changes to the `user_data.proto` file, the following command is enough:

```
$ git diff --name-only HEAD HEAD~1 | grep user_data.proto
```

This command validates whether there is any difference in the file between the current commit and the previous commit. Moving the command to a CI and creating a validation script is enough to apply signature tests in this case.

Monkey tests

Monkey tests are usually automated tests with random values that target identified errors in the application. Normally, the errors that emerge in this type of test are due to a failure of treatment in the input or slowness in the treatment of input owing to the stress of the application.

It is common to see the monkey tests used alongside a test technique called **Fuzzing**. Fuzzing relies on providing invalid, unexpected, and random data as input to computer programs. The program is then monitored, analyzing exceptions such as runtime errors.

In general, the monkey test is useful for identifying out-of-the-box errors.

Chaos Monkey

Chaos Monkey (`https://github.com/Netflix/chaosmonkey`) was created by the Netflix engineering team, and as its name suggests, it is intended to generate chaos in a random manner. The process will randomly choose servers in their production environment and deactivate them during business hours in order to measure application resiliency.

With Chaos Monkey, we can identify how to better distribute servers, look for more efficient monitoring systems, and develop resilient patterns.

Imagine an application that implements CQRS. Imagine what would happen if a Chaos Monkey test shut down the server from the writing database, as shown in the following diagram:

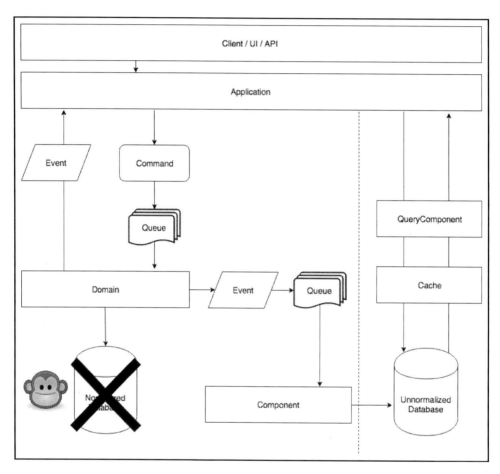

The answer is nothing serious. The process of writing the information will be interrupted, but the reading process will not be interrupted. If the queue used is transactional, the information consumed by the domain that is not registered will return to the queue until the `CommandStack` database instance is restored. With a good monitoring system in the application, a new instance of the database is re-established and the anomaly is solved without major impact.

Evolving an application to the point of using this type of pattern is only possible by testing with Chaos Monkey.

Chaos Monkey has the following test categories:

- **Chaos Gorilla**: This simulates the unavailability of an entire zone of availability
- **Conformity Monkey**: This closes instances that do not adhere to best practices
- **Doctor Monkey**: This performs performance checks (similar to a CPU)
- **Janitor Monkey**: This searches for unused resources and deletes them
- **Latency Monkey**: This creates artificial delays in client-server communication
- **Security Monkey**: This encounters security vulnerabilities, such as non-security groups configured properly

Summary

Throughout this chapter, we studied many test possibilities and applied the knowledge gained in real cases. We went from the simplest unit testing scenarios to the popular and powerful Chaos Monkey.

In the next chapter, we will study monitoring, security, and deployment. There will be many new concepts and strategies to further expand our knowledge of microservices architecture.

13
Monitoring Security and Deployment

So far, we have our application logic built. Throughout this process, we applied DDD, internal design patterns, and design patterns of communication between microservices. We looked at the concepts of scalability, anti-patterns, and good development practices.

Now, it's time to learn how to keep our application in production. We will cover a wide range of topics, such as:

- Monitoring services
- Understanding metric numbers
- Authentication and authorization services
- Single Sign-On
- Security data
- The human factor
- Identifying attacks
- The API gateway
- Continuous integration/delivery
- The deployment pipeline
- Multiple service instances per host
- Service instance per host
- Service instance per VM
- Service instance per container

No doubt it will be a great chapter with many new aspects to understand.

Monitoring microservices

Some microservices fail to come into production due to lack of monitoring. Even with tests in controlled environments, it is very difficult to get a true picture of a microservice's performance. The production numbers will give us a final view of the scalability, availability, and performance of an application.

Not having alert systems and constantly collecting metrics from the microservices can cause a higher number of hits, override the application, or cause some instability in some segments of the system. Unmonitored instability is the most dangerous case because it is a silent error and difficult to detect; it will probably be too late by the time we find it.

In some cases, microservice instabilities happen because the development team did not understand the monitoring metrics of the application or did not know how to properly collect them.

Monitoring a single service

Application monitoring, in general, seems simple. However, it implies a great capacity for analysis and knowledge of what to monitor. Firstly, we will cover the monitoring of a single server and then understand how the monitoring of multiple servers occurs.

There are two major general aspects of monitoring. The first aspect is machine monitoring, that is to say, measuring the availability, health, and performance of an application's servers. The second is monitoring the application, as it may be that the server machine is fully functional, but the application is not.

Within the scope of monitoring, there are two ways to do it—passive monitoring and active monitoring:

- **Active Monitoring** is when the server that is to be monitored sends the status information to the monitoring tool
- **Passive Monitoring** is when the monitoring tool requests information about the state of the machine or application from the server

Note this flow in the following diagram:

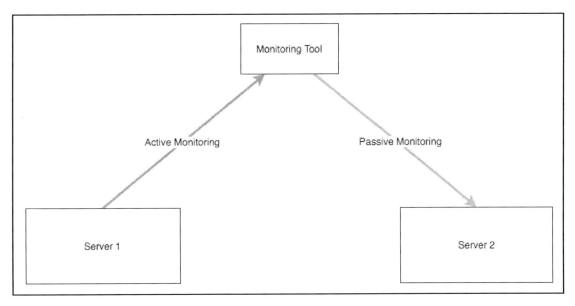

A very simple approach is the creation of endpoints that demonstrate the health of the application, also known as **health checks**. Let's create an endpoint of this type inside the UsersService microservice to understand it better.

In the app.go file of the UsersService microservice, we will add a new route to the initializeRoutes method:

```
func (a *App) initializeRoutes() {
        a.Router.HandleFunc("/all", a.getUsers).Methods("GET")
        a.Router.HandleFunc("/", a.createUser).Methods("POST")
        a.Router.HandleFunc("/{id:[0-9]+}", a.getUser).Methods("GET")
        a.Router.HandleFunc("/{id:[0-9]+}", a.updateUser).Methods("PUT")
        a.Router.HandleFunc("/{id:[0-9]+}", a.deleteUser).Methods("DELETE")
        a.Router.HandleFunc("/healthcheck", a.healthcheck).Methods("GET")
}
```

Then, we'll create the handler for this new route. We start with the name of the method, along with its parameters:

```
func (a *App) healthcheck(w http.ResponseWriter, r *http.Request) {
```

Next, we'll write a variable to collect the errors, search for a `Pool` connection from the cache, and prepare the return of the connection to the `Pool`:

```
var err error
c := a.Cache.Pool.Get()
defer c.Close()
```

Let's do the first validation, which is to check whether the cache is active:

```
// Check Cache
_, err = c.Do("PING")
```

Then, we make a second validation, which is to check whether the database is active:

```
// Check DB
err = a.DB.Ping()
```

If one of the components is unavailable, we will return an error to the monitoring tool:

```
if err != nil {
        http.Error(w, "CRITICAL", http.StatusInternalServerError)
        return
}
```

If there is no error within the components of the application, we return a message stating that everything is normal:

```
    w.Write([]byte("OK"))
    return
}
```

In the end, our health check handler has the following formatting:

```
func (a *App) healthcheck(w http.ResponseWriter, r *http.Request) {
    var err error
    c := a.Cache.Pool.Get()
    defer c.Close()

    // Check Cache
    _, err = c.Do("PING")

    // Check DB
    err = a.DB.Ping()

    if err != nil {
            http.Error(w, "CRITICAL", http.StatusInternalServerError)
            return
    }
```

```
      w.Write([]byte("OK"))
      return
}
```

Monitoring multiple services

In the *Monitoring a single service* section, we saw how the monitoring of a single server works, but when we are talking about the architecture of microservices, we can have a huge number of servers. How do we monitor all these servers? The answer is by *automation*.

It is humanly impossible to monitor so many servers. We need to make use of tools that help us in this work. In this sense, there is a range of tools that can help us. Some are paid for and some are free, but Nagios Core (`https://www.nagios.org/downloads/nagios-core/`) deserves a special mention. It is a flexible, customizable tool that handles the main use cases with regards to monitoring. Obviously, there are paid versions of Nagios that greatly simplify operations.

The following is a demonstration of the Nagios Core server monitoring interface:

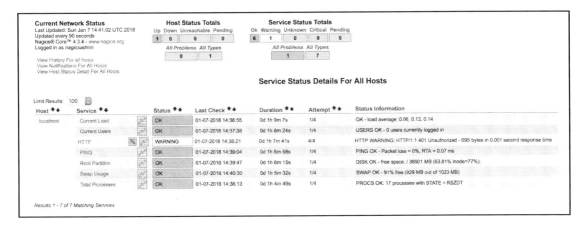

Now, here is a screenshot of how the result is presented when monitoring servers passively:

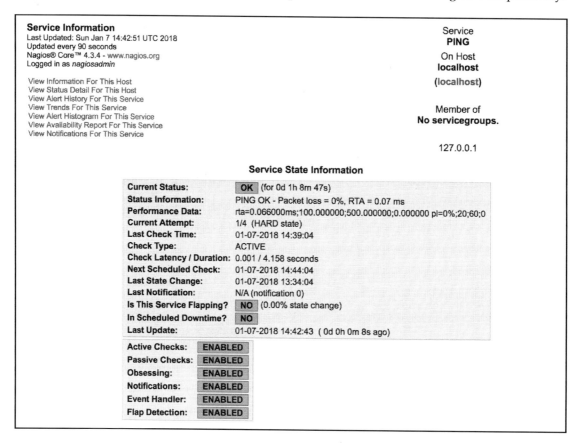

While not as complete and easy as other versions of Nagios, Nagios Core is very flexible and has good documentation.

Looking at the logs

Observing the behavior of an application through logs is something that many software developers are accustomed to, but when it comes to microservices and large-scale applications, monitoring manually is almost impossible.

In this context, where checking logs manually is extremely complex, using tools that parse logs and provide information in a simple way can be very useful.

There are some tools designed for this purpose. Among these tools, I would like to highlight Splunk.

Splunk has a free version, but with limited user capacity and quantity of MBs of logs per day. However, this version is very useful for getting acquainted with the tool. Overall, Splunk offers a system of queries to perform searches on the millions of lines of logs we can have. The following is a screenshot with a search example using Splunk:

This graph is only for demonstration purposes

Learning from the errors in the application

When we talk about software development, we have the certainty, at some point, that the software will fail. There are many variables that can make errors happen in an application. There may be extensive testing coverage and monitoring, but at some point, something will fail.

The first point is—do not be afraid to fail. Mistakes happen, but it is important is to keep a history of these errors. Tracking history is directly linked to how a failure is documented and how this documentation can be quickly recovered to assist in the recovery of production applications.

It may seem a bit old-fashioned to write documentation about crashes. However, up-to-date and well-written documentation is one of the most efficient forms of communication. In addition to generating historical data, it provides non-dependence to the memory of a specific person.

Documenting how an application works is a very good thing, but documenting the flaws is simply fantastic. A good tool for writing documents that are easy to edit, and that offers intelligent search features, is Sphinx.

Sphinx has the ability to provide documentation in a concentrated, indexed, HTML format with a dynamic search. It is not tied to any specific text editor.

Another very good tool for catching errors and keeping history is Sentry. With simple code instrumentation, all serious errors can be reported to Sentry. One interesting thing about the tool is that, in addition to maintaining history, it also provides the frequency of the error that occurred.

Let's apply Sentry in our `UsersService` microservice. In the `main.go` file, we will add the necessary `import` to communicate the failures to Sentry:

```
import (
        "flag"
        "log"
        "os"
        "github.com/jmoiron/sqlx"
        _ "github.com/lib/pq"
        raven "github.com/getsentry/raven-go"
)
```

In the `main.go` file, let's write the `init` method. This method runs before the `main` method and every time we start the application. In this method, we will include the configuration that indicates where errors should be sent:

```
func init() {
        raven.SetDSN("<YOUR SENTRY ROUTE>")
}
```

After the Sentry is configured, I will create a new handler for didactic purposes that always generates an error because it tries to open a file that does not exist. Obviously, we'll first create the new route in the `app.go` file:

```
func (a *App) initializeRoutes() {
        a.Router.HandleFunc("/all", a.getUsers).Methods("GET")
        a.Router.HandleFunc("/", a.createUser).Methods("POST")
        a.Router.HandleFunc("/{id:[0-9]+}", a.getUser).Methods("GET")
```

```
        a.Router.HandleFunc("/{id:[0-9]+}", a.updateUser).Methods("PUT")
        a.Router.HandleFunc("/{id:[0-9]+}", a.deleteUser).Methods("DELETE")
        a.Router.HandleFunc("/healthcheck", a.healthcheck).Methods("GET")
        a.Router.HandleFunc("/sentryerr", a.sentryerr).Methods("GET")
    }
```

Then, still in the `app.go` file, let's write the handler that generates the errors for Sentry:

```
func (a *App) sentryerr(w http.ResponseWriter, r *http.Request) {
```

The following line will create an error because the file we tried to read does not exist:

```
        _, err := os.Open("filename.ext")
```

Now, we catch the error and send it to Sentry, while we return an error in the HTTP response:

```
        if err != nil {
                raven.CaptureErrorAndWait(err, nil)
                http.Error(w, err.Error(), http.StatusInternalServerError)
                return
        }
```

If no error occurs, the response will be positive:

```
        w.Write([]byte("OK"))
        return
    }
```

In the end, our method created to send errors to Sentry has the following formatting:

```
func (a *App) sentryerr(w http.ResponseWriter, r *http.Request) {
        _, err := os.Open("filename.ext")
        if err != nil {
                raven.CaptureErrorAndWait(err, nil)
                http.Error(w, err.Error(), http.StatusInternalServerError)
                return
        }
        w.Write([]byte("OK"))
        return
    }
```

To generate the error in Sentry, just access the URL that ends with `/v1/users/sentryerr`. If we look at Sentry, there will be an error, as can be seen in the following screenshot:

This screenshot shows errors in the code

When we click on the error link that is reported in Sentry, we are faced with the following dashboard:

This screenshot represents an on-path error

As you can see, the dashboard is very detailed and gives us a complete view of the error. If we repeat the call to the endpoint that generates the failure, let's see whether what Sentry identifies is the same error and if it shows how many times the same fault has occurred in a period of time:

This screenshot represents an overview of all the errors

The important thing is to understand that keeping track of errors in the application is key to knowing how to recover faster and faster.

The metrics – Understanding the numbers

Metrics are very useful, but if we do not understand them, we can deceive ourselves. A common way of looking at metrics is to look at the numbers by the average. When we are dealing with microservices architecture, this is a big mistake.

The average value of a metric camouflages possible anomalies. Note the following numbers:

```
    4 threads and 50 connections
    Thread Stats   Avg      Stdev     Max     +/- Stdev
      Latency     28.68ms   67.34ms   1.55s    98.58%
      Req/Sec     554.47    154.04    1.06k    73.50%
    22085 requests in 10.01s, 3.45MB read
    Socket errors: connect 0, read 4, write 0, timeout 0
  Requests/sec:   2206.44
  Transfer/sec:    353.28KB
```

If we look at the latency average, apparently everything is fine as we have an average of `28.68ms`. However, if we look at the maximum latency, we see that there is something wrong. The maximum time is `1.55s`. This means that one request took almost two seconds to complete.

Being able to see this kind of anomaly in numbers helps us to better understand the metrics that the tools provide us. In addition, we can establish, through the numbers, a better scalability strategy.

Security

There are several ways to attack an application. Understanding how to protect microservices is paramount to not having the credibility of the software destroyed in seconds.

Understanding JWT

When we are working with APIs, we need to think about the security of data traffic and especially the level of permission that each user should have. There are many ways to do this, but the one that currently stands out is **JWT (JSON Web Token)**, mainly because it is safe and easy to implement.

JWT is a data transfer system that can be sent via URL, `POST`, or in an HTTP header. This information is digitally signed, for example, signed with the HMAC algorithm or public/private keys using the RSA algorithm.

The structure of the JWT is divided into three parts, separated by dots. The three parts are header, payload, and signature. The following example shows the creation and reading of a JWT token made in Go. Like all Go code, we start with the package declaration and the `import` statements:

```go
package main

import (
        "fmt"
        "log"
        "time"
        jwt "github.com/dgrijalva/jwt-go"
)
```

In the preceding code, we have the declaration of the `jwt-go` package, which is responsible for providing us with everything needed to create and use the token. Now, let's declare the method of the `struct` that will be a part of the token. Note that the `struct` method is a composite between the data we want to send and the default JWT struct:

```
type MyCustomClaims struct {
        UserID int      `json:"ID"`
        Name   string `json:"name"`
        Rule   string `json:"rule"`
        jwt.StandardClaims
}
```

After writing the `struct` method, let's start with the `createToken` function. The first step is to declare the function name, together with the token signature key:

```
func createToken() string {
        mySigningKey := []byte("AllYourBase")
```

Now, let's compose the `struct` method with the data that should go to the token payload:

```
        // Create the Claims
        claims := MyCustomClaims{
                1,
                "Vinicius Pacheco",
                "Admin",
                jwt.StandardClaims{
                        ExpiresAt: time.Now().Add(time.Hour * 72).Unix(),
                        Issuer:    "Localhost",
                        IssuedAt:  time.Now().Unix(),
                },
        }
```

With the `struct` method created, we will pass the same to JWT and then compose the token with the signature string. If no error occurs, we will return the token:

```
        token := jwt.NewWithClaims(jwt.SigningMethodHS256, claims)
        ss, err := token.SignedString(mySigningKey)
        if err != nil {
                log.Fatal(err.Error())
        }
        return ss
}
```

Let's create the `readToken` function. First, we declare the name of the function and the parameter that it will receive:

```
func readToken(tokenString string) {
```

Now, let's run token parsing:

```
token, err := jwt.ParseWithClaims(
        tokenString,
        &MyCustomClaims{},
        func(token *jwt.Token) (interface{}, error) {
                return []byte("AllYourBase"), nil
        },
)
```

After executing the token parsing, we validate if the token is intact and valid. If all is well, token values will be displayed:

```
if claims, ok := token.Claims.(*MyCustomClaims); ok &&
token.Valid {
        fmt.Printf(
                "%v %v %v %v\n",
                claims.UserID,
                claims.Name,
                claims.Rule,
                claims.StandardClaims.ExpiresAt,
        )
} else {
        fmt.Println(err)
}
}
```

In order to actually execute the process, we must write the `main` function:

```
func main() {
        token := createToken()
        fmt.Println(token)
        readToken(token)
}
```

The simplicity of JWT is really impressive. With the implementation of this type of technology, a range of authentication and authorization practices have been created.

Single Sign-On

We may not realize it, but the **Single Sign-On** (**SSO**) is much more present in our day-to-day lives than we can imagine. A good example is when we use the user account of a service to log in to another totally different service.

With JWT, which we looked at in the previous topic, it is entirely possible to create an application that provides SSO. In the following diagram, you can see the general behavior of the SSO using JWT:

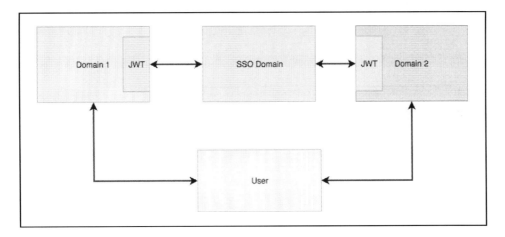

With SSO, we can provide more dynamics to the application, and not only as a product; we can also offer the authentication and authorization service.

Something important to understand is that a specialized microservice in authentication needs to be very optimized as it can become a bottleneck on a large scale. To reduce the friction that can be generated by an authentication microservice, it is common to separate the authentication microservice into two parts. The first part is responsible for token validation, and the second is responsible for token generation.

The following diagram shows two distinct streams, one for creating the JWT token and another stream to verify that the received token is valid:

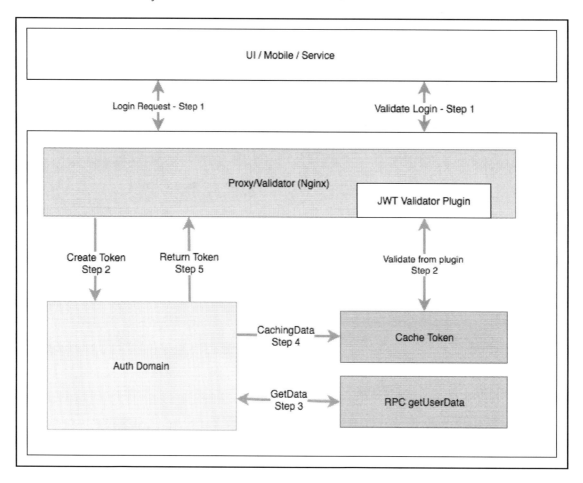

As you can see in the preceding diagram, we are using Nginx with a plugin to do the validation part of the token. This type of strategy reduces stress on the logical layer, thus reducing bottlenecks.

Security of data

Securely isolating the data layer is something that every development team has in mind. However, even though the data is well isolated behind a firewall or any other type of strategy, there is sensitive data that is not always properly stored.

Passwords are sensitive data; I know this seems obvious. But many development teams apply reversible encryption over passwords for database storage instead of applying irreversible hashes. Reversible passwords are a major security breach.

Another good practice with regards to data is avoiding sequential numeric IDs. This is a great gateway to identify and steal user data. Adopting hashes or skipped numbers as IDs in the database is safer for an application. If possible, always use hashes.

Adopt HTTPS, even below the API level. It is very common to see applications with HTTPS only for the external communication layer of the application.

Defense for malicious requests – Identifying attacks

Based on the microservices architecture, the most common type of attack is **Distributed Denial of Service (DDoS)**. This type of attack is the most common because it is simple to do and requires the microservice's high computational capacity. Know that computational resources are not infinite, especially if the application is facing an attack.

The first step to protect yourself is to identify attacks. There is a certain pattern for identifying an attack. The first is the human factor. In this case, calculate the time of calls to the microservices. The speed of calls is an excellent identifier, whether it is an attack or not. Very fast calls or calls with constant standard time, sequences, and repetitions do not represent human behavior, and attacks are possible.

Once the requisitions are identified and validated by the tests, the following mitigation strategies are suggested:

- Produce an architecture that minimizes the dependency between microservices. If one service fails, it should fail in isolation, without breaking others.
- Understand how services use each other and how services are invoked. For example, limit the batch or request execution size of objects.

- Provide feedback from the backend services to the application firewall. This passes on additional information regarding the use of API call features, which would not be identifiable.
- Monitor the lack of cached objects. A high volume may mean that the cache is not configured properly.
- Use various customer resiliency standards, for example, circuit breakers and timeouts.

These practices do not prevent attacks, but they certainly minimize the side effects.

Explaining the interceptor

The purpose of the interceptor is to include, within the code stream, a class responsible for collecting/manipulating information passed through the HTTP request, such as the authorization header, URL, and credentials provided by the HTTP agent. The concept is presented in the following diagram:

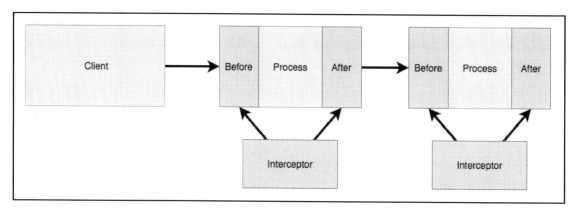

An interceptor is added before or after the call to the process responsible for handling the declared logic within the application. This interceptor involves your code and will act as a security guardian.

Any type of data that is not in the interceptor's processing policy causes some action to be taken within the application. The actions can be from a simple log to even interrupting the operation of a node of a microservice to maintain the overall integrity of the application. It is important to clarify that this type of technique does not help against socket exhaustion, for example.

Web container

The web container is the component of a web server that interacts with Java servlets. The web container standard is very useful and provides a range of tools that increase the security of the application, as well as helping to centralize rules and access policies. Here are some examples of how a web container might operate:

- It enables the **Secure Socket Layer (SSL)/Transport Layer Security (TLS)** security layer to encrypt the data exchanged between the HTTP agent and the server
- It configures mutual TLS
- It restricts access to web resources by using a security constraint associated with a user's role

The web container is positioned ahead of the application, serving as the first level of security, especially when it comes to message encryption. The following diagram demonstrates the positioning of the **Web Container** in relation to the application:

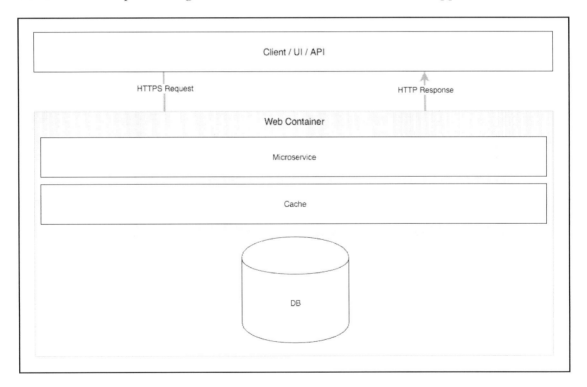

The API gateway

If you imagine microservices as a great orchestra, the gateway API would be the concertmaster. The gateway pattern instruments microservices.

The **API gateway** is positioned ahead of microservices. Some benefits we get from adopting the API gateway are optimized endpoints and centralized middleware functionality.

Imagine that our application, which uses the microservices architecture, has three different types of clients. The first is a web frontend, the second is a mobile application, and the third is another service external to our application. Each of these clients expects a different response to their respective requests. Without the gateway, each client should know directly the microservices responsible for delivering the information and know how to manipulate them. However, the API gateway can take on the role of optimizing an endpoint and handling the response.

Centralized middleware functionality means that levels of security, permissions, authentication, and other validations are at the gateway level.

The placement of an API gateway in relation to microservices can be seen in the following diagram:

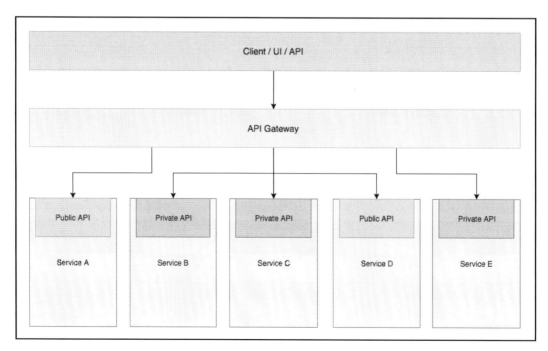

Deployment

We have the application working and we understand how security items work for microservices. Now, let's understand the patterns of deployment, thinking about the microservices architecture.

Continuous integration/continuous delivery/continuous deploy

Continuous integration is a practice where developers merge their changes back into the main branch as often as possible. Developer changes are validated by creating a compilation and running automated tests against the build. When performing the process of continuous integration, the problem that usually occurs when developers wait for the release of a new feature to merge their changes in the launch branch is avoided.

Continuous integration places great emphasis on automated testing to check whether a new feature is in trouble when new commits are being integrated into the core business.

Continuous delivery is an extension of continuous integration to ensure that you can quickly release new features to your customers in an agile and sustainable way. This means that in addition to automated testing, it has also automated the release process and you can deploy an application at any time by clicking a button.

In theory, with continuous delivery, it is possible to decide to make daily, weekly, bi-weekly releases, or whatever is appropriate to business requirements. However, if we really want to reap the benefits of continuous delivery, we must send production features as early as possible to ensure delivery in small batches, which are easy to solve in case of a problem. It is important to remember that the final process of sending a version of an application for production depends on human intervention, as can be seen in the following diagram:

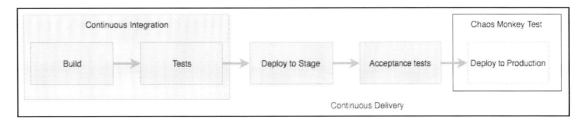

Continuous deploy goes one step beyond continuous delivery. With this practice, every change that passes through every step of your production pipeline is released to your customers. There is no human intervention, and only a failed test will prevent a new change from being implemented in production.

Continuous deploy is a great way to speed up the feedback loop for your customers. The delivery of new features does not have technically-structured planning as there is no release day anymore. Developers can focus on building software, and they see their work in production minutes after they finish development. Of course, reaching this release model requires stupendous automated testing coverage and a high degree of maturity from the development team.

In this model, unlike what happens with continuous integration, there is no human intervention to send new versions of the application for production, as can be seen in the following diagram:

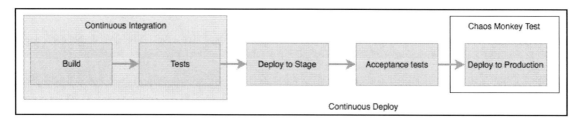

The blue/green deployment pattern and Canary releases

The deploy blue/green pattern is very simple in its concept, and it is very efficient to send new versions of software for production. For the implementation of the deploy blue/green pattern, the API gateway, with microservices architecture, is of great help.

In a monolithic application, generally, deployments are slower because every time a new version of the software is to be released, it must run the deployment of all the monolithics again. As the monolithic grows and becomes larger, it can become slow and problematic. With microservices, we can deploy individual components several times; it is usually faster and easier because of the size of the application thread itself being sent for production.

It is in the process of sending a new version of a microservice for production that the blue/green pattern is used. For example, if we have a microservice in version 1.0.0 and want to deploy version 1.0.1, an API gateway can know the location of both components and then provide an interface to switch traffic from the previous version to the new. The following diagram demonstrates very well the work of the **API Gateway** to make the change of versions using the blue/green pattern:

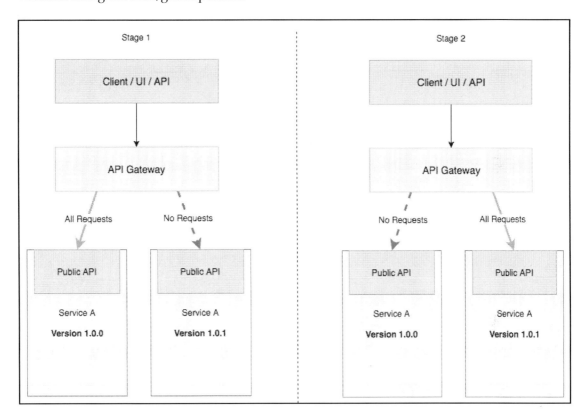

However, some deployments may entail a greater risk to the business of the application. In this scenario, a full version turn, as in the blue/green pattern, may not be the most appropriate. What would be interesting would be to run deploy, but direct the requests to the new version of the software in a controlled way.

As a solution to this type of situation, we have the pattern called the Canary release. The process is very similar to what is executed in blue/green patterns, and the difference is due to the gradual redirection of requests for the new version.

The requests control can be executed directly at the gateway. In this way, the impact in case of an error on the release of a new version will be much smaller. Take a look at the following diagram for an overview of this process:

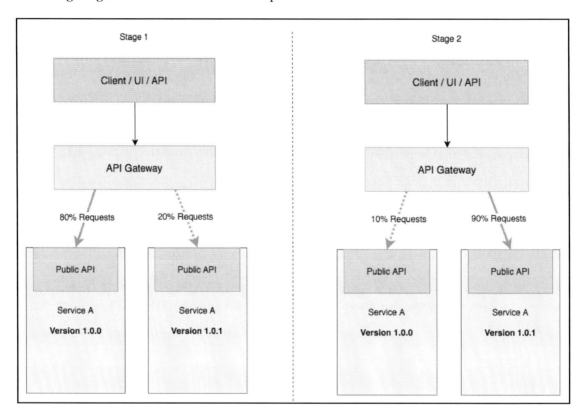

The progress of the number of requests redirected to the new version of the application will depend directly on how confident the development team is. This process is gradual and does not have a predetermined time. The goal is to transfer 100% of the requests to the new version of the application.

Multiple service instances per host

Using this pattern, we provide one or more physical or virtual host and run multiple instances of microservices on each. This is the traditional approach to deploying applications. Each microservice instance runs on a well-known port on one or more hosts.

The following diagram shows the structure of this pattern:

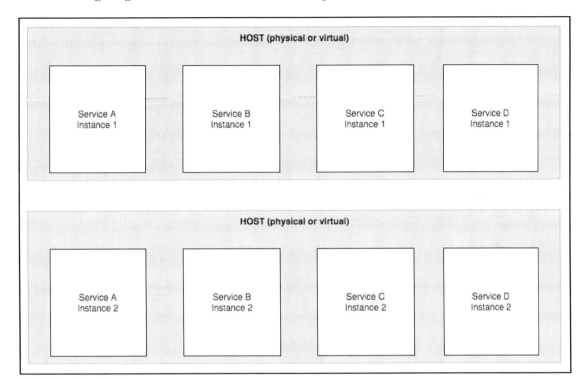

The multiple service instances per host pattern has benefits and drawbacks. One of the key benefits is that it uses resources efficiently. Multiple instances of the service share the server and its operating system. Another benefit of this pattern is the relatively rapid deployment of a microservice instance.

Despite this feature, the instances in this pattern have some significant drawbacks. A major disadvantage is that there is little to no isolation of instances of the service unless each service instance is a separate process. If the instances are not separated in different processes, an instance with errors could compromise the entire process, besides making the individual monitoring of instances impossible.

Service instance per host

With the service instance per host pattern, we run each microservice instance in isolation on its own host. There are two different models in this pattern—service instance per VM and service instance per container.

Service instance per VM

In this specialization of the pattern, we involve each microservice as an image of the **Virtual Machine** (**VM**). Each instance of a microservice is a VM, and the execution of this VM enables the microservice to work.

The service instance pattern per VM has a number of benefits. One of the main benefits of VMs is that each instance of microservice runs in a completely isolated manner, having fixed CPU and memory consumption, without competing for resource consumption with other microservices. Another great benefit of this pattern is the encapsulation of the technology used in the development of microservices.

Obviously, there are also disadvantages. A disadvantage is the less efficient resource utilization. Each service instance has the overhead of a full VM, including the operating system. Another disadvantage of this approach is that deploying and booting a new version of a microservice is often slow because the cost of booting operating systems using VMs can be high.

The following diagram illustrates this strategy:

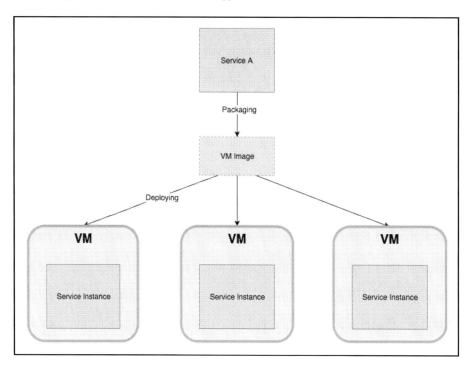

Service instance per container

When we use the service instance per container pattern, each microservice instance runs in a container unique to the instance. Containers are a virtualization engine operating at the system level. A good example of a container is Docker, which we are already using in our project for local development.

To use this pattern, we need a container image of a microservice. After the container is created, we release one or more containers. Multiple containers are usually run on each physical or virtual host. You are advised to use a cluster manager such as Kubernetes to manage the containers.

The service instance per container pattern has benefits and drawbacks. The benefits of the containers are similar to those of virtual machines. They isolate their instances of microservices from one another. Containers are easily monitored. In addition, similar to the VMs, the containers encapsulate the technology used to implement microservices. Unlike the virtual machines, the containers are lighter. The container images are usually very fast to build and initialize.

There are some disadvantages to using containers. Containers are not as secure as VMs because they share the host operating system kernel with each other.

Another disadvantage of the containers is the complexity of the infrastructure if they are not using any cloud platform that offers interesting mechanisms to manipulate the containers.

The following is a diagram illustrating how the pattern uses containers:

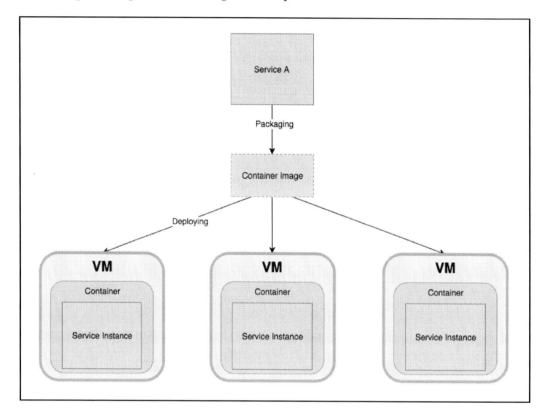

Summary

It has been a long journey. Over the course of 13 chapters, we presented numerous, distinct patterns. We even covered best practices and anti-patterns. We went from the definition of the technology adopted in this project to how to deploy and maintain the application in production.

I hope this book has been a pleasant read and has helped you develop your knowledge. The concepts and patterns of the microservices architecture are constantly evolving. My advice is keep studying. Thank you.

Other Books You May Enjoy

If you enjoyed this book, you may be interested in these other books by Packt:

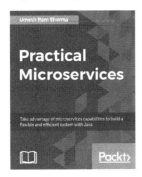

Practical Microservices
Umesh Ram Sharma

ISBN: 978-1-78588-508-2

- The role of a discovery service and externalized configuration in the overall architecture
- Use of message brokers for event driven microservices
- How to intermix data management strategies across components
- Implementing different types of tests in Spring Boot environment
- Applying CI to our microservices style architecture
- Walk through of monitoring and scaling the sample application

Cloud Native Python
Manish Sethi

ISBN: 978-1-78712-931-3

- Get to know "the way of the cloud", including why developing good cloud software is fundamentally about mindset and discipline
- Know what microservices are and how to design them
- Create reactive applications in the cloud with third-party messaging providers
- Build massive-scale, user-friendly GUIs with React and Flux
- Secure cloud-based web applications: the do's, don'ts, and options
- Plan cloud apps that support continuous delivery and deployment

Leave a review - let other readers know what you think

Please share your thoughts on this book with others by leaving a review on the site that you bought it from. If you purchased the book from Amazon, please leave us an honest review on this book's Amazon page. This is vital so that other potential readers can see and use your unbiased opinion to make purchasing decisions, we can understand what our customers think about our products, and our authors can see your feedback on the title that they have worked with Packt to create. It will only take a few minutes of your time, but is valuable to other potential customers, our authors, and Packt. Thank you!

Index

HTTP API 267

I

independent deployment 15
independent upgrade
  about 15, 16
  rules 16
integration test
  about 204, 299, 301
  containers, preparing 298, 299
  writing 204, 205
interceptor 330
interchange context 11
internal communication, microservice
  message broker 240
  sequential 240
  threads 240
Internal Services 172

J

Janitor Monkey 311
Java 39
JavaScript 40
JWT (JSON Web Token) 324, 326

K

Kafka 57, 58

L

Latency Monkey 311
layered services architecture 122
light weight communication
  about 22, 23
  asynchronous 24
  synchronous 23, 24
Load Balancer 187, 222
locale proof performance
  AB 69, 70
  about 68
  Locust 73, 74
  WRK tool 71, 72
Locust 73, 74
logrus
  reference link 44

logs
  viewing 318

M

Memcached 60
message broker
  about 187, 240, 241
  ActiveMQ 56
  applying 194
  containers, working 194
  Kafka 57, 58
  proxy/load balancer, updating 196
  RabbitMQ 56
  used, for async communication between services 54, 55
MessagePack
  about 49
  URL 49
metrics 323
Microservice Aggregator 239
microservice communication
  about 187
  message broker, applying 194
  orchestrator, building 188
microservice domains
  identifying, for business 30
microservice encapsulation 202
microservice frameworks
  about 41
  Go 44
  Python 42, 44
microservices structure
  about 79
  app.go file 84, 86, 87, 89, 93
  main.go file 93
  models.go file 79, 82, 83
microservices, monitoring
  about 314
  application errors, learning from 319, 323
  logs, viewing 318
  metrics 323
  multiple services, monitoring 317
  single service, monitoring 314
microservices
  app, executing 158

96954104R00202

Made in the USA
Lexington, KY
25 August 2018